TIME

A Pastor's Story

TIME AND GRACE
A Pastor's Story

BY

MICHAEL KASTING

www.bookstandpublishing.com

Published by
Bookstand Publishing
Morgan Hill, CA 95037
3743_3

Copyright © 2012 by Michael Kasting

All rights reserved. No part of this publication may be reproduced or transmitted in any form or by any means, electronic or mechanical, including photocopy, recording, or any information storage and retrieval system, without permission in writing from the copyright owner.

ISBN 978-1-61863-371-2

Printed in the United States of America

AUTHOR'S FOREWORD

I began to write this story many years ago for my children. I wanted to give them a glimpse of the world before they were born and of us parents when we were young.

Inspiration for the task came in reading my children the 'Little House' books by Laura Ingalls Wilder. Those books transported us to another time and place with a striking everyday realism. Her books portrayed the very sort of detail I would like to have known about my own parents and grandparents, but waited too long to ask them. What were the rhythms of daily life (mealtimes, school, work, interaction with neighbors)? How did family relationships play out before people wandered into cyberspace? What did my parents and grandparents fear and hope when they were children? What was it like for them to grow old, and how did they react to changes in their world?

I undertook to answer those questions about myself for my children. As I did so, I found myself reflecting on my life and appreciating it as a gift from God. Writing about it has become a springboard to thanksgiving.

Lately I have felt another reason to write. I'd like to tell people about the life and work of a pastor, something that remains largely unknown to most folks. When pastors appear on the screen, they are often in the background, officiating at a wedding or at a funeral, while the main story line unfolds in the heads or the bride and groom, the grieving widow, or the people standing nearby preoccupied with their own thoughts. Pastors and priests in literature are sometimes caricatures – a wildly profligate Elmer Gantry or a detective like Father Dowling who is ostensibly a priest but whose true vocation emerges as he follows a criminal's trail. Jan Karon's Father Tim at work in Mitford comes closer to my own experience of the pastor's life. I hope that an honest telling of my story will offer a window into the funny, sad, perplexing ways of human beings and the mysterious and gracious ways of God with us.

The story you're about to read is true within the limits of my own imperfect memory. It was supplemented with the help I received from others who have reminisced with me. With gratitude I acknowledge the assistance of those who provided encouragement or correction in the writing of this book. Among them are Professor Francis Rossow, Kathy Sievert, Sharon Durham, Pastor Mark Bertermann, Brian Pierson, and my daughters Melanie Hoffman and Christa Zellar. Along the way I enjoyed many phone visits with people in the book as I held my memories alongside theirs. Thanks to them all!

Out of respect for the feelings and the privacy of several people in this book, I have taken the liberty of changing some of the names and places. Mrs. Elliott, Brad and Leah, Arnold and June Rutherford, Jim and Marlene Norris, the Ernst children, Robert Schwabe, Vicar Bob and Chloe Raedeke and daughter Tessa, Pastor Ron and Wanda Blumhorst, Gary Stone, Ben Alfredo, Don Nicola, and DCE John and Donna Zimmermann are all pseudonyms, and Flint Creek, Alaska, is a fictitious name for a real place.

"Everyone has a story," I heard author Jane Kirkpatrick say during a visit to the church I served in Oregon City. Her words helped prompt me to take a serious stab at sharing mine. Perhaps this book will help you do the same with yours.

PROLOGUE

REFLECTIONS IN AN OIL FIELD

A few miles north of Casey, Illinois, there's an oil field mantled with acres of tasseling corn. The first commercial wells began producing more than a hundred years ago. Here and there are islands in the fields where scattered 'nodding donkey' pumps still bob up and down with a tired, but steady rhythm, pulling up what crude oil is left in this nearly depleted field.

Casey is where Sue and I live now. We've pulled off the expressway of helter-skelter fulltime ministry onto the small country road of part-time service. We're in the slow lane. Throttled back. There's time to reflect and let our spirits catch up.

We drive visitors up here now and again. Like us, almost none of them have seen oil wells in a cornfield. The smell of petroleum that greets our noses feels out of place here in corn country. The tiny restaurant on nearby highway 49 that invites customers to come and enjoy a porkburger, fries, and a piece of pie seems unappetizing. Would anyone want to grab a bite at 'Oilfield'? Or at 'Moonshine,' twenty miles south of here? Quite a few folks want to, as it turns out, including us.

Not long ago I drove up the road by myself, parked the car, and walked, reflecting on how I came to be here in this tiny town by the oil field. In my sixties now, I feel like one of those pumps, slow and steady, still working to extract another barrel or two out of my personal tank of crude before it runs dry.

For forty years I've been a pastor. It has been a journey of unexpected turns to a fascinating assortment of places. A Tlingit village in Alaska. A monastery in Minnesota. A row house in a Chicago ghetto. The prow of a fishing boat in Port Angeles, Washington. The edge of a trench in Jericho, staring down at the remains of the oldest human construction on earth. How did an ordinary Hoosier boy touch all those bases and wind up in a cornfield right next door?

How did I ever get into this work that takes me to the joyful and sorrowful poles of human experience? I preside over the marriages of couples with stars in their eyes and referee the acrimonious divorces of others who have lost the love they once treasured. I administer the first taste of Communion wine for a seventh-grader and observe the DTs of an alcoholic in a detox center. I laugh with first-time parents as I hold their tiny baby, and my insides churn as I hear the news that a distraught man has just shot himself to death. Being a pastor is a romance stranger and sweeter than any movie. "People really have no idea what it's like for us," a veteran fellow pastor told me.

It was my childhood dream, but I had no conception of what would meet me on this vocational road. Faces and voices float back across the years. "You leave my son alone!" bellowed the father of a delinquent member I was pursuing. Startled and angry in my turn, I hung up on him. "I've murdered three people" said one hollow-eyed woman, "and I've never been able to tell my husband or my mother." She, the superintendent of our Sunday School, was confessing three abortions. "I need to talk to you, pastor," said a man in his fifties, struggling with his homosexuality. "I'm so lonely I want to kill myself."

Nor did I imagine the exquisite joys that would spill over from lives touched by the Gospel. "I think," one older woman wrote me, "that I finally understand it. I'm the sheep found by the Shepherd." "It's fun being a Christian!" beamed a man who had lately returned to church after years away. Over and over there have been tears of joy. Tears of the newly-baptized and the newly-married and the newly-absolved. "I feel a hundred pounds lighter," said that hollow-eyed woman with tears after speaking a painful, private confession and hearing the words of absolution that washed over her.

Sometimes the tears were my own. I preached at one daughter's wedding and recalled her 'dolltown' marriages in our basement and trembled with the exquisitely sweet recollection. When my son, who had been through some hellish years as a teen, began to weep before me at his wedding, I found tears in my own eyes. On the morning I commissioned my other daughter to her year-long mission in Kenya, my fatherly pride brought such a lump in my throat that I could hardly speak. In what other vocation is one allowed such a mixture of delight and sorrow?

I return often to a question I cannot answer except by faith: Did it all do any good? On many a Sunday after church, walking in an empty sanctuary, I replay the sermon I preached earlier that morning and wonder whether the seed will take root or be plucked from the pathway by the birds. Whether the people with whom I preached and prayed and played will stay on the narrow path or wander off to some sad end.

How does a pastor evaluate his ministry? It is tempting to employ what can be seen and counted. How many people in church today? Are we meeting our budget? How many attended Bible School this summer? How many were gained (or lost) on the church rolls this year? By now I've learned how little such things really reveal. What one sees happening to people as the years of life run through the hourglass is more telling. Jesus described it in the parable of the two sons who said one thing but did another. Paul Harvey called it 'the rest of the story.' I think of a seminarian I mentored for a year who called it the greatest year of his life, but later left his marriage and his ministry and committed suicide. I think of the aging pastor who took me aside at a conference. "You're an in-your-face pastor," he told me, and then added, "and I mean that as a compliment. You saved my grandson's life!" He proceeded to tell me that I had gotten in his daughter's face when she was pregnant out of wedlock and contemplating an abortion. She had changed her mind and kept that baby, who was now grown and the apple of grandpa's eye. I didn't remember any of it.

That's how it usually is. We pastors plant like Paul and water like Apollos, but most of the results remain hidden until the final judgment. Years ago I was in Rose Hill Cemetery in Akron, Ohio, after finishing a graveside committal. The mourners had all gone, and I sauntered among the headstones, reading names and dates and the occasional epitaphs engraved there. Suddenly, unexpectedly, I saw a familiar name. It was the headstone of J. Franklin Yount, the founding pastor at Concordia Lutheran Church, where I was then serving. It caused me to shudder, as if I were standing at my own grave with my name written there.

That day is closer now than it was then. What would I choose as my epitaph? I think of a portion of the confirmation verse (Romans 1:16) that Pastor Ed Albers gave me back in May of 1960:

NOT ASHAMED OF THE GOSPEL

That's what I'd want written on my headstone. There is, of course, much of which I am ashamed as I look back over these years in my life and ministry. My wife and children (and my successors) could provide the unpleasant details. The Gospel is the one sure, solid thing of which I'm not ashamed. It proclaims to me that because of Jesus, God keeps on forgiving and washing away the shameful things that have stained my life and work. Through Him I know grace, the undeserved kindness of God. I hold on to that.

I get into my car and head back home to Casey. The sun's going down. It's suppertime and Sue's in the kitchen. As usual, there's plenty to talk about.

TABLE OF CONTENTS

Author's Foreword v
Prologue: Reflections in an Oil Field vii

PART ONE – CHILDHOOD YEARS (1947–1964) 1

A Tap on My Shoulder 3
The Family Circle 7
Sundays and Wednesdays at Calvary 11
Mr. Schwark's Domain 15
Paper Boy 21
Hail to Southport High 25

PART TWO – COLLEGE AND SEMINARY (1964–1972) 31

Into the System 33
The Promised Land 41
Eyes Newly Opened 45
The School for Character 51
Sharpening the Sword 55
Vicarage Times Two 61
Frailty and Fatherhood 67

PART THREE – STATIONS IN PASTORAL MINISTRY (1972–PRESENT) 71

Memorial Lutheran Church, Vancouver, Washington (1972–80) 73

An Extended Apprenticeship 75
Youth Pastor 83
Missouri's Civil War 87
Larry Gantka 91
Playful Times and Deep Friendship 95
A Prophecy and an Explosion 99

Concordia Lutheran Church, Akron, Ohio (1980–1988) 103

Something Like a Wedding 105
Gothic in Goosetown 109
At Home in Firestone Park 113
A Collision in Values 119
Getting Organized 125
Journey to Israel 131
A Procession of Vicars 139
Roses and Thorns 145

Faith Lutheran Church, Sequim, Washington (1988–1999) 149

Not Quite the End of the World 151
Ministry Snapshots 157
Helpers in the Vineyard 165
The LOGOS Program 171
Our Darkest Hour.. 175
Letting Go... 181

Trinity Lutheran Church, Oregon City, Oregon (1999–2010)............ 187

On the Oregon Trail.. 189
Shadows on the Wall 193
Farming the Field.. 197
Multiple Staff Matters.. 201
Sabbatical Journeys.. 207
Mission Fits and Starts... 217
Fighting and Fainting... 225
Decision to Downsize 231
Grace Notes.. 235

Trinity Lutheran Church, Casey, Illinois (2010–Present)................... 239

The Rhythm of the Heartland... 241
Epilogue.. 247

PART ONE

Childhood Years

(1947-1964)

A TAP ON MY SHOULDER

It began simply. No angelic vision. No burning bush. I don't even remember the day God administered His tap on my shoulder to enter the ministry. I have only my mother's remembrance as witness to it. She was tending to her home-maker's chores while my younger brother Danny and I played. Out of the corner of her eye, she spied me in an unexpected pose. I strutted before her like a tiny rooster, holding the family hymnal up before my face. My head was back, my steps measured in childlike solemnity – a four-year-old's tiny processional through her kitchen.

"What are you doing?" she said, bending low, nose to my nose.

"I be pastor!"

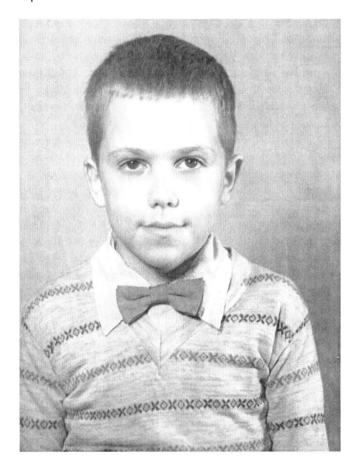

It was an unexpected revelation to my parents. There were no pastors perched in our family tree. Dad was employed at Eli Lilly, a pharmaceutical company in Indianapolis. His father, Harry, had worked for Chevrolet. Great-great-great-grandfather Gerhard Hermann Heinrich Kasting was a farmer who emigrated from Dielingen, Germany, to Jackson County, Indiana, in the 1840s. There were flax growers and linen weavers among my ancestors in the old country. There were several centuries of staunch Lutherans, but no pastors that we ever discovered.

Nor did any of my pastors recruit me. None took me aside for a shepherdly talk or asked me the question I later asked a number of young men, "Have you ever thought about being a pastor?" The call was simply there in my toddler's heart. It remained fixed there as I grew up. I was as certain of it as I was of sunrise and sunset. God's gentle, persistent tap on my shoulder.

In my grade school years, I daydreamed about what shape that ministry might take. Sometimes I pictured myself as a missionary in the South Seas. I envisioned grass shacks, hula girls and gulls crying overhead as a reverent congregation of native folk gathered to hear the Word. Later images were less romantic. I saw myself sheperding a stateside church where I preached and taught and fielded questions. I would be a peacemaker, helping reconcile people who were at odds.

For me, an important function of the faith was to provide answers to questions. I was a child curious about God and all things religious. I wanted to know about the people peddling religious tracts who knocked at our door. Why did Dad have us scurry to find a catechism when he saw them coming? I was at a loss to explain eternity, the idea that time had no beginning and no end. For my child's mind, time was something like a very long clothesline, like the one my father had affixed to the metal posts in our back yard, only much longer. But how could it be infinitely longer, with no fixed beginning? And if there were no beginning, how did we ever get to this place on the clothesline? The Holy Trinity was another puzzle on my mystery shelf. How could God be three distinct 'persons,' yet only 'one divine being'? I resolved that the congregation I served one day would be a place where people could ask anything they wanted. I hoped I would have found my answers by then.

Some of my questions were more than academic. I wondered about death. Was it painful? What came afterward? I often bore a fearful knot of emotion in my belly. There were the deaths of pets and stories of horrors I read in the newspaper. Then death came closer. A neighbor boy named Pat Schmidt was my occasional playmate. One night his father was killed in an accident on Highway 31 coming home from work. It was the same route my father used! For a long time afterward, I watched anxiously each evening until I saw Dad's car turn into our driveway.

On Halloween night of 1963 death brushed my own family. I had just gone to bed after baby-sitting my brothers. Mom and Dad were away seeing the "Holiday on Ice" show at the state fairgrounds coliseum. Near midnight I was awakened by a chillingly surreal sight. My parents stood in the bedroom doorway – their faces shaken, their clothes blood-stained. Together they narrated what had happened. There had been a propane gas explosion at the coliseum that night. More than 70 people were killed and at least 400 injured. There were frantic attempts to help in the ensuing chaos. They had made a trip to the hospital with an injured man in the car. There was a remnant of shock in their faces. And there was shock in my heart when they told me that the section which exploded was just a few rows in front of where they were sitting.

If I became a pastor, would it help me get some handle on death? At church, the death of Jesus was clearly at the center of the message. It was especially so in Lent, when we sang hymns that touched me deeply and bespoke this death that was like no other. Most vivid were the poignant words of Johann Heermann's hymn:

What punishment so strange is suffered yonder!
The Shepherd dies for sheep that loved to wander;
The Master pays the debt His servants owe Him,
Who would not know Him.

For me! His death was for me. And God had called me to follow that Savior and hold Him out to people. That conviction grew stronger as I grew older. I would learn all I could about the mysteries of eternity and God and death. I did not yet know what 'ministry' was about and what it would take to shape me for His service. Nor did I yet know the truth about myself and the depth of my own need for redemption.

Time would make those things painfully clear.

THE FAMILY CIRCLE

In a speech to the Toastmasters' Club in the 1950s, my father explained his approach to family planning: "There were three children in my family and five in Mary's. We thought we'd aim somewhere in the middle and have four..." That's how it was. I was the second of four children born to my parents, the oldest boy.

Arthur George Kasting was an outwardly unremarkable man of average height and weight. Born at the end of World War I, he had the virtues that marked his GI generation – he was honest, hard-working, and frugal. His self-control was a comfortable counterpoint to my mother's often mercurial disposition. Even when he administered a spanking, it was done under control, the way a police officer politely administers a ticket.

"You look more like your father all the time," my wife tells me. She observes my expanding belly and the way my mouth hangs open. But I am like my father in ways deeper than genetic endowment. It was because of Dad that I grew up Lutheran. He and Mom took me to be baptized at St. Peter's Lutheran Church in Indianapolis where he had been baptized in his infancy. He spoke admiringly of old Teacher Yunghans, and he remained a faithful churchgoer all his life. If it was Sunday, we knew we'd be in church unless providentially hindered. At Dad's funeral, the pastor's message was fittingly titled 'It's Sunday!' What he confessed on Sundays, he lived on Mondays. He was faithful in his marriage and kind to his neighbors. Only once in all my life did I hear him utter the word 'damn.' My brother Jeff summarized his life simply: "He never did anything to make us ashamed."

My mother, Mary Katherine (nee Pritchard), three years his junior, was one of five children born to Guy and Edith Pritchard on the east side of Indianapolis. Early pictures of her reveal a cute, dimpled child with dark hair and striking eyes. The one cloud in her otherwise happy childhood was the death of her father when she was eleven years old. Her mother kept the family together and took them faithfully to the Westminster Presbyterian Church. The Word of God had its impact on Mom. Her love for the Lord was as earnestly held as my father's.

Mom and Dad met at Eli Lilly, where both worked and both tried out for the same play. It was a forgettable play, but a memorable romance, though Mom later confessed to me, "I didn't like your father at first." World War II came before marriage did. Dad enlisted in the army and completed basic training at Camp Perry, Ohio. While he was home on leave in 1942, they married at St. Peter's on Christmas Day. He soon returned to duty and shipped out for France, landing at Normandy a few weeks after D-Day as a member of General Patton's army. Their wartime correspondence fills a large shoebox.

After the war Dad returned to Lilly's and Mom became a full-time homemaker, occupied with meals and laundry and making sure we children made it out to the school bus on time. If we rose early enough on winter mornings, we went to the kitchen to sit in front of the register and keep warm while we watched Dad finish his cup of coffee before he drove off to work.

My father's script in the family drama called for him to be the breadwinner, activity planner, photographer, and Mr. Fix-it. He mowed grass, cut hair, administered corporal punishment, repaired whatever broke, and did the driving whenever the family traveled, which was often. There were short hops to cross over the 'fun bridge' at Garfield Park, to watch airplanes take off and land at Weir Cook Airport, or to get cones and Dilly Bars at the Dairy Queen on Madison Avenue. There were evenings at the Greenwood or Meridian drive-in theaters for double features. There were longer days spent at Riverside Amusement Park, a rustic place that would be dwarfed by today's theme parks, and at the Indiana State Fair, where we gawked at the Percheron horses, Brahma bulls, and enormous sows with their litters of hungry piglets. There were lengthy vacation trips to Florida, California, and Massachusetts, fun that was doubled by the slides Dad took and later projected as we watched, mesmerized.

He had a silly side that provided laughs and occasional embarrassment. He liked to recite snatches of a frivolous song from the 1920s called '*Ain't We Crazy?*' He made 'napkin bunnies' in the restaurant to surprise the waitress as we rolled our eyes. He laughed until he cried watching Victor Borge at the piano.

God designed that faith be caught more than taught. Dad's actions were the pattern for my faith's formation. A memory that stands out sharply for me took place on a Saturday afternoon as he and I drove down a two-lane road. We got behind a car that weaved unpredictably over the roadway. My father stayed behind the man, flashing his lights at oncoming traffic. When the other driver stopped at an intersection, Dad jumped out, ran to the man's window and said something I could not hear. Then he jumped back in our car and we continued following for a mile or so until the man finally drove into his own driveway and lurched to a stop. The man got out and stumbled toward his door. Dad opened the car door, stepped out and watched to make sure he was OK. Just then the man turned and cursed my father. I was shocked at the unexpected outburst and hurt for him. But Dad simply got in the car and drove us home without a word. It was his enacted creed that the love of God was to be demonstrated in the treatment of our neighbors.

If Dad's script was actions, my mother's was decidedly words. She did much of the explaining, exhorting, praising, and scolding. She liked sit-down talks and folksy advice. Over the years she reminded me often,

"Remember to write a thank-you note." More than once she wrote me a special note of her own with some piece of motherly wisdom. During my eighth grade year, I was a contestant in the Central Indiana Spelling Bee. In my pocket was an envelope with a small letter she tucked in just before we left the house. She wrote me:

This week is a tense one, just before the finals of the spelling bee. Do not spend time worrying about how someone may get ahead of you. Think not of the prizes, but of being well-prepared and calm. Make your contribution to the spelling bee as a representative of your school one that will be remembered for quality and good sportsmanship. "Trust in the Lord with all thine heart, and lean not unto thine own understanding. In all thy ways acknowledge Him and He shall direct thy paths" – Proverbs 3:5-6

Dad and Mom taught us children to pray by daily example. At almost every meal we spoke the Common Table Prayer that was a Lutheran staple:

Come, Lord Jesus, be our guest
And let Thy gifts to us be blessed.

Bedtime prayer was also learned by rote:

Now I lay me down to sleep,
I pray the Lord my soul to keep.
If I should die before I wake
I pray the Lord my soul to take.

Dad's one memorable failure in our spiritual training was his attempt to institute family devotions as we sat at table for the evening meal. He brought out a large book and read from it while we were expected to sit still and listen. It didn't work. Before supper we were too hungry. After supper we were full of pep, still wanting to play. Nevertheless, I admired him for trying.

My parents were products of a generation that knew privation first-hand. We rarely ate out, and when we did, it was an unspoken rule that we got the cheapest item on the menu. Both of my parents liked books and music. Dad brought home 78-rpm recordings of the Indianapolis Symphony. As we listened together to great choruses, there awoke in me a life-long love of choral music. Mother enjoyed reading and kept us children supplied with books.

I shared their attention and affection with three siblings. My sister Natalie was the oldest child, a girl both strong and capable. I envied her ability to speak a secret language she called 'alfalfa' with her friend when they wanted to hide their conversation from me. She possessed enough strength and skill to hold her own in sports, but she did not like snakes. The only time I was the victor in our skirmishes was when I found a dead garter snake and chased her triumphantly, holding it aloft.

Younger brother Danny arrived at our home on a snowy, winter day in 1950 while I sat on the windowsill watching the car come down the driveway. Early on we were playmates, riding broomstick horses and shooting rifles fashioned from horseweeds. He enjoyed tinkering in the garage more than doing his homework. Sadly, our relationship eroded as we grew older. He became increasingly a sort of prodigal son who wanted out of the family circle to follow his nose, and I became the elder brother who dutifully pointed out his misdeeds.

Brother Jeff was the latecomer, a gentle, peace-loving boy who eventually grew to be the tallest of us siblings. Because eight years separated us, he was not so much a playmate as a protégée, especially in basketball. Years later I thrilled to hear that he had indeed become a center for Southport High School's team, and that during his career, the team rose to be among the top ten in the state. Mom furnished me the clippings.

Natalie eventually graduated from Lutheran Hospital School of Nursing in Ft. Wayne and became a nurse for an eye doctor. Danny navigated through some personal crises, served as sound man for the Manhattan Transfer, and later settled into a stable marriage and work with the local school district. Jeff became a corporate jet pilot for Eli Lilly and coached girls' basketball for the CYO. I became a pastor. All of us had children of our own.

We survived and thrived because of the steady commitment of our parents, whose marriage stayed strong through fifty-seven years. On the wall above the washing machine hung a triangular plaque made of plaster of Paris. When I got old enough, I climbed up to investigate. On the back I found an inscription from Dad to Mom.

"What's this triangle for?" I asked.

"That's the symbol we chose for our marriage," Mom explained. "It stands for your father and I and the Lord."

We saw the picture fleshed out before us, an incarnation of grace lived over time as St. Paul described it in Ephesians 5 - Dad's Christ-like, sacrificial love for Mom, Mom's respectful submission to Dad, and the presence and forgiveness of Jesus healing their times of hurt. Their shared faith in God was the fountainhead of my own faith and a great part of the reason I finally became a pastor.

Having godly parents who stayed married and stayed in love was a gift I did not fully appreciate until many years later.

SUNDAYS AND WEDNESDAYS AT CALVARY

It was a cloudless Sunday morning in June. Our family was packed into our green '53 Ford. Little Jeff was in the front with Dad and Mom. We older three children sat elbow to elbow in the back seat for the 2½-mile drive to church.

"Here we are," Dad announced as he parked the car beneath the tall shade trees that ringed Calvary Lutheran Church. Our parents were glad to go to church, and their attitude was infectious. The services could be dull at times, but I never rebelled against going. If it was Sunday, that's where we were.

We children tumbled out of the car but didn't get far.

"It's crooked," Mom observed as she bent down to straighten Danny's bow tie while he fidgeted. Everyone dressed up for church: dresses and hats for the women, shirts and ties for the men.

Calvary Lutheran Church was a beautiful brick church with a bell tower for a steeple. It sat nestled on a generously wooded lot on the corner of Shelby and Dudley Streets. The church building had an A-frame roof, a narrow nave with a center aisle and wooden pews, and a basement which provided space for both Sunday school classes and a fellowship hall for our occasional potluck meals. Of special interest to me was the north entrance. It offered three options. A step up to the right was the pastor's office and a pull cord that rang the bells in the tower. I often hoped someone would invite me to pull it, but the ushers held that duty and guarded the cord. To the left was a stairway to the basement. Straight ahead the door opened into the sanctuary right beneath the pulpit. During the hottest days of summer a huge, black fan was placed by that doorway, aimed at the congregation. Air-conditioning was still years away. Hand-held fans from the G. H. Herrmann Funeral Home were distributed to folks for relief as they sat perspiring in the pews.

We went to Sunday school first. The classes were spread out through the basement, with dividers separating classes by age. My class convened in the kitchen under Mrs. Wetzel's tutelage. As we wiggled in our wooden folding chairs, she directed our attention to a flip-chart by the gas stove. On the stand was a giant picture of the Tower of Babel. While Mrs. Wetzel's voice droned on in the background, I was lost in the picture, tracing the slow ascent of someone climbing the circular stairway up the cone-shaped tower. The top was hidden in the clouds, and I imagined God up there, just out of sight.

"Has everybody got a leaflet?" Her voice roused me from my daydream. The boy next to me handed me a folded sheet with a picture to color and label. As we colored, we could smell the natural gas from the kitchen stove.

As I got older, I preferred sitting in the adult class with my father upstairs in the sanctuary. We sat in the front pews. Pastor Barth stood before us, notes on a stand. "Would it be better to be a good Baptist or a poor Lutheran?" he asked one day. I didn't know what a Baptist was, but judged that to be a good anything was better than to be a bad anything. I discovered that I was wrong. Pastor Barth went on to explain that to be any kind of Lutheran was better than to be any kind of Baptist. "Why?" I wanted to ask, but, surrounded by all those adults, I was too timid to hold up my hand.

After our church's move to a new location, I became a regular in the adult class, preferring its substance to the disorder of our teens' group, where Mr. Rothkopf would routinely ask, "What would you like to study today?" *You're the teacher, aren't you?* The largest adult class was taught by Gerhard Hasz, who seemed unusually knowledgeable for a layman. I learned later that he had graduated from Concordia Seminary in St. Louis during the Great Depression. Since few churches had enough money to pay a living wage, not a single call into the pastoral ministry was available that year. Most of those fellows had dispersed to farms and factories. Teaching Sunday school was as close as Hasz would get to pastoral work. His teaching modeled the investigation of detail I came to love in Bible study.

After Sunday school it was time for worship. We made our way to a pew and squeezed in, taking bulletins from the ushers on the way. Pastor Barth, now robed in his black cassock with a white surplice covering it, led us through the liturgy in *The Lutheran Hymnal*. Page 5 (non-Communion Sundays) and page 15 (Communion Sundays) were nearly identical in wording, and since we used those two services almost exclusively, the result was a kind of reverent monotony. "Decently and in order" was St. Paul's dictum for worship in his letter to the Corinthians. We Lutherans specialized in the orderly. Fortunately, not everything at church was scripted! One Sunday in springtime, a squirrel bounded through the open door and leaped nimbly onto the baptismal font. After a moment of mutual surprise and inspection, our visitor turned, dismounted and raced out.

Though the liturgy was orderly to the point of sheer boredom, the repetition served to embed the words of the Apostles' and Nicene Creeds in my brain. The liturgy taught me snippets of the Psalms and ushered me into the treasury of the ancient church's faith enshrined in its hymnody. It was my theological skeleton. The flesh was added over time.

There were no children's sermons in those days, nor any blessing for them at the altar. The sermons targeted the adults. Since Lutherans did not employ 'children's church' (dismissing the little ones to a separate room for the sermon), what remained for us kids was to listen as hard as possible. That proved tiring. So I began to invent ways to pass the time, like imagining the word *SERMON* hanging in midair above me – each letter a hollow tube slowly filling with sand in its turn. I tried to time things so that the word was filled as the sermon ended. Another choice was to study the architecture, counting the concrete blocks in the archway or the wooden ceiling beams. The stained glass image of Jesus kneeling in Gethsemane over the altar was worth an extra look. One Sunday I discovered that a woman sitting nearby had a fur piece around her shoulders, with little minks biting each other's tails in a perpetual chase.

When our parents went up to the communion rail, we children were left waiting in the pew until they returned. When they came back, I leaned close to smell the mysterious aroma of wine on their breath.

Things could be seen from a different perspective from the choir loft. Located in the left transept, the loft offered a side view of the pulpit, the congregation, and the doorway out. Organist Lorenz Kropp took his seat at the organ bench in back and the choir was arrayed in the three rows in front of the loft. When I grew older and sang in the grade school choir, I got to sit with the other boys in the back row, where we could watch Mr. Kropp's feet dance on the pedals.

Wednesday nights in Lent were markedly different from Sunday mornings. It was dark outside. Fewer people were in attendance. The mood was somber. The paraments (altar cloths) and the pastor's stole were deep purple. Without Sunday school and with a shorter service, it was easier to stay awake. Now and then came something unexpected. I was impressed one Lenten season to see that Pastor Barth had printed out a sheet with questions – dozens of them. Before the worship began, he strolled out before us, his own copy in hand. "Anything on this list you'd like to ask?" *Wow! How does he know all those things?* That small exercise introduced the idea that a pastor was an answer man. That's what I wanted to be, I decided.

The focus in Lent was narrow, concentrated on Jesus' final days. The sermons and service were tightly thematic and bunched in sevens. The seven words from the cross. Seven characters from the Passion Story – Judas, Pilate, Herod, the Penitent Thief, and others paraded before us. The hymns of Lent spoke to me of a sweet and indescribable sadness. Dad chose to sing the bass line in some of those hymns, and when my voice began to change, I followed him, imitating his ups and downs, memorizing the part without consciously trying.

Changes came. Pastor Barth moved on and Pastor Ed Albers replaced him in 1955. Ed was a taller man with fuzzy hair and eyes that looked two directions at once. He bore himself with an easy dignity – a man to be taken seriously. But one of my most vivid memories of Pastor Albers was not an austere but a playful one. It was the memory of him hamming it up downstairs at one of our congregational potlucks. After the meal he strolled to the piano dressed in a tuxedo adorned with gaudy sequins. He had morphed into Liberace, flapping his coattails out in back and sitting at the bench with a flourish. Then, as I stared wide-eyed, there came my own parents, cross-dressed. Mom was Nelson Eddy, and Dad was Jeanette Macdonald! They sang *'Ah, Sweet Mystery of Life'* as Liberace Albers played accompaniment.

A bigger change came in the 1960s when the whole congregation moved to new quarters by the grade school a mile south on Shelby Street. It was a church, but it looked like a gym. The men of the church had disagreed about what to build first. In the end, they decided on a building that could be used as a sanctuary and converted to a gym later.

The people were the same. Mr. Kropp still played the organ. Mr. Huck still handed out bulletins. The liturgy remained familiar. But I missed the old brick church and the cozy feeling I had there. The new church had no little round window above the altar, no dark trees standing like sentinels, and no rock for us to climb and play 'king of the hill.'

That all happened decades ago. In time, that gym-church became a real gymnasium with a hardwood floor and basketball goals at each end. A new sanctuary rose – a lovely, expansive place with heavy, metal crosses suspended from the ceiling to draw the eyes and minds of a new generation. New hymnals brought a richer variety to worship.

The old brick church is still where it was. It was bought by another congregation and remodeled. I drive by on visits home to see the relatives and relive churchly memories. A look inside reveals that the chancel's been stripped down and the pulpit moved out. The name has been changed to Tallwood Chapel.

I stop to reminisce. The voices and familiar hymns of my boyhood are still echoing in my mind.

MR. SCHWARK'S DOMAIN

Most of my grade school days began with a race down our long driveway to intercept Mr. Epler's yellow school bus. They ended with a slower, longer walk from where that same bus disgorged us a half-mile east at Meridian Street. In the winter months, when the wind was whining in the telephone lines and Mother Nature was calling, it was a very long walk, indeed.

Calvary Church opened its own parochial school in 1950. When I started there, the school had already grown to nearly 100 students. The building was of solid grey stonework. Eight grades were sandwiched into three classrooms. A long hallway connected the two lower-grade rooms on the left with the upper-grade room on the right. A boiler room, restrooms and a library flanked the hallway.

An ample plot of ground would allow expansion in the years ahead, but in the fall of 1953, when I began, there wasn't much out back – a basketball hoop, swings, a teeter-totter, and some drinking fountains just beneath the restroom windows. We relished our two recesses a day, each brought to an end by the ringing of a loud bell in the hand of our school principal, Mr. August Schwark. His residence sat just a stone's throw south across a field from the school.

My first teacher was Leona Eisele, a proper, kindly woman with grey hair and a soft voice. She directed us to hang our coats on hooks in the back closets and place our lunch boxes in the grid of cubbies in the back of the room. My standard fare was a peanut butter and jelly sandwich (wrapped in wax paper), an apple, and perhaps a Twinkie or a Hostess pie. Our milk came in little half-pint cartons distributed daily and paid for with 'milk money.'

Mrs. Eisele was a peaceable enough person, and I was no trouble-maker, but I recall two incidents by which I managed to make a very bad impression on her. The first took place on the playground during recess. It was a winter day with a wet snow falling, just the right kind for a snowball fight. I made and heaved only a few snowballs, and by accident one of them managed to smash her squarely in the face. With a sinking feeling I watched her crying and trying to wipe her granny glasses. On another occasion, as we were poised to take our achievement tests (administered in grade two), I held my packet at eye level to see how thick it was. For that I earned a sharp reprimand from Mrs. Eisele, who assumed I was cheating.

That test, though I did not know it, was about to change my life. Three other boys and I did well enough on it that the school gave our parents the option of skipping the remainder of grade two and passing directly into the next grade, the next room, and the next teacher, Mrs. Abdon. At the time, I was elated. Not until high school did I realize it meant being at a disadvantage in going out for sports and having to wait a year longer than classmates for my driver's license.

Maxine Abdon was more businesslike than Mrs. Eisele. She was shorter, with a face both square and grim. It seemed only fitting that her husband Russell operated a funeral home and that another relative, Horace, was our family dentist. She had a fearsome reputation among the students and was the subject of occasional whispered rumors like the one that reached my ears one day: "Mrs. Abdon slugged Jackie!" I had not seen it, but I believed she could do it.

Mrs. Abdon taught grades three through five. She struck fear in me one morning when she called on me to come forward and read to the class my social studies assignment. We were to write about how we might make a trip from Indianapolis to New York. I had completely forgotten! Now what? Fake it or confess? I chose to fake it, and I came forward holding several blank sheets of lined paper. While the class gazed vacantly at me and Mrs. Abdon settled herself against the chalkboard, I proceeded to narrate my imaginary trip. It didn't take long for her to smell the ruse. Slowly she walked toward me, until she stood just behind, where she could plainly see my empty paper.

"Why, Michael Kasting, you've been deceiving me!"

She said it with genuine hurt. In that moment I saw that she was no ogre, but a teacher who cared, and I had let her down – the worst of punishments. I also realized with shame how easily I lied to her. It was the first crack in my haughty self-image.

Soon enough, I entered Mr. Schwark's domain. He served as principal, taught grades six through eight, and stayed on after school to do custodial work with the help of his wife Mabel. He was a wiry, intense man who wore suspenders and rolled up the sleeves on his white shirt like a man on a mission. He had, we swore, eyes in the back of his head, and the frightening knack of appearing at the most inopportune moments.

One was the day I stood with several boys at the drinking fountain under the girls' restroom window. The day was warm, and the window was ajar. We could hear the girls on the other side of the wall, giggling and squealing with their adolescent gossip. We took pebbles and began tossing them through the open window, hoping for the payoff in their screams of surprise. Instead, it was I who got the surprise of discovering Mr. Schwark at my elbow, peering at me with hawklike eyes.

"What do you think you're doing?"

My erstwhile companions had all conveniently disappeared. I stood alone before him wordless. Inside he marched me, where I was to stand for the next twenty minutes at the chalkboard, concentrating aim with my nose at a chalk circle while the class watched and snickered.

It was in Mr. Schwark's room that I first experienced music performance. The school had contracted with the Gary Davis Music Makers to come up from Columbus weekly to conduct a beginning band. I elected to play drums, and in short order I learned to tap a waltz beat on a snare drum (rest-tap-tap, rest-tap-tap). Mr. Schwark himself directed a choir that sang three-part harmony. After having sung bass with my father in church, finding the harmony line was a piece of cake. We boys with the low voices got the best seats when we sang in church – the back row by the organ.

Basketball was, as seemed fitting in the Hoosier State, our serious sport. Our school team practiced at nearby Edgewood School. At our evening practices, we entered by the basement door, wound our way through the boiler room to the gym, and then ran our drills under the watchful eyes of our coaches. The Lutheran school gyms where we played came in a laughable variety. Emmaus had a tiny, boxy one. Trinity had a spacious new one. Grace's gym had a low ceiling and a tile floor. St. John, out in farm country, had a second-floor gym with a raised stage under one basket. St. Paul, where we played our home games, had a balcony overlooking the gym on two sides, and nice rows of wooden bleachers. Our colors were red and white, like the local high school. The team name was 'Redskins.' No one then conceived how politically incorrect that name would become. Practically every girl in school was a cheerleader, and the cheers were utterly simple:

Two bits, four bits, six bits, a dollar,
All for Calvary, stand up and holler!

I see random pictures of those grade school years, as from on old photo album. Standing at attention to start the day, saying the Pledge of Allegiance. Standing again at the end to recite the Mizpah Benediction from Genesis: "*May the Lord watch between me and thee, while we are absent one from the other.*" Gathering erasers from the chalkboards and beating the dust out on the stone wall outside. Bringing stacks of newspapers for the bins lining the circular drive. Taking my turn hoisting the two flags – the American flag on top, and under it the green Herman Hoglebogle pennant we got for school safety from *The Indianapolis News*. Painting Christmas scenes with tempera paints on the inside of the windows. Doing excruciating penmanship exercises on lined paper sheets (my worst subject).

On Saturdays during our final two years, the school became the site of our confirmation instruction. Pastor Albers, dressed in a black clergy shirt with clerical collar, met with us on Saturday mornings. We sat in rows just as we did for school. There were lessons consisting mostly of filling in worksheets based on Bible readings. Each week we were assigned the memorization of a portion of *Luther's Small Catechism*, a tiny blue book with enormous importance for Lutheran children. Along with the Ten Commandments, the Creed, the Lord's Prayer, and the 'What does this mean?' questions and answers Luther had penned more than 400 years earlier, we were served a generous helping of Bible verses from Dr. Schwan's lengthy explanation section of the book. My impression of confirmation instruction was like my estimate of medicine – unpleasant at times, but good for you. One Saturday a girl in our class was called on by Pastor Albers to recite her assigned verses. She stood, gulped in a panic of forgetfulness, then burst out crying. All of us had such forgetful moments. Years later, I found that the verses I had crammed into my brain often came tumbling out at need:

*There is not a just man upon earth that doeth good
and sinneth not.
For the wages of sin is death, but the gift of God is
eternal life through Jesus Christ our Lord.
I am fearfully and wonderfully made, and that my soul
knoweth right well.*
The great capper of them all was from Ephesians 2:8-9
*For by grace are ye saved through faith, and that not
of yourselves; it is the gift of God, not of works,
lest any man should boast.*

Confirmation day came in the spring of my eighth grade year. We robed in white and sat trembling before the assembled congregation for the traditional public examination, designed to demonstrate that we had the answers to life's crucial questions. Students A and B stood up. Pastor Albers asked Student A his question.
"How do you know that you are a sinner?"
"By the Ten Commandments. These I have not kept."
With the question answered, A sat and C rose. This question was for B:
"What is the Holy Trinity?"
"The Holy Trinity is three divine persons in one divine being or essence."
Student B sat and student D rose. And so it went. Apparently, the experience of occasional speechlessness and embarrassment had helped Pastor Albers make the decision to tell us all ahead of time what questions we would get so that we could be prepared. We would look good, and so would he!
After the examination, we sang our class hymn, *"Let Me Be Thine Forever."* Then, one by one, we knelt beneath a curved arch wrapped in

greenery and topped with a stuffed white dove. Pastor Albers' hand was heavy and warm on my head. After the word of blessing over me, he gave me my own special verse, as he did with each confirmand. Knowing that I intended to become a pastor, he had chosen words from Romans 1:16:

I am not ashamed of the Gospel of Christ; for it is the power of God unto salvation to every one that believeth.

That verse was more than words on a certificate. It was etched into my heart and became a vehicle by which God routinely called me out of myself, out of my pride, and out of my failures, back to the power source, the Gospel.

PAPER BOY

When I was in seventh grade, I got a job as a paper boy for *The Indianapolis News*, one of three daily newspapers in our city. At the time I thought the job's chief benefit would be the extra spending money I'd earn. My parents reasoned it would teach me discipline and responsibility. God had something more in mind. He used that paper route to prepare me for one of my chief tasks in the ministry. I learned to visit people without fear, appreciate their fascinating foibles, listen to their stories and laugh at their jokes. I also learned something urgently important about myself.

The equipment for the job was simple. I already had a maroon bike with a metal basket attached to the handlebars. My supervisor gave me a canvas bag for carrying the papers, a two-ring receipt book with a page for each of my 42 customers, and a coin changer I could wear on my belt when I collected the money on Saturdays. My father built a square, wooden box with a lid and set it at the end of the driveway. My distributer left the papers there each afternoon.

The customers were spread along a three-mile route. Most requested that the paper be put into the mailbox or, in some instances, into a special newspaper tube beneath. A few asked for special delivery onto porches or behind screen doors. By the time I got home from school each day, the papers were in the box, bound with brown wrapping paper and secured with a loop of wire that had to be slid off with care. Once unwrapped, the papers had to be counted. Sometimes there were extras. At other times I was short, usually by only one paper, necessitating a phone call to the circulation department. I stuffed the papers into my canvas bag, wedged the bag into my bike basket, and pedaled off.

Up Rahke Road I went, dodging the chuckholes. Stop. Pull out a paper, fold it, slide it into the box or toss it to the porch, then move on to the next house. I turned east on Epler Avenue, then south on Garden Drive, working through my list. All told, it took less than an hour.

Saturdays were set aside for collecting. Customers paid 40 cents a week, and I had to stop at each house to collect my money, after which I tore out a tiny dated receipt from my receipt book to give them. Most of the people were kind to me, and I enjoyed stopping at their homes. The Speichers were well-to-do and somewhat brusque, as if they had a million things on their schedule. I never stayed there long. A customer named Al would come to his door with a liquor bottle in hand. He had a small green Alpha Romeo in his driveway. Mr. Renier was a very poor man who spent most of his days in the grimy greenhouse on the back of his lot. To find him I had to shout repeatedly into the greenhouse. Eventually he would emerge from the gloom, wearing faded overalls and sporting a stubby growth of whiskers. I was startled to discover that he wore no underwear – nothing but the overalls and a red beret. He squinted at me, reaching wordlessly for a tiny leather coin purse in his pocket. It seemed, as with the biblical widow, that he had almost nothing left after handing over his 40 cents in coins. Mrs. Gee was a talker who regaled me with tales of her husband's fishing trips and her son's academic progress. Some Saturdays, before I knew it, I had spent three hours and covered only half the homes. I enjoyed visiting with people and hearing them talk. I sometimes wonder what they thought of this paper boy they couldn't easily shoo off the porch.

It was on my paper route that I displayed one of my ugliest eruptions of temper. One afternoon as I made my way down Garden Drive, I rode past two smaller girls playing with sticks. One of them pitched a stick at my bicycle wheel as I passed, and it bounced harmlessly off. Angered that she was trying somehow to flip me off my bike, I skidded to a stop. The girls backed away. I reached to the road, grasped a medium-sized rock, and threw it at them. To my dismay, I hit one of the girls in the leg! She screamed. Frightened by what I had done, I mounted my bike and sped for home. Mom and Dad weren't home yet, I realized. So I turned abruptly into the Wallaces' driveway. I stashed the bike behind their house, then crept under one of the bushes in their front yard to watch the street. Beads of sweat trickled down my forehead. Flies buzzed nearby, but I stayed in hiding. Soon a car with that girl – and her father – raced past, headed for my house. I stayed put. A few minutes later, the same car went past the other way, slower this time. In a few minutes, when I judged the coast to be clear, I retrieved my bike and rode home.

I crept into my house with a sense of relief, but no sooner had I come in the front door than the phone rang.

"Hello," I squeaked with a trembling voice.

"Mrs. Kasting?" *He thinks he's talking to my mother!*

"Yes."

"Isn't your boy the one who delivers the papers around here?"

"Oh, no," I lied. "You must mean Mike Green. He lives up on Epler Avenue somewhere." I hung up.

A few minutes later my parents came home. They could see something strange in my eyes. "What's wrong?" Dad asked in a way that could not be put off. The story came out, and I was in tears. I hadn't really thought I would hit the girl, just scare her. Would her father come to get me?

"Well, you know what you have to do," Dad said matter-of-factly. A feeling of dread rose in my throat as we got into the car and drove to her house. I walked like a robot toward the front door. Walking the plank! Taking my place in front of the firing squad! It was the worst moment of my young life when that door opened. There was the girl, with her father towering behind her. "I'm…sorry…" my voice quivered and tears ran down my cheeks. But there was no triumph on the girl's face, and there was no anger, only pain, in the father's voice as he looked at me. "She has hemophilia," he told us soberly. "If that rock had cut her, she might have bled to death. You'd better stop and think about what you're doing." His words were a mirror held before my face, showing me the danger of giving vent to my temper.

The incident brought a life lesson from my father: God hates sin and makes us face it. Wrong must be confessed and the consequences accepted. But there was a compassionate note included. My father's presence beside me modeled how God was there, helping me tell the truth and speak the fearful, but necessary apology. I learned confession and absolution there on the front porch of a neighbor's home. Dad embodied the sternness and steadiness of God's grace.

In after years, as I stood at the door of someone new or someone with reason to be angry at me, I was able to walk forward and face it. I learned to do it on my paper route.

HAIL TO SOUTHPORT HIGH

Southport High School was a huge complex on a vast tract of acreage eight miles south of Indianapolis. Its red brick buildings were solid and Midwestern, formed into an immense two-story 'L.' To the east was a spacious parking lot where the marching band drilled on summer evenings. Further east, across Shelby Street, was a concrete-walled football stadium and cinder track. To the south were baseball fields and tennis courts. To the west, across an asphalt lot where a fleet of yellow buses loaded students every afternoon, was a rambling wooded estate where our cross country teams stretched their legs.

More than 2500 students roamed Southport's tiled hallways and chattered beside its beige lockers. In the anteroom outside the ample cafeteria, boys would match pennies after lunch as they waited for their teachers to pick them up for the next class. The school had a wood shop, an auditorium, and a swimming pool. But the school's pride and joy was its gymnasium, a monument to Hoosier Hysteria. Many a university might have envied this blue-windowed sports palace, which boasted more than 7100 seats. Blackie Braden's Cardinals played to capacity crowds and did not disappoint. Louie Dampier, who later became all-time leading scorer in the American Basketball Association, was our brightest star.

But it is the teachers who remain most vividly in my memory. Since I aspired to be a pastor in a denomination with a German heritage, it behooved me to take as much German as I could. Anna Megnis, my German teacher for three years, was an immigrant from Latvia. Her husband, pressed into service in the Russian army, had been swallowed up in the maelstrom of World War II and never heard from again. Periodically, she would digress from her lesson to reminisce how she and her children made a desperate flight to freedom 'with the bombs falling all around.' For all the drama of her life, she was a simple teacher with a woodenly predictable routine. Every day began with the same exchange:

"*Guten Tag, Klasse.*" (Good day, class.)
"*Guten Tag, Frau Lehrerin.*" (Good day, Mrs. Teacher.)
"*Wie geht es ihnen, heute?*" (How are you today?)
"*Danke, gut. Und ihnen?*" (Good, thank you. And you?)

Mrs. Megnis, having learned of my vocational plans, showed a special interest in me. She urged me into the German Club, rewarded me with performance ribbons, and wrote a saying in my yearbook by Friedrich

Nietzsche, one of the God-is-dead philosophers, as a sample of the pride and unbelief she thought I might encounter later along the way.

I was advised to take Latin too. So in addition to three years of German, I took three years of Latin. My two Latin teachers were memorable characters. Elsa Majors was an older woman with faded orange hair and an oft-discussed slip strap that tumbled out of her blouse onto her bare arm. She kept track of our recitations in a book, and I made sure to hold my hand in the air every day to translate at least one section. My other Latin instructor, Miss Mary Reed, hobbled down the classroom's rows with her wooden leg creaking and swinging. She stared at us with a walleyed gaze and liked to remind us that since we could not tell where she was looking, we should be careful to behave. "And my name is MISS Reed!" she puffed. "Don't call me Mrs. Reed until I meet a man named Mr. Reed and marry him!" It was said with a smile – her favorite joke about her spinsterhood.

Mr. Routh, my social studies teacher, strode to class each morning, face and shoulders jutting forward, all business. In class he barked out the lesson in a way that generated fear in us. But there was one redeeming feature in his method. He posted test scores on the hallway bulletin board outside after each exam. All class sections were posted side by side so that one could compare his performance, not only against his own class, but against every other section too. I found the challenge exhilarating. I came to know my competitors: Dale Sidebottom, Carol Miller, Bill Parmenter, and Suzanne Rodebaugh, a girl in whom I would later take special interest.

Richard Dart, our economics teacher, had a round face, an even rounder belly, sandy hair cut in a burr, glasses, and an old Civil War uniform he occasionally wore to class after his club had re-enacted a battle. He also sponsored the chess club. I had just begun to learn the game at home, reading and replaying games from Fred Reinfeld's *Chess in a Nutshell*. The club provided the game experience I craved. Mr. Dart posted a chess ladder and urged us to come in before school to challenge each other. One was allowed to challenge one or two spots above, and if victorious, take that person's spot on the ladder and move him down.

Tom Hathaway was a biology teacher who doubled as track and cross-country coach. He was boyishly handsome, with dark hair, a cheerful smile, and a perpetually hoarse voice. My track involvement began by accident after my P.E. teacher noticed that I had done well in the broad jump skill test. At his urging, I stayed after school one day to try out in front of Coach Hathaway. Since he was well stocked with jumpers, he asked me to try a 220 and then a 440. "We'll find a place for you," he encouraged. A few days later, I saw some hurdles left on the track and I leaped over a few for fun. Coach Hathaway noticed. "Do that again," he suggested. From then on, I was a hurdler. My initial races were embarrassing. Competitors pulled away with ease, while I lurched clumsily over the hurdles. But Coach Hathaway was perpetually positive. His approach was not to compare me with other runners, but to give me a challenging, reachable goal for myself. Near the end of the season, after I had run my best time of 16.4 seconds, coach smiled at me and said, "Next year 15.5!" It was a prophecy both inviting and remote, like a mountain to climb. Spurred by his optimism, I did extra work over the winter in the gym, and my times dropped. In the very last race of my high school career, in the sectionals, I ran 15.5. It wasn't enough to place – I had finished fifth – but Coach Hathaway greeted me as if I were state champ. "You did it!" he shouted. I felt like shouting too.

High school years provided my first small opportunities to practice the kind of speaking and praying that is expected of pastors. These came courtesy of teachers who learned of my career plans and opened tiny doors for me.

Chuck Robbins was a math teacher who doubled as football coach. He was built like a tank and had a friendly fire in his eyes. Everyone in his classes was a 'sportfan.' Robbins arranged that on the team's road trip to Jeffersonville, I would be an impromptu chaplain. We stopped at a restaurant for a postgame meal. Coach Robbins turned to me with a grin and said, "Michael, my boy, how about you say grace for us?" With my heart in my throat and forty football players listening, I stumbled through my first public prayer.

Lois Lichtsinn, a member at my home church, gave me an opportunity of a different sort. As a part of her English class, she structured debates for which students could prepare by reading, then discussing their ideas. One of the subjects often debated within our church body was creation versus evolution. My introduction to serious thinking about that subject had come via the play *Inherit the Wind*, which I had read earlier that year. The play was a portrayal of the Scopes Monkey Trial in which the creationist was made to look decidedly silly by his opponent. Miss Lichtsinn arranged for a class debate on the subject. She assigned me to represent the creationist perspective. My friend Steve Powers was to be spokesman for the evolutionist's point of view. I knew almost nothing of the science behind evolution. That became painfully obvious as we sparred over this complex topic. I was relieved when our debate was over.

Kathleen Ritchie, the speech teacher, provided another venue for speech-making. She assigned speeches to inform, then speeches to persuade. She gave us exercises in extemporaneous speech, with topics handed to us and less than a minute to prepare a few thoughts before addressing the class. It was a useful art to learn.

At mid-year she announced the senior play, *One Foot in Heaven*. I was one of many who auditioned, and I was assigned the role of narrator.

Strangely enough, the play, written by a minister's son named Hartzell Spence, was a kind of preview of my own future. It portrayed the home and church life of a pastor's family – their life in a fishbowl with the congregation watching every move. As narrator, I emerged between scenes to stand alone in the spotlight behind a podium, explaining the joys and sorrows of such a life. There was a sweet sort of terror that I both hungered for and dreaded in that spotlight, the moment when I walked out, blinded by it, unable to see any of the hundreds of people who were watching me, to speak my lines about a pastor who had "One foot in heaven, and one foot on earth, not daring to plant both feet solidly either way…" I would find out later what it was like to live the part.

My life was about to change in a way I had not dreamed as I sat in the front row, center seat, of Mr. Timmons' U. S. History class. Mr. Timmons, a genial Quaker whose mild manner would have made his spiritual forbears proud, sat sweating at his desk before me. Giant wet circles spread from his armpits as he tried to warm us to the Stamp Act and the Dred Scott Decision, but he did not have my full attention.

Behind me sat a girl who did. Her name was Suzanne Rodebaugh – a girl with a round face, a good mind, a sweet smile, and liquid brown eyes. I had chosen the very worst place in the row, squarely in front of her, facing Mr. Timmons, who was squarely in front of me. Like a dial on a compass, I rotated constantly on my seat, turning now and again to whisper to her and fetch a glance at those eyes.

I remembered her as one of several at the top of Mr. Routh's test charts, so I saw her from that angle as a competitor. But as the weeks passed, I discovered more. She had a pleasant manner, interested, but not overbearing. Then came a new revelation. Early in December of my senior year, I was working at one end of the gym making decorations for the Christmas Dance. At the other end, the school choir was rehearsing for the annual *Messiah* sing they did jointly with the nearby college choir. Suddenly, across the gym floor and up the stairs where I knelt by my poster board, there floated the angelic tones of a lovely soprano voice. I was suddenly Ulysses tied to the mast, listening to the sirens' cry with unstopped ear! It was Sue, singing as I had never heard another sing.

Now in Mr. Timmons' class, I was increasingly drawn to her. But what did she think of me? Not until years later did she reveal that she, on her part, noted a significant hole in my knit shirt. Fortunately, that wasn't all. Mr. Timmons was assigned a student teacher whose opinions roused in me some primal fighting instinct, and I stayed to debate with him after class. Unnoticed by me as I sparred with him, Sue stood near the door, doing some admiring of her own. She too was interested, but knew her manners well enough to wait. It was the boy who was supposed to take the initiative.

In February I finally invited her to accompany me to (what else?) a basketball game. Southport was playing dreaded rival Columbus. While the Cardinals got trounced on the playing floor, our more momentous encounter was in the stands and then afterwards at the Southern Circle Drive-In Restaurant. We ordered hamburgers and fries. Sue, fearful that I would regard her as dull, decided to let me know that she was both exciting and unpredictable. Waiting for a moment when my back was turned, she poured her remaining ice cubes down my shirt. It was an unforgettable first date.

Sue's parents, Myron and Gerry, mirrored my own in some ways. Nearly the same age, they were also faithful churchgoers and happily married. Myron was a funeral director at the Jordan Funeral Home in Indianapolis. Gerry was a stay-at-home mom who had done some teaching and was a great cook. I discovered that Sue was the beneficiary of her parents' musical abilities. Myron had considered becoming a concert pianist before marriage necessitated his taking up work at a mortuary. He had been the organist at the Cadle Tabernacle in Indianapolis and was often heard on their radio broadcasts. Gerry and her mother, 'Granny' Gilliatt, were both fine singers. I admired Sue's mind and voice, and I was increasingly drawn to her. Now and again I accompanied her and her father when they provided music at a wedding.

Early that summer we rode home from the senior picnic in the back seat of our friends' car, groggy from lack of sleep. Sue sat cradling my head in her lap, stringing my hair as her granny had often done to her. Looking up at her, I said, softly, "*Te amo*" (Latin for "I love you"). "Tell me in English," she asked. So I did.

Not all was moonlight and roses. We visited one another's churches. That provoked occasional theological disagreements. I poked fun at her teetotaler convictions. "Haven't you read that Jesus made wine?" I asked. Besides enduring my pompous observations, she saw me make some astonishingly uncouth choices. One occurred on a picnic at Brown County State Park, where I accidentally rolled our hot dogs off a grill into the dirt. Waste a hot dog? No siree! I retrieved the rag from under the front seat, wiped the dogs off, and put them back on the grill. Sue was mortified. This was worse by far than having holes in my shirt.

On that same trip home, as we drove north on a two-lane road, the left front tire blew, pulling the car across the center line as I frantically pressed the brake pedal. No one was coming the other way. The tire was duly changed and we made it home.

Protecting grace had shielded us on the road. It was one of several moments that made us both feel that ours was a relationship 'meant to be.'

From that summer on, we had marriage on our minds, but marriage would have to wait on a long stretch of schooling for each of us.

PART TWO

College and Seminary

(1964-1972)

INTO THE SYSTEM

Young adults, like rockets, must be launched if they're to accomplish anything. My launch date arrived in the fall of 1964. On a sunny Saturday, my parents drove me to Ann Arbor, Michigan, where I entered 'The System,' the unofficial name given to the network of schools founded by the Lutheran Church-Missouri Synod to train its pastors and teachers. Concordia College, opened the year before in Ann Arbor, was one of eight junior colleges that fed students into a seminary or teachers' college.

Concordia's lovely campus hugged the shore of the Huron River. At the center of the campus rose an exquisite pyramid-shaped chapel topped with a slender spire and cross. Its windows formed a narrow band of stained glass, its pulpit featured a burning bush sculpted in metal, and its voice box was a modest, but adequate Schlicker pipe organ. Around the chapel in a semi-circle lay the academic buildings. At opposite ends of the campus were dormitories named for great people of the Bible. On the west were Hannah, Esther, Ruth, and Miriam for the women. The men lived at the east end in Paul, Timothy, Stephen, Barnabas, Titus, and Silas. Nestled in a grove of trees was a mansion dubbed 'The Manor House,' once occupied by the people who had donated this land to the church. Across Geddes Road were two farmhouses with additional housing, athletic fields, open acreage, and a subdivision up the hill for faculty families.

I was assigned to Stephen Dorm. My roommate was Louis Kief, a pre-ministerial student from Michigan. Louis was cleanly and courteous to a fault, the perfect counterpoint to my slovenliness. Now that I was away from home, I discovered the inconvenient necessities of laundry and cleaning. I did as little of these as I could manage. As the weeks rolled by, dust balls accumulated under the bed and rings grew around my collars. Saintly, selfless Louie would often be left to sweep and dust when he couldn't stand it anymore. Our suitemates were sophomores Keith Lonsberry and Fred Jordan, who had roomed here the year before. Most of the time, it seemed, they were hunched together over a cribbage board attired in T-shirts. Now and then they labored in a frenzy over their Greek translation of 'Polycrap' (so they had renamed *The Martyrdom of Polycarp*) and warned us of the rigors we would face in Professor Nissen's Greek class.

The daily routine of college life was a dramatic departure from the uniformity of the high school schedule. Meals were on my own, and I had to wake myself on time if I wanted to eat at all in the morning. Classes met on an irregular basis, so I taped a schedule to my wall and carried another folded in my pocket. There was a morning chapel service daily. A professor led, a student played the organ, and a sizable proportion of the student body attended. Free time between classes was spent either in the library or in the dorm, where I studied religiously. Late afternoons were devoted to athletic practices, the evenings to more study.

My professors were all male, and possessed of a variety of personalities and teaching styles. Wilbert 'Pappy' Rusch stalked the classroom with a shuffling gait, moustache twitching, as he directed us to dissect our *platyhelminthes* in invertebrate zoology class. I earned his wrath when I tried to wheedle another point on a test. I had written 'culex' for a question whose required answer was 'culex mosquito.'

"But that's what I meant," I told him. "I knew the answer."

He wheeled on me. "I can't read your mind, Kasting!"

For Principles of Biblical Interpretation, I had Willie Hassold, a dwarf-like man with a crew cut who loved to squeeze his face into a massive wink. He was a single man who cared for his elderly father at his apartment. Hassold frequented the dorms and spoke with students, seeking our trust and urging us to pour out our struggles as he listened.

The most formidable of my professors was Eugene Nissen, dubbed 'Ho Nous' (Greek for 'The Brain') by his students. A fortyish man with wavy hair and piercing eyes behind his heavy glasses, he was our bridge into the fascinating world of New Testament Greek. The first day we learned the entire alphabet: "alpha, beta, gamma, delta, epsilon, zeta, eta, theta…" I drilled it into my brain, hungry for the challenge. The second day we opened our red, hardcover Greek New Testaments, purchased for $2.25 in the bookstore. Gospel of John, first chapter. *En archee een ho logos...* "In the beginning was the Word…" It was only the second day in class and already we were translating the Bible! I was enthralled. Nissen had the unique practice of administering take-home tests, which we took on our honor and then returned to a manila pocket on his office door – vocabulary lists, declensions, principal parts of verbs, and more. There were nine in all, and no one cheated. 'The Brain' was sure to find out.

Sue and I stayed connected by letter. Trips to the mailbox were rewarded several times a week with envelopes smelling of perfume, bearing postage affixed upside- down and coded messages on the flap (S.W.A.K , I.L.Y, I. M. Y!). My own letters back were less frequent but no less passionate. Long-distance phone calls were viewed by both of us as a luxury too expensive to be indulged regularly.

In one of her letters, Sue mentioned a set of books she had been reading by an author new to me. "It's a space trilogy," she told me, "by a writer named C. S. Lewis." Lewis, an Oxford don who had been converted from atheism to Christianity, had died the same day as President Kennedy, but with far less fanfare. In due time I acquired and began to read *Out of the Silent Planet*, the first book in the trilogy. I was fascinated, and read on through all three. Lewis had the ability to do what no other writer had done

– make eternal life an almost tangible reality to me. He addressed my fear of death by opening a door through which I could see and feel the life on the other side. More than any professor, or any other author, it was Lewis who became the mentor of my intellectual life.

One of the primary differences college life presented to me was life without fences. I knew where my boundaries were, but my parents were no longer the border guards. Such accountability as I had was to my conscience. My conscience was to be tested, because I had been launched into a world more vulgar and openly wicked than I had anticipated at a church school.

Some other students did not, apparently, have the strict conscience I had. Our suitemates cursed amidst their cribbage games. I found a six-pack of beer cooling in the toilet tank. "Isn't that against the rules?" I asked naively. My suitemates laughed uproariously. Worse were the rumors of sexual encounters between students living in the farmhouses across Geddes Road. Several were later expelled, proving the rumor true.

In my second year, I signed up to be a dorm proctor, a student who represented the administration and enforced campus rules. I was to work closely with the faculty residence counselor who lived in a home nearby. Being a proctor was a position of honor I readily took on. My growing sense of pride was being served.

The position furnished me a delicious taste of authority. For the first time in my life, I had an almost parental power over my peers. The proctor was allowed to make dorm cleanup assignments, organize the dorm schedule, and mete out punishments for infractions. The ultimate punishment was to confine someone to quarters for an evening or an entire weekend, and I was not shy about doing that to students who seemed rebellious. In the process, I learned three truths:

a) Students are exceptionally clever at hiding their misbehavior,

b) Students with a rigid proctor love to rile him intentionally, and

c) Proctors who enforce the rules too rigorously will pay for it.

Breaking the rules became a game for the men in my dorm, who soon discovered how easily perturbed I became. Answering a knock on my door one morning triggered a booby-trap that pulled boxes of tin cans down with a crash into the dorm's central area floor. I returned from a weekend away to a stack of Polaroid pictures of students sliding down the stairs on an ironing board. Toward the end of the spring, my charges had their grandest triumph. One evening I looked up from my desk to see my dorm-mates sauntering into my room, smiling broadly. Swiftly they grabbed me, stripped my bed down to the springs, and carried both me and my bed outside. There they tied me to the bed frame with cords. Thus immobilized, I was carried in the dark on their shoulders to the Manor House. They stopped short at the pond. Out into the midst of the water they bore me, like Israel's priests bearing the ark into the Jordan. They lowered me ceremoniously into the chilly waters of the pond, which left just enough clearance for me to breathe as I held my head up off the bedsprings, struggling to get free while they laughed. I spluttered for a bit. Then I laughed too. I was taking myself way too seriously. Launched out of my childhood, I had made splashdown in a different world.

I checked my appointment time on the bulletin board in the music building. There was plenty of time. Too much time! I paced nervously, clearing my throat and hoping something respectable would come out. I was trying out for the college choir.

My experience was limited. Our three-part choir in grade school had sung easy hymns learned by rote. More useful were my Sundays in church, seated by Dad, listening to him sing bass and getting a feel for it, even though I couldn't read music.

Down the hall a door swung open and a student exited. I was next. Doctor Paul Foelber, the director, welcomed me to the rehearsal room, put me at ease, and invited me to stand by the piano. He was short and trim, with a pleasant, intelligent face. On the music stand was a hymnal, opened to a familiar hymn. He had me sing it, melody line first, then the bass line. My voice felt uncertain and pitifully weak. "That's fine," said Foelber. "Now let's do this one." Another hymn, this time with the tenor part, which I struggled to follow. That was all. He told me that results would be posted next day on the bulletin board if I wanted to check. I was downcast. It had not gone well. But the next day I saw to my surprise that I had made the choir as a second bass.

Doctor Foelber inspired awe from the very first rehearsal. Everything from the neatness of his suit and tie to the sternness of his gaze communicated competence. His discipline became our discipline. He never settled for a so-so rendering of any piece. It must be crisp, on pitch, and delivered with energy, whether piano or fortissimo.

Our diet of music was heavily classical. As Lutherans, we were bound to learn our share of J. S. Bach, including the entire motet *'Christ Lag in Todesbanden,'* accompanied by a string ensemble. We also learned a hauntingly beautiful setting of *'Behold a Branch is Growing'* by Hugo Distler, the *'Our Father'* by Alexander Gretchaninoff, and pieces by Heinrich Schuetz and Hans Leo Hassler. Every tour stop would begin with Hassler's *'Cantate Domino,'* a Latin version of Psalm 96. Almost everything was to be sung a cappella.

Our first tour, at winter quarter break, was to Florida. On a snowy Michigan morning we loaded our tour bus, stowed risers, instruments, and robes in the cargo hold, and we were off. On the way south we made a single concert stop at a church in Cincinnati before re-boarding the bus for the all-night drive to Florida. My parents were in the audience, Dad recording our presence on his trusty camera. To be part of such music was so emotionally moving that I sang at times with tears in my eyes and a lump in my throat.

The days that followed took us down to Miami, then back up through Tampa-St. Petersburg. The routine became familiar: a long bus ride, punctuated by spontaneous singing as we rode, arrival in the afternoon, unloading and setup, a sound check and directions for processing, then supper together, robing and warm-up in the basement as we heard the concert-goers arriving and the floorboards creaking overhead, a prayer time together, and then the concert. Some nights went better than others. On one occasion, the boy who sounded our note with his pitch-pipe had forgotten it, and I was momentarily alarmed. But Dr. Foelber, gifted with perfect pitch, simply hummed the right note for each piece.

The next year's tour was closer to home – a circuit through Midwestern towns large and small like Jackson, Michigan, and Defiance, Ohio. On this trip I roomed with Rob Drews, a friend I had made in my first day on campus the year before. Our favorite stop was a home with a ping-pong table. We played until long after our host family had gone to bed.

Sixteen years later, shortly after I had come to Akron, Ohio, to serve as pastor of Concordia Lutheran Church, I was rummaging through a four-drawer file when I happened across a folder marked 'choir tour.' Naturally, I had to have a closer look. Inside were lists of names on yellowed paper, students to be paired up with congregation members. "So they hosted a choir once too," I mused, looking at the names, listed two by two. A tingling sensation went down my back, for I recognized many of them. Then I saw my own pairing:

14. Robert Drews and Michael Kasting

We had been here to this very church, but I had not remembered it. I went back into the sanctuary, down the long, red-carpeted aisle. There in front I imagined the choir, standing poised on our risers. I sang here with the choir. Now I'm the pastor! How little we know what's in store as we march down the aisles of our lives.

High school years had given me a taste for and the thrill of athletic endeavor, but it was not until college that I learned what St. Paul meant by 'pummeling the body.' During college years I was a three-sport athlete, an exercise in discipline I needed badly.

Cross country, coached by Walt Harting, came first each autumn. I found it a grueling sport. The physical challenge was considerable. The weather grew colder, wetter, and windier as the season progressed. It was not unusual to run in 40-degree temperatures with a stinging rain. Even in our sweat clothes we shivered as we walked the various courses, observing the placement of directional flags ("Red is LEFT, white is RIGHT, and blue is THROUGH"). Then the dreaded words, "Runners, remove your sweats!" There was a near total absence of fan support. Except for a smattering of cheers at the start and finish, the races were run in silence, the only sound being the rhythmic thumping of spiked shoes on turf or gravel. There were occasional surprises, like the startling eruption of a pheasant from the bushes, or a sudden tumble over an exposed tree root. There was plenty of time to think. *Why am I doing this? I must be crazy!* I even toyed with faking an injury so that I might drop out of a race. Of the three sports in which I participated, cross country proved to be the most like daily life.

Fall yielded to winter and cross country yielded to basketball. In a high school of 2500 students, I had not even made the first cut. Here at a small junior college, I made the team as a reserve forward. Coach Dave Wenzel's optimism was a necessary starting point for us, because we faced some high-caliber athletes who were biding their time in the junior college hoop world waiting for admission to bigger schools like Eastern Michigan.

One wintry night, after a home game, the students scattered for a holiday weekend. Everyone but me, it seemed. I trudged to the dorm across a nearly-deserted campus in swirling snow. Cold and lonely, I called home and whined like a stray puppy. I went to bed feeling sorry for myself. The next thing I knew, I was being wakened by a soft kiss on my cheek from Sue. There she was, and Dad and Mom beside her. They had driven all night to surprise me. It was a gift I never forgot.

Winter thawed into spring, and basketball gave way to the year's final sport, track and field. Here at least I had high school experience. To my chagrin, I learned that high hurdles in college were three inches higher. But the conditioning I had received in the two prior sports gave me a head start. After being drubbed in basketball, it was a pleasure to inflict some defeats on rival schools.

The following year, at the senior college level, I eliminated basketball from the cycle. Studies had become too demanding. Cross country was now four miles instead of three. Track was a special challenge, for the campus in Ft. Wayne had no track at all, and only eight men went out for the sport, which meant we all had to do as many events as possible. I wound up in seven events, often stopping between events to lie motionless on the grass, retching and exhausted. Though few in number, we managed a conference championship.

So why did I pummel my body and subdue it for those four years? My ribbons and clippings lie fading in a storage box these days. The world did not long remember our moments of glory. But I remember. I learned I was capable of more than I had imagined because I endured a discipline. I learned that there can be satisfaction even in defeat and that a prize requires sacrifice.

The memory of those college days proved to be a model for the race I am still running year after year.

THE PROMISED LAND

My second stop in 'the System' was Concordia Senior College in Ft. Wayne, Indiana. The campus was a feast for the eyes. Eero Saarinen, the world-renowned Finnish architect, had designed every building and every diamond-shaped brick to direct the eye upward to heaven. Each building had an A-frame roof line. Highest of all was the magnificent Kramer Chapel. Photographers came to capture the campus's beauty, mirrored in the man-made lake beside it.

Beautiful it was, but lonely. Ringed by acres of field and forest, it had an insulated, austere feel that was heightened in winter months by frigid winds that swept the campus. But its loneliest aspect was that the college was all male. The sight and sound of coeds, which had made Ann Arbor a homey sort of place, was missing here. Like army recruits, many of the men adorned their walls and closets with pin-ups. Women made occasional appearances on campus, but for the most part we lived a monastic existence.

The dorms themselves were not named but simply lettered – A, B, C, and so on. They were arranged into four groupings, each of which got a nickname. I was assigned to Dorm P, and my village was dubbed 'The Promised Land.' The students, funneled in from a wide array of junior colleges and state schools, were largely strangers to me and to each other. In our dorm a contingent of fellows from Portland, Oregon, brought with them an air of craziness. They were perpetually popping corn, strumming guitars and telling jokes.

Our proctor, Mark Hoelter, normally appeared with a pipe in his mouth and was a calming influence. For evening devotions, he liked to lead us through compline (the last order in the monks' daily devotional cycle) with its haunting prayer:

Guide us waking, O Lord, and guard us sleeping, that awake we may watch with Christ and asleep we may rest in peace.

Academic life at Ft. Wayne was a step up in intensity from Ann Arbor. We began the study of Hebrew. Professors Rehm and Spomer introduced us to the 'silent schwa' and the strangely-named tenses – qal, niphal, piel, pual, hiphil, hophal, hithpael. I found it more forbidding than the familiar Greek and Latin. Additionally, each of us at the college had to choose an area of concentration. I chose philosophy since I was fascinated with the history of ideas and because philosophy and theology had points of tangence. Not a few of the great thinkers we studied (Aquinas, Augustine, and Kierkegaard) were both philosophers and theologians. But the readings assigned were often dusty dry and mind-numbing. I could plow through forty pages of an assignment with my mind on auto-pilot and remember almost nothing.

The library became both a place of study and a place of part-time work. My supervisor was an unforgettable person named Margaret Hermes, a single, friendly woman in her fifties with her hair pulled back in a bun. Diligent in her responsibilities, she expected the same in her workers. Each day's task list was typed neatly on a card and tacked to a bulletin board. My assignments were to do shelf-reading and to run sets of book cards on the compact mini-graph machine for distribution to trays according to author, title, and subject.

Miss Hermes fit no customary mold, and she was blithely unaware of the jokes some students made about her spinsterhood and her buxom frame. One day she threw me a curve.

"Would you like to see my knockers?"

"I…I guess so."

She invited me into her office and, turning, gestured toward her wall, where there was a large framed collection of door knockers made of brass, silver, and wood on a mounted wall box with a red velvet backing. Each one was identified with its type and date on a metal plate beneath. I breathed a sigh of relief.

Students went off campus to worship at churches in the Ft. Wayne area. I joined a team of students who taught Sunday school class at a small, impoverished church. Our organizer and encourager was classmate Hank Simon. That classroom, the tiny chairs, the leaflets like I had once received, and the children with their tattered clothes and distractible eyes, seemed light years removed from the theological intricacies of the college. It was a salutary dose of reality.

I continued singing in the choir at Ft. Wayne. Director Herb Nuechterlein (dubbed 'Nicky' by the students) had decided to make a brief drama part of the pre-concert presentation to church youth groups while we toured. I volunteered to participate in the playlet, entitled *'Are You Joking, Jeremiah?'* I played Jeremiah, a youth chosen by God to be a prophet to the nations. In each scene, my cries to God were answered by a smart-aleck kids' chorus that spoke the world's cynicism. Finally, God answered to comfort me and remind them that He is still at work in the world.

Sue and I, meanwhile, entered a more serious mode in our courtship. Ft. Wayne was far closer to Indianapolis than Ann Arbor, and my grandfather Harry had sold me his 1951 Pontiac for $100. I had wheels! As often as I could manage it, I drove the 130 miles home for a weekend. On two occasions, she came north on the bus and I picked her up at the town's ancient Greyhound depot.

We wrestled mightily with the issue of chastity. The calling of our hormones pitted themselves against the very strong scruples implanted by our parents and reinforced by our loyalty to the Lord. We talked about our commitment to abstinence, but the flesh put up a mighty fight. For the first time, I experienced prayer as a battle, and I began to get a sense of what Saint Peter meant when he counseled resistance against Satan. An unexpected ally in the struggle was dorm residence counselor, professor Milford Brelje, a veteran pastor who listened long and sympathetically to me. He reaffirmed the need to observe boundaries, but he did not condemn my longings. I was experiencing pastoral care – as a recipient. He became a model of what I hoped I could do for others later.

The Ft. Wayne years brought experiences that enabled me to sharpen the Spirit's sword, my use of God's Word. One was a two-year stint as copy editor of *Triangle*, the student journal. I evaluated the initial copy turned in for publication and made recommendations for revision. With the role came a growing desire to do some writing myself, resulting in articles on Lutheran-Catholic relationships, a response to the Black Manifesto, and two experimental orders of worship. Another experience was the opportunity to do some public Scripture reading. One memorable moment came at Redeemer Lutheran Church in Indianapolis, where I was asked to read for an evening service while some of my peers watched. I finished the reading, congratulating myself on how articulate I had been, then promptly tripped and fell on my face as I descended the chancel steps. There must have been laughter in heaven.

In that moment and other more serious ones, God was opening my eyes to some of the less-than-noble motives at work in my desire to serve in the pastoral ministry. The clearest and most painful of those insights was delivered by my roommate. I had begun my senior year rooming with Lane Seitz, who was my opposite in several ways. I was dark-haired and slim. He was a chunky redhead. He was a humble fellow who was neither an athlete nor a notable scholar. I, on the other hand, saw myself as both. After a few months together, there came an afternoon when Lane asked, "Can I talk to you a minute?"

I sat opposite him on my bed, unaware of the emotion that filled his chest that day. "So what's on your mind?"

"I want a different roommate," he told me simply.

It was a lightning bolt. "Why? What's wrong?"

"Because," he spoke slowly, measuring his words, "I never met anyone so arrogant as you." As soon as he said it, I knew it was the truth.

It was the first time anyone had named my besetting sin - the sin of pride, which C. S. Lewis called 'the great sin.' Lane had drawn back the curtain I had carefully draped over my own eyes. For the first time, I saw myself as others must have seen me all along – a pompous know-it-all who had to prove himself right by showing others they were wrong. It was the attitude that had fueled my debates with the student teacher in high school. It was the reason I argued for a better mark on Pappy Rusch's zoology test. It was behind the repeated religious conversations with Sue in our courtship.

It would have been wise to sit with Lane to listen, to let him paint the picture of what he had seen in me. Instead, I left the room emotionally numb, simply seeking to escape. We never had another talk, and I lost an opportunity to hear the full explanation of a brother's rebuke.

In the days that followed, I walked the campus in a cloud of shame and gloom. I entered the chapel and sat quietly in the dark, pondering the enormity of what he had told me. How many of my classmates could see it but had said nothing to me? On the sidewalk, I lowered my eyes as I passed others. A veil had been lifted, exposing my motives. I saw many of my behaviors in a new, unpleasant light.

Even my call into the ministry was colored by arrogance. One reason I wanted to be a pastor, I could now see, was because I wanted a position of distinction, of honor, of respect. Who had more of that in the church than the pastor? My ego had hijacked my calling. Where was the servant's heart so necessary for this vocation? It was the opening salvo of a quiet but deadly conflict in me. God had gone to war with my pride.

EYES NEWLY OPENED

The broken glass crunched under my tires as I came to a stop at the Division Street intersection. While I waited for the light to turn, I felt the stares of the black men who lounged against the utility poles or squatted on the steps of the liquor store. *What are you doing here, white boy?*

It was mid-June of 1967. A few months before, I had sat in the student commons at the senior college listening intently to Walt Reiner, the director of Prince of Peace Volunteers, describe a summer ministry opportunity in a Chicago ghetto called Cabrini. A joint Roman Catholic-Lutheran endeavor, its primary focus was to teach remedial reading and math to grade-schoolers. Volunteers would be hosted by black families in the neighborhood for seven weeks. I sat, Isaiah-like, hearing the voice: "Whom shall I send, and who will go for us?" Without so much as five minutes' reflection, without any discussion with my parents or friends, I raised my hand (or did God raise it?). "Here am I. Send me."

Now here I was, a trembling 20-year-old from the suburbs, plunked down in the heart of a black ghetto. The Cabrini-Green housing project on Chicago's near north side was almost a city in itself, with 15,000 people living in more than 3600 apartments in row houses and high rise buildings. I felt I was entering a human anthill.

My first night in Cabrini was spent in the attic of a Roman Catholic rectory. It was a strange sensation after growing up Lutheran and learning about the tangled hostilities between Lutherans and Catholics after the Reformation. Catholics were on 'the other side,' weren't they? Yet here I was sleeping under the erstwhile enemy's roof! It was a strange and wonderful phenomenon.

I was also a suburban boy planted in the heart of a huge city. Lying awake in the dark, jarred from sleep by the noises in the street below, I could hear harsh cries, the sounds of a bottle breaking, feet running. I shuddered as I recalled the dark eyes at the intersection, watching me. This was an alien world with its littered streets, its barred storefronts, and its omnipresent graffiti. What folly had possessed me to volunteer for this?

The next day came orientation. The project involved about three dozen volunteers, most of whom were Lutheran ministerial students like me, along with some Roman Catholic students (seminarians and postulant nuns), and a few people from the community and local charitable agencies. Walt Reiner was there, as were a couple of priests and pastors who assisted him. We met in the Community House, a school building that had become a community center. By the door was a poster that read:

*If you're not part of the solution,
you're part of the problem.*

My tiny piece of the solution would be teaching a class of grade school boys. Aside from Sunday School classes in Ft. Wayne, I had done no other teaching, nor taken any education theory or practicum courses. An older nun, a grizzled classroom veteran, gave us some basic directions and simple lesson plans, helped us assemble our materials, and shared some strategies for getting acquainted. Each evening we were to debrief and plan the next day's lesson.

After supper it was time to meet our host families. I bundled my suitcase and sleeping bag into my car and headed down Cambridge Street. The growing darkness made it difficult to distinguish the numbers above the pale green doors on the row houses. I was looking for '844,' the address of the Whitaker family.

As I approached the door, I felt squeezed, oppressed by my surroundings. These houses were more like barracks, one side of the street mirroring the other. They were squat, grey buildings, double-storied, with cement steps jutting out like swollen tongues every few yards. There were no trees. Except for the house number, each door, each plain window, was like the next. *I'm going to live here?*

I knocked. Momentarily, the door swung open to reveal an angular black youth who returned my sheepish smile. "You must be Mike!" I nodded awkwardly and entered. At the bottom of the steps were two younger boys with eyes wide as saucers, and next to them a largish woman in a brown-and-white checked dress. She began the introductions. Hugh, the eldest, had greeted me at the door. Norman, round-faced and plump, wearing an irrepressible grin, was the middle son. Demetrius (Meetchie), the youngest, had an impish face and was scrawny by comparison. They were so eager that I burst out laughing, and that broke the ice. "My name is Mae," my hostess said softly, leading me to the bedroom that was to be mine. The only other bedroom was occupied by the three boys. I realized she had given up her room for me. "Where will you sleep?" I asked her, and she pointed to the couch. "I don't mind," was all she said.

The boys followed me like puppies and watched me unpack. The questions began.

"Are you married yet?"

"No, not yet."

"Why do you have so much hair on your legs?"

I smiled. "I guess that's how God wanted it."

Norman, ever mindful of the next mealtime, wanted to know, "Do you like Puffa Puffa Rice?"

Mae watched amused. "Those three gonna wear you out!" she said with a shake of her head.

The next morning when I set out for the Community House, I was flanked by Norman and Demetrius, who introduced me to the neighborhood kids, winning me an acceptance I would not have had otherwise. When I arrived at my classroom on the second floor, I found a group of eight boys awaiting me.

What does one do with 10-year-old boys bursting with energy? They will not sit still, I soon learned. Each day was a test of wits and wills. Read. Have a chalkboard relay. Recite numbers or the alphabet. Take a potty break. Make a collage (and clean Elmer's Glue off pants and the floor). Tell Reginald he cannot go to the bathroom again since he was just there ten minutes ago. Reginald pouts for twenty minutes. Referee a fight. Play a game. Repeat as necessary. The bell mercifully sounds and we say our goodbyes. What in the world am I going to do tomorrow? I discovered how little I knew about teaching.

Each day was an eye-opener. In addition to the instruction, I was to meet the families of the boys, most of whom lived not in row houses but in the mammoth 15-story high rises north of the Community House. The projects teemed with children, and I was astonished at how street-wise even the youngest seemed to be. They told me matter-of-factly how a small girl had been killed just days earlier by a pop bottle dropped on her head by some unknown hand many stories above. They amazed me with their ability to entertain themselves with discarded popsicle sticks and bike tires.

One day little George Cowan brought me a note written in crayon on a half-sheet of lined paper:

We had a fire last night. Our apartment burned and mostly all our clothes burned up too. George won't be able to come to school for a while.

The note from George's mother was simple and direct, and George stared at me impassively as I read it – no tears, no show of emotion. It was just another pothole in the bumpy road of life in the projects. Our volunteers coordinated a gathering of clothes for the family.

As the weeks passed, my eyes were opened to the joyful possibilities hidden in each day. On a hot afternoon under the Chicago sun, children frolicked in the spray of a leaky fire hydrant. Others gathered around a cart operated by whiskery Mr. Colladay, who sold snow cones and dispensed wisdom with soft whoops of laughter. In the evenings people came out on their tiny stoops to sit in faded lawn chairs and banter. It was the neighborhood's social hour. Later when the three boys had gone to bed, Mae would sit with me to get an account of the day's lessons. She laughed as I described a walking trip a mile east to Lake Michigan, and how the boys in my class loved the silly rhythm song I used, repeating each line after me:

Du-bop-duh-bo…
DU-BOP-DUH-BO!
Re-bop-duh-bay…
RE-BOP-DUH-BAY!

She laughed harder when I told her how, upon arriving to go wading, we had discovered the beach inundated with millions of tiny dead fish (alewives) washed up in heaps and rotting. "All that way you went," she giggled, "and you didn't even get in the water!"

Mae was reticent about her own days, spent cleaning houses in Evanston, a long bus ride north. Back home it was more of the same for her – washing, ironing, meals, bedtime routines. The family received ADC (Aid for Dependent Children) money, and Mae received a small wage. I could see they barely made ends meet. There was no husband in the picture. I never asked what had happened to him. It was humbling to be in the presence of someone so simple, hard-working, and uncomplaining. My eyes were opened to a new view of the poor and to how very much I took for granted in my life.

The three boys educated me. I learned that blacks and whites were more like each other than I had thought. Blacks weren't all naturally rhythmic. They had the same fears and laughed at the same jokes I did. They could even get sunburned, just as I could, Hugh informed me. Week by week the neighborhood felt more like a home, and my neighbors were no longer black, but just people like me.

Sunday mornings were happy times for the Whitakers. After breakfast came a blessed scurrying to wash and dress for church. The boys always seemed to be missing a sock or putting a shirt on backward. There was an occasional yelp as Norman or Meetchie got a solid whack on the bottom. There were no whacks for Hugh. He alone called his mother 'Shug' (short for 'Sugar'). We went together to Holy Family Lutheran Church in Cabrini, a fair but not forbiddingly distant walk. The pastor, Fred Downing, had the respect of Mae and her boys.

Times with other staffers were eye-opening too. After years of observing the Roman Catholic Church from a distance, I now rubbed shoulders with future priests and nuns on a daily basis. One young woman, a novice my age, rode with me to Milwaukee for a staff enrichment weekend. She described to me how, in taking her vow of chastity, she felt she was exchanging marriage to an earthly husband for marriage to Christ. She showed me a ring she called "my wedding ring to Jesus."

I was taking time to reflect on my journey toward pastoral ministry. One evening while sharing some dissatisfaction about the traditional liturgy with a visiting pastor named Fred Reklau, he pulled me up short. "Do you think you can do better? Do you think it's easy preparing a service that can be used by the wide array of people who show up for church? Why don't you give it a try?" So I tried. The result was what I called "A Service of Celebration of Our New Life." Fred and others who read it said it might be fine for young people like me, but not so much for older folks or children. I emerged with a greater respect for the tradition I had received and an awareness of the difficulty of creating widely usable contemporary worship orders. It was easier to criticize than to create.

Suddenly it was over – the hectic Sunday mornings, the affectionate good-night hugs from Norman and Meetchie, the clowning with my class, the talks with Mae. I packed my suitcase into the car, waved good-bye and drove away from a house that had become my house, a black family that had become my family.

I had brought ignorance and some unexamined prejudices with me seven weeks before. I was challenged to look in a new way at people on welfare, at blacks, and at Catholics. I learned that I didn't have all the answers and that wisdom is more than knowledge. I looked in the mirror and saw again my haughtiness. I could see that pastoral ministry would be a complex, frightening, and rewarding profession.

Upon returning home, I wrote Mae a note of thanks. Sometime later there came a letter back. She wrote:

Dear Mike,

Everyone was glad to hear from you. Some of the neighbor had ask if we got a letter from you. We told them as soon as you had time, you would write. Norman still going around with open zipper and not getting any better about his school work. Hugh still being Mr. Know-All. Demetrius still crying and saying give me this and that. I don't think I have change too much. We all miss you and be glad when you have time to come again.

With love always,
The Family

THE SCHOOL FOR CHARACTER

Sunday, June 16, 1968, dawned sunny and warm. Everything was ready for our wedding that afternoon at the University Heights EUB Church across the street from Indiana Central College where Sue had completed her elementary education studies. Dr. Robert Koenig, long-time pastor and friend to the Rodebaugh family, was to officiate. My own pastor, Robert Meier, would assist.

Over several years of courtship, we had come to know one another's families well. I was a frequent guest in the Rodebaugh home and the beneficiary of many a good meal. Myron was a funeral director at G. H. Herrmann mortuary and he regaled us with stories sometimes poignant and sometimes funny about his work there. He and Gerry were kind-hearted people and patient in caring for Granny, widowed by her husband's sudden heart attack years before.

Sue and I were more than ready for marriage, we thought. Though both only 21 years old, we had finished college and, with a brief separation to test our commitment, we had persevered through more than four years of courtship. We expressed our passion with frequent love letters in perfumed envelopes adorned with stamps turned upside-down. We knew all about love, and we hoped soon to know all about love-making. We had weathered the testing of our chastity and survived with our virginity intact, barely. We knew all about virtue! Now, with the restraints removed, we could almost taste the 'skyrockets in flight' of the coming honeymoon.

Sue asked me not to wear my glasses ("You're so much cuter without them") and so, quite literally, the wedding day was a blur in my memory. The service seemed exceedingly brief, though a full half-hour elapsed by the time Dr. Koenig said, "I now pronounce you husband and wife" precisely at 4:00 p.m. I remember the chimes outside ringing the hour. Sue's grandmother sang 'Savior, Like a Shepherd Lead Us,' and as we recessed, Dr. Koenig read the poem by Elizabeth Barrett Browning that Sue chose:

How do I love thee? Let me count the ways
I love thee to the depth and breadth and height
My soul can reach when feeling out of sight
For the ends of being and ideal grace...

The reception was in the church basement, a simple gathering with cake and punch, mints and nuts, and lots of well-wishing. Afterward, we exited through a shower of rice and did the obligatory ride around the neighborhood in our 'just married' chariot, with best man Rob Drews driving and maid of honor Chris Blumhardt in front with him.

The spot I chose for the honeymoon sounded idyllic. It was, chamber of commerce folders exuded, a 'romantic log cabin' on the shore of Glen Lake near Traverse City, Michigan. Our first night's stay was at the Howard Johnson Motor Lodge in Ft. Wayne, about halfway to Glen Lake. The next morning, Sue accepted my suggestion that we stop briefly to see Professor Brelje and his wife to express our thanks for their encouragement to wait till marriage, although in truth our wedding night was unexpectedly awkward and decidedly lacking in the marital fireworks department.

Our lakeside cabin was dubbed "Deer Lodge" because of the deer heads (and stuffed squirrels) mounted on the walls. We reveled in the joy of sitting in the breakfast nook sharing simple meals with no distractions and no assignments pending. The main room had a pot-bellied stove which was, we discovered, the only source of heat. That was important for the brochures did not tell us how very COLD it could be there in the middle of June. By day we took walks by the dunes or tried paddling our canoe in the chilly wind. Then we raced back to the relative warmth of the cabin, where we finally had to move the bed in beside the stove, realizing that even love wasn't enough to keep us warm. Nor was it enough to stave off the loneliness Sue was feeling in this remote place. I did not appreciate how hard it was for her to leave family and friends for the first time. Our days at Glen Lake showed me that marriage was not going to be one long date. It would require some painful daily adjustments.

Our first home was a ground-level apartment on Elm Avenue in Maplewood, Missouri, three miles south of the seminary where I was to begin in the fall. Sue's parents went with us to assist in the move, and I carried her across the threshold into our love nest. We bought a cheap set of bedroom furniture to supplement the bookshelves from college and the eclectic mix of chairs we brought from home.

Life in an apartment was a different matter altogether from life in the suburbs. Since our income was minimal, entertainments were necessarily simple. We discovered the Maplewood Theater, where movies could be seen for 75 cents by anyone willing to endure the sticky, pop-splattered floor. Now and then we made the short drive to Grant Park to feed the mallard ducks. We tuned in our 17-inch TV to watch *Mission: Impossible.* We also hunted roaches. Early on we discovered them, scuttling into crevices and behind canisters when the kitchen lights went on. Sue was horrified by the discovery, since she associated roaches with filth and poverty. She obtained some roach spray from a co-worker and we used it liberally. Shortly thereafter we could hear the tiny pattering sounds of roaches scurrying, then falling dead beneath the sink.

We discovered another unpleasantness due to the thin walls and floors of our building. Just above us resided a young woman who was decidedly promiscuous. The nights (and sometimes days) were punctuated by groanings and squeakings from her bedroom as she entertained a sequence of lovers, some of whom we observed through the window as they made their way up and down the stairs. Her behavior offended against our sense of morality. It was discouraging to hear her enjoying her passionate coupling while we continued to struggle with our own. Was it fair that the intimacies of marriage should be so hard for us after all our waiting?

Not all the neighbors were so disturbing. Some took a kindly interest in us and stopped in the stairwells to chat. Some were humorous, like the man across the alley who kept two hound dogs which bayed at the moon and a pet raccoon that liked balancing on his slat fence. We learned that investing time in talk was an important ingredient in making friends.

Sue found a job teaching second grade at a school in Warson Woods. While I attended classes at the seminary, she was earning her PHT degree ('Putting Hubby Through'). The setting was ideal – a fine principal, a low teacher-pupil ratio, and children highly motivated to achieve. Nevertheless, perfectionist that she was, Sue found the task almost overwhelming. Each evening she was the last to leave the school. Once at home, she stayed up until the wee hours making projects for the next day, and I was drafted to assist with art work or laborious cutting. It was one of the many small tests that began to strain our young marriage by pitting my needs for homework time, sleep, or relaxation against her need for a job well done. Selfishness versus service was still another lesson in this living laboratory called marriage, what Martin Luther called a 'school for character,' a school in which one's spouse was one's professor.

There were just two of us in the marital classroom then. In the final year of seminary there came a new arrival, and harder lessons to be learned about life together arrived with her.

SHARPENING THE SWORD

In the fall of 1968 I began my studies at the seminary.

While not as stark and crisply-lined as the senior college in Ft. Wayne, Concordia Seminary in St. Louis displayed an older, earthier beauty. The Tudor-Gothic buildings, constructed in 1926, were laid out in rectangles and faced with tan-colored stonework. A magnificent tower that practically shouted 'Mighty Fortress!' dominated the center of campus. Inside was a wondrous carillon, and just beneath it by the parking lot stood a statue of Luther himself, grim-faced and resolute, unflinching in the face of the pigeons that settled on his head. On the west side of campus sat a log cabin replica of the denomination's very first seminary in Perry County, Missouri, where the synod's immigrant ancestors established their first settlements. Further west sprawled athletic fields trimmed with forest land, an old-style field house, and radio station KFUO, which for decades already had broadcast *The Lutheran Hour*, among the earliest religious radio programs in the nation. South of the campus proper was an older neighborhood of two and three-story brick homes where many of the married students resided.

I chose to come to the seminary in St. Louis, in part, because of the reputation of its faculty. That faculty was both a great treasure and a source of increasing consternation in the church at large. The years I studied on campus were spent under a gathering cloud of disagreement over our approach to the Bible. Alfred O. Fuerbringer was in his last years as president, and lately he had come under fire from conservatives in the church who were worried about the theological latitude evident at the seminary. Our church body had, for generations, held a mostly literal understanding of the Bible and resisted the modernist (also called liberal) trend that discounted its historicity. Some in the church feared that liberal teaching would erode the authority of the Bible. Most of the suspected liberals were in the department of exegesis (biblical study). These included Norman Habel, Ralph Klein, Everett Kalin, Robert Smith, Martin Scharlemann, and Edgar Krentz – formidable scholars all. Habel, an Australian with a Crocodile Dundee accent, wrote books of drama for youth I very much enjoyed. He regaled us with stories of his pet albino dingo and did occasional kookaburra imitations to keep our sessions light. Edgar Krentz was a walking encyclopedia of biblical and bibliographical information. A precise, dignified man, he began every class session with a prayer and was always courteous and on task. Because Martin Scharlemann was ill, I took 1 Peter from Ed Schroeder, a substitute instructor from Valparaiso University who played word games at every opportunity. His explanation of 1 Peter 1:4 transformed 'imperishable, undefiled, and unfading' into 'won't rot, spot, or go to pot.'

Besides exegetical theology there were three other departments which offered both required and elective classes. In the department of historical theology, my favorite instructor was Robert Bertram, who taught the Reformation. "Scholars debate whether Luther nailed the 95 Theses or merely mailed them," he quipped, "but in either case he posted them!" Besides being a fine lecturer, Bertram took more than a passing interest in us students.

The department of systematic theology introduced us to *The Book of Concord*, our Lutheran confessional writings. I was destined not to get deeply into them because Ralph Bohlmann was my professor. Bohlmann, who later became president of the synod, attempted to answer every question, no matter how trivial or far afield. Students soon found clever ways to derail him, sending Bohlmann off in all directions except toward completion of his planned lecture.

My better systematics teachers during seminary years were two writers, C. S. Lewis and Dietrich Bonhoeffer. I delved into Lewis's *Mere Christianity*, which began with a thought-provoking look at what all people have in common. We all have a standard of right and wrong, and all know we've violated the standard, wrote Lewis. He then went on to explain why not merely 'theism' but 'Christianity' was the necessary and sufficient remedy for what had gone wrong with mankind. Bonhoeffer's *The Cost of Discipleship* was stunning in its critique of the 'cheap grace' so common among us Lutherans and urgent in its call to come and die with Christ. Never had a book so challenged my complacency and issued such a stirring summons to a genuine following of Jesus. I returned to those books often at the seminary and later in my early years of the pastorate.

The fourth department, practical theology, had the weighty assignment of equipping us with the skills we needed for preaching and pastoral care. In homiletics we practiced our preaching in front of a video camera. Professor Lester Zeitler gave us sheets on which to record our critique of each other as we watched the sermon replayed. The dean of the faculty, Richard R. Caemmerer, had written the definitive text *Preaching for the Church*. I got one of my sermon manuscripts back from him with the comment, "This looks like the way Peter Marshall wrote his sermons." Marshall was the former chaplain of the U. S. Senate. I had, in fact, begun to imitate his stair-step writing style after getting a book of his sermons from my aunt Martha Jean.

The department's course work took all of us off campus for some hands-on ministry experiences. I was assigned to a detoxification center where men arrested for public drunkenness were taken. Chaplain Charles Knippel assigned us to talk to some of the men and provide a listening ear and prayer, if desired. After each conversation, we were to write up 'verbatims' of our visits and then discuss what we had learned in the small group he led. I found it a daunting task to remember the course of a 15-minute (or longer) conversation. Knippel's most frequent comment to me was "Didn't you hear what he was telling you there?" The ministry of listening, he told us, was a crucial and challenging part of pastoral care.

All seminary students chose a field work church in the St. Louis area where they would worship and assist the local pastor with tasks he might assign. Because of the experience I'd had in Cabrini, I chose St. Michael Lutheran in Kinloch, an all-black suburb. Though a small congregation with a cramped, shabby building, it was staffed by two full-time pastors, Dick Sering and Joe Mensing, along with Deaconess Joan Cole. Mensing was prone to be dramatic in the pulpit. One Sunday he brought a chunk of firewood and held it before his face as he preached on the log and the speck from Matthew 7. His simple device made the message unforgettable.

Unfortunately, so many other students chose this same church that I can remember preaching only once. Most of my work was teaching Sunday School, mingling with the people at worship, and attending community meetings. There was an easy informality at St. Michael's that stood in sharp contrast to the culture in which I'd grown up. Children chewed sunflower seeds and left the remnants on the floor, earning no reprimand from nearby adults. Worship itself might start 10 or even 15 minutes late, and no one seemed in a hurry. Sue and I made friends with the McCray family, and I found a chess partner in the oldest son, Pleasant. Soon after our acquaintance, he was drafted and shipped off to Viet Nam, where he was killed in action after just weeks of service. The war, often an academic debate subject on campus, became more personal to me. I grieved for Pleasant and his family.

Midweek worship at the seminary brought its own share of learning experiences. The preaching by the professors was often memorable. Robert Bertram's sermon on loving one's enemy (from Romans 12) has remained fixed in my head. He told us how to spell 'Enemy':

E — is for **Evil**.
An enemy is someone who does you evil.
N — is for **Nobody Wins**.
Nobody wins if you try to get even.
E — is for **Entrance**.
Jesus entered into the world, enters this relationship with your enemy
M — is for **Mealtime**.
If your enemy hungers, feed him!
Y — is for **Yield**.
Yield to the Spirit's work to bring change as you pray.

The spirit of thankful joy at the sacrament was expressed in smiles such as I had never seen at the rail while growing up. Students and faculty frequently 'passed the peace' going to and from the altar rail. At one outdoor service in the quadrangle, Dr. Krentz reminded us that quarrels were to be mended before we communed. Then he stopped and waited for us to do so! That very morning I had engaged in an unkindly exchange in the dining hall with another student. It was unresolved. Now that student was in plain sight on the opposite side of the altar. The words burned in my heart, and I made my way to him and spoke an apology. Others were doing the same. It would not be the last time I needed to make amends before the sacrament.

Students were allowed to lead worship as well. When the time came for me, I saw it as an opportunity to strike a blow for newness and creativity. Remembering the challenge of Fred Reklau in Chicago earlier, I collaborated with fellow student Jack Flachsbart on a service called 'Dying and Rising,' for which I wrote the liturgical text and Jack supplied music to be sung by a small choir. We submitted the order to Professor Robert Bergt, the chapel dean, who criticized what we produced as 'campfire music' with 'seventeenth-century harmonies.' Hot with anger, I penned a torrid defense. We did not change Dr. Bergt's mind, but we were allowed to do the service in the chapel.

Afterward, I visited Dr. Caemmerer, who I supposed would be a more sympathetic listener to my concerns about the dullness of Lutheran worship. Dr. Caemmerer listened patiently for a while before making a simple comment, "Mike, do you know what your problem is?

I grew silent. It was a question I didn't expect.

"You don't know how to worship. You'll never get anywhere until you learn to submit yourself to whatever is presented to you, and then use it for God's glory. Your order in chapel yesterday wasn't what I would personally choose, but it was offered to me. So I submitted to it and used it. You need to learn to do that."

I was humbled. Caemmerer cut to the core of what worship was to be and moved the spotlight from the form used to the heart of the worshipper. In the worship wars that spread in later years, congregations would have done well to hear his advice and learn such mutual submission.

The growing controversy in the synod was painfully apparent to all of us. In 1969 it intensified when President Fuerbringer retired and a new president was called. The new man was John H. Tietjen, a pastor who had earned his doctorate at Union Theological Seminary in New York and written a book called *Which Way to Lutheran Unity?* During a preliminary visit to the campus, Tietjen asked to meet with several of the students. Someone included me in that group. I was struck by his boyish good looks, his gracious manner, and his articulate speech. I did not know that within five years, a major rift would take place that would split our church body and the seminary itself, taking most of the faculty and student body to a 'seminary in exile' off campus. What we DID know was that he faced a time of serious trial and that he needed our prayers for wisdom.

Life at the seminary was not all academics. While Sue worked as a teacher at Warson Woods School, I took a part-time job at the Concordia Historical Institute on the seminary campus. CHI was officially the synod's department of archives and history, and my work there was chiefly to file the mass of donated material that came in. Two factors complicated my work. First, the material itself was so diverse as to defy categorization. I sorted through old tracts (William Dallmann, a prolific tract writer, became a familiar name), church bulletins, a box of flags from a missionary in Ceylon, books of all descriptions, correspondence, teachers' lecture notes, Sunday School handouts, anniversary booklets, and much more. Second, our director, Dr. August Suelflow, a rotund, chain-smoking former pastor, seemed intent on keeping everything anyone cared to donate, even if it was the 23rd copy of an old German songbook. He wrote effusive letters of thanks for all contributions, no matter how insignificant. The rest of us on the staff had to decide where to put things in stacks that were crammed to the point of bursting.

It was, in spite of the frustration, an interesting place to work, with a quaint cast of characters. Suelflow was sequestered in his smoky office. Proper, old-fashioned Anna Dorn manned the reception desk and gave tours. Suelflow's research assistants, Marv Huggins and Tom Manteufel, were bookish and all business. The rest of the staff was a playful and gossipy lot. My conscience needled me when I joined the too-frequent complaints about the work and the boss. I was especially ashamed later on when Suelflow commended my work and promoted me to help with giving tours. When finally I finished my days in the stacks at CHI, I realized that I had learned much about the history of my church. Far from being a bunch of stodgy, inflexible Germans, our synod did pioneering work in radio ministry and outreach to the deaf and disabled. Jokes portrayed us as unwilling to change even a light bulb ('How many Lutherans does it take...?'), but we had the flexibility to adopt new understandings about engagement, dancing, life insurance, and women as teachers.

My classmates and I were soon to learn much more about pastoral ministry in the best of all settings. For our third year of seminary education, we would be scattered across the country to separate congregations for a year of internship called vicarage.

VICARAGE TIMES TWO

The third year of our seminary education was called vicarage. It was a year of internship served in a local congregation under the supervision of a veteran pastor, who taught the student by giving him a wide array of experiences in pastoral ministry. Most of my classmates were destined to experience a single vicarage. I was privileged to have not one, but two, and the first was to be in Canada.

I made application for a summer opportunity at St. John's Lutheran Church in Pembroke, Ontario, and was accepted. In June, 1970, Sue and I drove across the border from Detroit to Windsor and then northeast to Pembroke, a town of 15,000 people situated on the Ottawa River a hundred miles or so from the nation's capital in Ottawa. Our first impressions of Canada were of a country wide, clean, and proud without being pompous. Pembroke itself was a quiet town, a good place to ease in to pastoral work at a relaxed pace.

The sanctuary at St. John's was a large, rectangular brick structure with a prominent steeple surmounted by a cross. The very ample nave, furnished with heavy oak pews, was adjoined to a fellowship hall equal in floor space. There was no wall between them, so the place felt cavernous. Next door was a two-story brick parsonage with an adjoining office. The quarters were more than adequate, with kitchen and dining rooms downstairs and the bedrooms on the upper floor. In one of them I saw the words 'Dickie Neuhaus was here' grooved into the wood near the ceiling. This was, in fact, the boyhood home of Richard John Neuhaus, a Lutheran pastor in Brooklyn who founded the well-known journal *First Things*. He had gained national notice when, with Daniel Berrigan and others, he opposed the war in Viet Nam.

Downstairs at the front of the building was the church office. There at the desk sat Kathryn Purvis, a no-nonsense woman who was to teach me the value of having a good secretary. I would be manning the fort alone after a brief orientation from resident pastor Ron Reisdorf, who was to be away for the remainder of the summer. After he left, I still had countless questions, but Kathryn proved to be a more than adequate survival kit. She knew where everything was, how things should be done, and who was who in the life of the congregation.

I relished having sole responsibility for the weekly conduct of congregational life. My main task was to be preaching. The pulpit at St. John's was massive and, in European fashion, elevated at least eight feet above the heads of the worshippers. It protruded from the wall like the prow of a ship and was entered by a door atop a stairway at the rear.

Though the people proved to be a friendly lot, the turnout Sunday mornings was disappointing, and all the more because the church was so massive. Most people sat in the very back, a fact that irritated me increasingly as the weeks passed. One Saturday I resolved to bring the people closer to the front. My idea was to stretch the ushers' purple cord over the back section of pews, forcing worshippers forward. But the next morning, the people simply ducked under the rope to reach their familiar places. *Those stubborn Germans!* My experiment was a flop.

Some, I discovered, were paying better attention to my preaching than I realized. One Sunday after church, one of the oldest couples pulled me aside. With faces wrinkled in concern, the husband said, "Vicar, did I hear you say 'gee' this morning?" I recalled having used that word. "Well," the wife interjected, like a granny taking a toddler on her knee, "that's short for 'Jesus,' and we would really like to ask that you not use that word again." It was a simple, kindly word of correction which did what they intended. I never used that word again.

There were no confirmation classes to teach that summer, and I had few hospital calls or emergencies, so there was an abundance of free time. I used it to explore fishing spots on the nearby Ottawa River alone or in the company of Mervyn and Joyce Buske, who invited Sue and me aboard their boat to fish for walleyed pike. Carl Baker, who had heard of my love for fishing from Mervyn, made a special stop at our parsonage door one evening. "Come out to the car," he invited, "and see something." When he opened the door, I stared dumbstruck into the fearsome maw of a huge northern pike. The teeth were a full inch long, and its body took the whole back seat and more. "Took me an hour to land him," he said proudly. His son David was soon to enter the seminary, and David stayed to talk about theological education and inquire about the conflicts brewing at the seminary.

Sue, meanwhile, enjoyed the company of the church's women. On a retreat we attended together, she was assigned the role of the elder brother in a Prodigal Son re-enactment, for which she donned a sport coat and tie and an uppity manner. The retreat site was made memorable by mosquitoes so numerous we could hear their malevolent humming in the darkness outside the trailer.

It was a light-hearted summer. One of the women taught Sue to make raspberry pie. We adopted our first pet, a tan and white dwarf rabbit we named Butterscotch. We played ping pong in the church basement. And a small company of new friends helped us celebrate Sue's birthday with a surprise party in August.

The end of the summer brought the end of this first brief vicarage and the beginning of the second. A trip across the country lay in between, for though I had requested a vicarage in New England, I was assigned to Memorial Lutheran Church in Vancouver, Washington. We bade a sad farewell to our bunny and to the friendly people of St. John's. Several, especially Kathryn Purvis, maintained their ties with us for long years afterward. For the present, we loaded our belongings in a U-Haul van and turned our attention westward. The morning we left, a skunk waddled across the driveway, much to Sue's delight. It was the last of many pleasant moments in Pembroke.

We drove west through the Badlands, across the Rockies, and finally into Washington, the Evergreen State. I had expected rolling green hills bedecked with apple trees. Instead, Sue and I encountered the rocky barrenness of the high desert. The temperature in Walla Walla that August afternoon was nearly 100 degrees. By nightfall we were making our way down the Columbia Gorge amid a sea of traffic.

A long while later we pulled up in front of a solidly built brick parsonage on East 28th Street in Vancouver. We had left the heat and desert far behind. The sky was brilliant with stars. The air was cool and the birch and fir trees were a welcome sight. The Schroeder family – Pastor Win, his wife Lois, and their children Gordon, Eunice, and Carol – gave us an open-armed greeting.

For the next year, Winfred A. Schroeder was my mentor and role model as I learned to do pastoral ministry. Then in his mid-fifties, Win had served churches in Tacoma and Honolulu before coming to Memorial in 1960. In Hawaii he had been an active force in mission work. Now he was first vice-president of the Northwest District. I was his third vicar. Victor Hippe, my immediate predecessor, had written me, "You have, without doubt, the best vicarage in the system." He described Pastor Schroeder as 'an exceptional man.'

Exceptional is just what Pastor Schroeder proved to be. Tall and slender in build he was, and nearly bald already. He stood with a slight crook in his back with head cocked, listening carefully. He was intelligent, precise in speech, disciplined in his personal life, and he possessed a dry wit. His middle name was Albrecht, but it could have been 'Organization.' Was there anyone so neatly and completely organized as he? His extensive file system bulged with notes, some neatly typed, others clipped from periodicals. Where some might have been content with a file folder on a Bible book, he had a separate folder on each chapter, sometimes on individual verses! The entire wall of his office was filled with books. When I opened one, I'd usually find summary notes with page references inside the front cover, along with a review article. His home was similarly organized. The Schroeders' large collection of records was cross-referenced by composers and piece names. His slide shows were legendary, each tray labeled so that he could, at a moment's notice, arrange a slide program for a group in need.

When we sat down to plan the year's ministry, that too was done in an orderly way, with a sheet of topics to cover over a three-day period. Some might have found this intimidating, but I found it extremely satisfying, even refreshing, after chafing at some professors whose lectures were brilliant but so disorganized I struggled to follow. Now I had a supervisor who laid out expectations clearly. I was to help teach confirmation class, preach twice per month, assist in extensive visitation, and be responsible for youth ministry.

My first assignment was, in retrospect, the one that most shaped my life and ministry. "I want you to spend the first hour of each day in devotion," Win directed. "Read your Bible first. Then spend some time reading other good books or devotional literature. Then finish the hour in prayer."

I had not been given much direction in my devotional life, nor had I established a regular time of prayer. Dad had tried to lead family devotions at the dinner table, but the effort met disinterest from us children and was soon abandoned. Though my parents set an example for me in praying regularly, we rarely talked about it and there was never a mention of what I later called 'Daily Quiet Time.' But Win made it my first assignment. My spirit drank in the opportunity as a parched field drinks in the rain. In that way, Win became a second father, providing a kind of devotional direction in my life that my own father had been unable to fill.

Win modeled good preaching. His sermons, always typed out on a single sheet, were clearly outlined, filled with illustrations and Scripture citations, and effectively delivered. When it was my turn, he asked that I turn in an outline and describe how I would translate the text into 'faith goals' and 'life goals.' Afterward, we de-briefed together. The two comments I heard most often: "You're spending too much time on your introduction" and "Where is the Gospel in this message?"

Visitation was taught by example. Win took me along to hospitals, nursing care facilities, and private homes. I was amazed at how much he could say in a few words, while still being an attentive listener. At the hospital, I learned to pay attention to other patients who might share the room with my parishioner and to pray for them as well. The roommates often expressed gratitude for being included. Another tip: "Keep the visit brief," he told me, "unless they ask you to stay longer." As the months passed, he turned me loose to visit on my own, but he continued to show great interest in the details of my experiences.

A special opportunity that year was a request from St. Joseph Community Hospital to serve as the Protestant/No Preference chaplain. My assignment was to inquire if those patients wished to see a pastor of their choice. Many were simply not interested in 'organized religion,' but almost all appreciated having a bit of company. All but a few were courteous. One of the few who were not was a middle-aged woman who dismissed me from her room with a triumphant shout, "You blew it! Now get out of here!" I struck up ongoing friendships with several, including a drug user in his late teens named Mike Gierke. A few days after making a visit at his bedside, I heard from the charge nurse that he had overdosed on methadone. Mike's was the first funeral I conducted.

My office at the church was a small, quiet corner of the old army chapel that had once been Memorial's sanctuary but was now its gymnasium. I could see out my window across 29th Street the duplex apartment we had rented for the year. Frequent visitors to both home and office were the kids from our youth group. The year's biggest venture was a trip by our young people to San Francisco to attend the Lutheran Youth Congress. A slide show of the trip might have included images of me sleeping on the floor of the bus on our all-night drive south, the saffron-clad Hare Krishna devotees chanting on the street corners, and the imposing figure of speaker Hal Lindsey. Lindsey, not a Lutheran himself, had been imported to present his thoughts about the end of the world (by the year 1988, he asserted, forty years from the founding of the nation of Israel!). I took feverish notes and later did a paper on his book *The Late, Great Planet Earth* upon my return to the seminary.

The Schroeders made sure we were properly introduced to the delights of the Pacific Northwest, taking us on little day-trips to Beacon Rock and the Horsetail Falls Trail on the Columbia Gorge, the Hood River Valley with its abundant fruit and its winding highway up to Mt. Hood, and the cold, rocky beaches of the Oregon Coast. Their enthusiasm for the beauties of the Northwest was infectious. "There's a banana slug!" Lois beamed, pointing to an immense six-inch mollusk on the path before us. "This is a trillium," said Win, pointing to a short green plant with a three-petaled white flower. Oregon grape, Douglas Fir, and sword ferns soon became part of our experience and vocabulary.

While I worked at the church, Sue experienced a challenge in her job at a local employment service. Her boss, Mrs. Elliott, required Sue to lie for her on a regular basis on the phone. Meanwhile, there was a constant backdrop of sniping comments by the boss and her employees behind one another's backs. Finally, she faced her boss: "I don't want to tell your customers what isn't true. If you want me to keep doing that, I'll have to resign my position." Mrs. Elliott, startled by Sue's unexpected pluck, backed down and agreed Sue need not do that anymore. It was a tiny, but significant victory for honesty.

At home together we fixed our meals, created a few homemade banners, and indulged ourselves in the guilty pleasure of watching *Days of Our Lives* at lunchtime. We also devoted ourselves to the serious business of starting a family. On the day Sue announced the news that I would be a daddy, I felt an odd mixture of pride and fear. The people at church rejoiced with us and gave Sue a baby shower. Pastor Schroeder surprised us all by giving a demonstration of diapering on a life-size doll while all of us laughed.

Our two-part vicarage year had been rich with growth. I considered it one of the best of my life. The next year, too, would bring growth, albeit with a greater measure of pain.

FRAILTY AND FATHERHOOD

It was hard to return to the seminary. A year in the beautiful Northwest and the challenge and fulfillment of daily ministry made the routine of class work and assignments seem tedious. But there was a baby coming, and the anticipation of that moment pushed us forward. It felt like the end of a cross-country race – a last agonizing push to the finish line.

Our final year's apartment on Bellevue Avenue was closer to the seminary and a bit roomier. What's more, we now had several seminary couples as fellow residents. Jim and Paula Barker, who lived directly above us, blessed us with simple acts of kindness like baked goods and homemade cards and inadvertently presented us with a spiritual challenge. One evening we heard unusual musical sounds coming from the Barkers' apartment. When we later asked them about it, Jim explained that they had been 'singing in tongues.' I had heard of speaking in tongues, but not singing in tongues.

To this point, the charismatic movement had been an academic curiosity in a lecture or a textbook for me. It was a movement viewed in our well-ordered church body with skepticism and, by some, with open disdain. Now it was incarnated in our neighbors, whom we loved and respected. They were neither pushy nor arrogant as they shared. For some time Sue wrestled with whether or not to pursue this gift, and she began to pray for God to give it if it were His will. The answer, apparently, was 'no.' Neither of us ever received the gift of tongues, though we grew in our respect for those who might exercise it.

As it turned out, one of my professors, Holland Jones, was involved in charismatic meetings. Jones, my advisor for my thesis on the symbolical acts of the prophets, was not a 'charismatic' personality. He had a gravelly voice, smoked a pipe, and was neither effusive nor energetic. He was a living reminder not to categorize people.

Soon there were more immediate concerns at hand. Sue's bulging abdomen reminded us of the approach of her due date, and we enrolled in a Lamaze childbirth class on the recommendation of my sister Natalie, now a registered nurse.

"It's great preparation, and you get to be there for the birth of the baby," she urged.

I didn't know if I wanted to be there or not. I felt somewhat squeamish. "It's bloody, isn't it?" I pictured Sue shouting in pain and myself panicked and helpless.

But we went. The class, conducted at St. Mary's Hospital just south of the seminary campus, had a dozen or so participants, and it proved a revelation to me. How much there was to know about childbirth, and how ignorant I was! The leader explained the wondrous combination of interlocking events that led to birth, deepening our appreciation of this everyday miracle. She taught us the skills of relaxing and breathing Sue needed to cope with her labor. I was her coach. "You'll do fine," our teacher assured half a dozen nervous husbands.

We finished just in time. On a Friday night in December, I took Sue to a movie. During the show, she quietly took my hand and whispered, "I'm having contractions." *Oh boy, here we go.* Back home we tried to sleep, but the contractions continued steady and ever stronger. By 5 a.m. we were headed for St. Mary's. Once there I timed the contractions and did my best to coach Sue in her breathing rhythm. The nuns on duty were experienced and gentle, and they provided an air of confidence we needed. After an hour's unexpected cessation, the contractions resumed, the doctor was summoned, and that afternoon our baby arrived – a fat-cheeked girl. After cleaning her, the nurse wrapped our baby in a blanket and laid her in a warmer. While Sue was in a semi-conscious haze from a shot of Demerol, I bent down over that sweet child. "Hello, Melanie!" That was the name we'd agreed on.

After years of being fathered, it was my turn to be a father. It was a very tall order. Babies don't come with instructions, and childbirth class did not take us past the delivery. Now what? I began parenthood with a mix of joy and fear. The joy was evident as we placed our new baby in a tilt-chair under the Christmas tree. Melanie was fascinated by the lights, and later that became her first word, spoken with wide-eyed enthusiasm - "Lights!"

The fear was there too, right from the start. Melanie was a generally quiet child, but even quiet children cry, wet their diapers, and demand feeding. *What am I supposed to do?* Beyond Pastor Schroeder's light-hearted diapering demo, I had received no training at all in ordinary parenting tasks with a newborn baby. I decided to step back and pass the responsibility to Sue. I offered little help when the crying came at night, preferring to stay in bed and let Sue struggle with parent duty.

Nor was I much help with other household chores. If I was not at the seminary in class or working out at the gym, I was absorbed in my own priorities at home, doing homework or listening to broadcasts of the St. Louis Blues on station KMOX. To make matters worse, as the months passed, I began to feel jealous of the time and attention the baby was getting. No time left for me, I complained with increasing volume. One night our tempers and voices escalated into a full-scale battle. Then the unthinkable. I shoved her roughly. She picked up a book and threw it at me. "You don't want a wife," she accused through tears, "YOU WANT A MAID AND A MISTRESS!" She fled the apartment, slamming the door behind her, leaving me breathing hard, alone with the baby. Her words echoed. A maid and a mistress? She had me perfectly pegged. Her words were the mirror in which God again showed me my immaturity.

Our early marriage's dream world evaporated. Disillusionment took up residence. Both of us, we admitted to each other later, contemplated the possibility of divorce for the first time. How could this be happening to us after all the waiting and love letters and promises? How could I, a divinity student and soon-to-be pastor, have said and done these things to her? Marriage and fatherhood had brought me face to face with my frailty and arrogance more powerfully than when I had been dumped by my roommate in Ft. Wayne, for now two other lives were intimately tied to mine. Later as we looked back, we observed that we had not established a 'couple time' for prayer as I'd done alone. Prayer together would have made a big difference, but at that point in our lives it was an important missing ingredient.

Sue came back an hour later, and we talked and reached a truce, but a settled peace and marital maturity did not come until years later. For now, our heart of romance had suffered a serious crack of uncertainty.

We finished the final year at St. Louis, working and worshipping with our daughter in our arms. We were no longer at the field work church in Kinloch. We had joined a small, mixed chorus of seminarians and wives who liked to sing, and we sampled a variety of churches where we could minister with our songs.

Early in 1972, the placement office summoned me and gave me two options for the immediate future. One was to be placed with the national church in Korea as a linguist. The other was to return to Memorial in Vancouver as their assistant. The request had come from Pastor Schroeder, who told the leaders, "Let's call Mike back; I can work with him." It was an easy choice to make. We would return to the Pacific Northwest.

Graduation took place on a sunny, humid evening in St. Louis. More than 150 of us gathered with hundreds more of our family and friends in the large quadrangle for the ceremony. Most would receive a Master of Divinity degree, the academic prerequisite for pastoral ministry in the Lutheran Church. For the last time we sat as a class before scattering to the four winds. Sue donned a bright floral dress and sat by my parents holding Melanie, who sported a tiny bow taped to her nearly bald head.

The speakers used glorious words about our vocation of shepherding God's flock. I sat listening with a growing sense of inadequacy and even some shame. I already knew that I fell far short as a husband and father. Now I would be a pastor too? I was, in Paul's words, a clay pot – potentially useful, but frail and breakable. God would have to teach me repeatedly that the only way I could remain useful was by His grace.

PART THREE

Stations in Pastoral Ministry

(1972–Present)

Memorial Lutheran Church

Vancouver, Washington

(1972–1980)

AN EXTENDED APPRENTICESHIP

Melanie was crying inconsolably and Sue was frantic. It was installation day at Memorial Lutheran Church, and the sanctuary was already crowded. I was, as usual, unavailable to assist, sequestered in Pastor Schroeder's office, robing with the other pastors of the circuit who would soon lay hands of blessing on me. As we donned our red stoles, Emil Jaech, the new Northwest District president, bustled in to join us. Win Schroeder took charge of the lineup, made sure that all had a bulletin, and asked which Scripture verse each wanted to use, lest one brother take another's intended verse and leave the second man groping for an alternative at the last minute. Finally, we made our way outside to the front entrance.

Meanwhile, in the still-crowded entryway, an angel of mercy in the person of Elizabeth Thompson spied Sue's distress. "Here, I'll take her," she said soothingly and enfolded our squirming daughter. Sue, cheeks wet with her own tears, took my arm and marched in. Back and forth Elizabeth paced as the songs and readings began. Our own parents were 2500 miles east in Indiana where, weeks earlier, I had been ordained at my childhood church, Calvary. Pastor Robert Meier and dear Professor Brelje, who had been such a support during my lonely times in Ft. Wayne, shared in my service of ordination with Sue's parents and mine looking on.

The solemn questions directed at me weeks earlier at my home church were now repeated by President Jaech:

IN THE PRESENCE OF GOD AND OF THIS CONGREGATION I NOW ASK YOU: DO YOU BELIEVE THE CANONICAL BOOKS OF THE OLD AND NEW TESTAMENTS TO BE THE INSPIRED WORD OF GOD?

I do.

DO YOU ACCEPT THE THREE ECUMENICAL CREEDS...

I do.

DO YOU BELIEVE THE UNALTERED AUGSBURG CONFESSION IS A TRUE EXPOSITION...

I do.

DO YOU SOLEMNLY PROMISE THAT YOU WILL PERFORM THE DUTIES OF YOUR OFFICE...

I do.

WILL YOU ADORN THE DOCTRINE OF OUR SAVIOR WITH A GODLY LIFE?

I will, with the help of God.

The questions tolled over me like the ringing of an ancient bell. When the hands of my fellow pastors joined to rest on my head, I felt the weight of an awesome responsibility. I was a pastor now. Seminary was over, and my education in ministry and life was about to begin in earnest.

The return to Memorial and the work with Pastor Schroeder was like an extended apprenticeship. As an ordained pastor, I could now officiate at weddings, consecrate the bread and wine at Holy Communion, and be given a larger role generally. Being on a team spared both of us the grinding demands of preaching every week and being perpetually on call.

Pastor Win Schroeder at the lectern

I settled into a routine, imitating Win's style and adopting his pace. Mornings were spent in the office ("so that people know where and when to find us"). I had prayer time, wrote letters, made phone calls, and planned class work and sermons. Afternoons were generally devoted to visiting shut-ins and hospital patients, usually 8-10 visits a week. The evenings brought meetings, classes and counseling of various sorts. Win took most of the difficult cases but would consult with me so as to offer insights, which I badly needed. To keep myself accountable, I reported my 'meetings, classes and calls' to the elders each month.

With Win's help, I began a filing system of my own. I learned to observe and mark weekly worship attendance, and especially to pay attention to people who turned up missing. "Most people won't tell you something's wrong in words," Schroeder explained. "They'll simply go missing. It's our job to notice and to inquire if things are OK." It turned out to be solid advice.

Memorial congregation was a large (more than 500 souls), vibrant, gifted group of people. Pastor Schroeder was the farmer who patiently tilled the soil with his persistent visitation and listening ears and planted the good seed in his richly-nourishing sermons and meaty Bible classes. The congregation had adopted the Bethel Series, an intensive course of Bible study authored by Harley Swiggum. Schroeder spent two years training a cadre of lay men and women as Bethel Bible teachers. A whole wing of classrooms was built and then filled with eager students. It was dubbed 'The Bethel Wing.'

We used every square foot of space, especially on Sundays. Each Sunday our schedule was a sandwich of three events -- two worship services with an education hour for all ages in between. Pastor Schroeder and I scripted the services with care. Whoever preached also planned the liturgy for the day. The partner served as liturgist and lector. No matter how carefully we planned, there came moments that defied planning. In the middle of one sermon I asked a rhetorical question I hoped would dangle dramatically in the minds of the hearers.

"Is there any one among us who would cast the first stone?"

The reverent silence was broken, as a very young, loud voice answered, "Yes!" It was little Darin Swan, who derailed that moment of somber introspection. There was an eruption of guffaws in the sanctuary.

It wasn't always the children who provided surprises. Sue Mark punctuated more than one service with her sneezes. No ordinary sneezes, these! More like small explosions that combined a laugh and a scream. A more serious moment came one Christmas Eve, when the adult choir stood before the congregation in soft candlelight singing a long-rehearsed cantata. Smiling and radiant in the center of the front row stood Kathy White, enormously pregnant, the embodiment of Mary in Bethlehem. The hour was late and we were in a semi-dreamy state of rapture when it happened. Without warning, Kathy fainted and pitched forward, smack on her bulging belly. There was a gasp from the watchers. Then an anxious hush as several of the men from the choir surrounded our fallen Madonna. When she rose, unhurt and practically unfazed, there was heavenly relief.

Pastor Schroeder was a tireless visitor. By observing him, I learned to prepare with prayer, take a bulletin or tract with me to leave behind ("They'll have something to think about after you've left"), and employ prayer whenever possible. He was especially insistent on seeing members who had grown delinquent in their attendance. "Let them go," he lamented, "and their habit will harden into concrete." Most such visits, alas, brought little visible result. Sometimes the success we had was not the success we had anticipated. One evening I attempted a visit on a young woman named Debbie, who had been missing at church for two years. I went to her home without phoning ahead (which would make it too easy to dodge me). At the door I was met by a tall, balding fellow. "No Debbie here," he explained. "We just moved in a few weeks ago. Who are you?"
When I explained that I was Debbie's Lutheran pastor looking for her, he brightened. "A Lutheran pastor? Well, come on in. We'd like to meet you!" Paul and Joyce Prigge and their children soon joined Memorial, and later Paul became congregational president.
One of the saddest visits I made happened at St. Joseph Community Hospital. Ken Thompson was there. He and Elizabeth had endeared themselves to us by stepping in as substitute grandparents for our girls. As head elder, his meekness put us all to shame. One evening at our elders' meeting Pastor Schroeder asked Ken to lead a closing prayer – something he normally did not do because of a sense of his limitations in public speech. But he ventured to obey. "O Lord," Ken began, "we come to you…" There was a pause as he searched for words, "…in high…humility." I thought of that prayer as I entered his room. The diagnosis Elizabeth had told us was ominous: Hodgkins Disease. But I wasn't prepared for what I saw. His neck had swollen grotesquely, as if he had an orange lodged in his throat. I stood staring, wordless. Ken looked at me with the faintest hint of a smile. "How are you, pastor?" It broke my heart. I managed a short visit and a brief prayer with him. As I left the room, I leaned against the corridor wall and wept. Vera Hoover, a member who worked as a nurse at St. Joseph, found me there and wrapped me in her arms. It was the last time I saw Ken before he died.
Pastor Schroeder took Ken's funeral, and most other funerals. Because of his experience, people called on him for most emergencies and the truly frightening, knotty problems that beset their marriages and families. The few funerals I took taught me how careful one must be at such a time of raw emotion. When Ken Bonnell, husband of our member Betty, died suddenly, she asked me to do his funeral. Ken had been uninvolved at church for years.

As Betty and I prepared, I asked her if I might be free to speak what I felt necessary in the situation, and Betty gave me permission. I preached from 2 Corinthians 6 ("Now is the time, now is the day of salvation"), urging listeners to let Ken's sudden death remind them of the importance of considering spiritual matters while there was time. The next day I received an angry open letter from one of his colleagues at Hudson's Bay High School where Ken had taught. The letter derided me for omitting all Ken's accomplishments and for failing to involve anyone from the faculty. Dozens of teachers had received it. Betty assured me that it was OK, but I was stung. It was a hard lesson about the gap that exists between the way the church and the public deal with death. It was important, obviously, to consider the wider web of connections of the person who had died.

Baptisms, while more predictable and vastly happier occasions, also provided some surprising moments. One Sunday, as Pastor Schroeder and I swung the side door open for the entrance hymn, my heart sank. There in the front pew sat a family who had come for the baptism of their baby. Baby herself was dressed in a long, white heirloom gown. But I had completely forgotten the event after making arrangements by phone earlier that week. While the congregation sang the hymn, I raced back to my office to gather an agenda, collared an usher to fetch a pitcher of water, and picked up a baptismal napkin from the office drawer. Heart pounding, I arrived at the font as the usher finished pouring and the hymn was ending. The family never knew that anything was amiss. On another occasion, the baptismal party made its way to the font, and I was prepared with the agenda, napkin, and certificate. But when the lid was lifted from the font, we could plainly see that the ushers had forgotten the water. The hymn ceased. All were waiting for my words. *What in the world do I say?* A moment's pause. "We will now have the filling of the font!" I said, flashing a look at the usher nearby. To his credit, he turned, unflustered, to get a pitcher of water, as I introduced the family and their fine new child. In short order, we were able to proceed. Whew.

Weddings, too, could surprise. Ralph Porter and Carol Bradford were standing before the altar. She was re-marrying, and her son David, age 10, was the ring-bearer. It was a hot day, and David was unwell. Right in the midst of the service, David vomited in front of everyone, right in front of the altar! Carol, a very proper person, was horrified. David was helped out by a groomsman and vomited again as he exited the sanctuary. "Well, Ralph and Carol," I said soothingly, "if this is the worst thing you have to face, you'll be fine." There was scattered laughter. The tension eased. We finished the ceremony.

Along with my first call came our first (and only) parsonage. This solid brick and frame house, which sat across a field fifty yards west of the church, had been the Schroeders' residence for years. They had now moved to their own home in Hazel Dell. The parsonage was surrounded by an escort of birch trees. A camellia bush and a row of crocuses in front heralded springtime. A separate garage framed with pyracantha bushes was just outside the kitchen door on the north side, and beyond it an old bus barn converted to the congregation's catch-all storage.

Between the garage and the bus barn Pastor Schroeder had tended a garden plot that I now inherited, a patch of tilled soil about twenty feet square with a row of loganberry bushes running north and south in the center. "Plant your rows north and south," he instructed, "to get the benefit of the sun." Gardening became one of my perennial enjoyments, with carrots, beans and berries the very first harvest.

We began to meet our neighbors. A widow with a gruff voice but a kindly demeanor named Marie Harris lived across the street. An older couple named Howard and Shirley Bales, who liked to sit outside in a pair of lawn chairs, would wave and "Halloo!" as I walked to my office. The neighbors were mostly pleasant, the neighborhood mostly quiet. Mostly.

There were unpleasant experiences. Persons unknown stole the clothing off our clothesline in back of the garage. On another occasion, I came out to start my car and found that the battery was missing. One afternoon when school was just letting out, I chanced to see out the back window a group of teens walking by, pitching their semi-full pop cans into our yard. In a rush of temper I raced out and, without stopping to consider the consequences, I began throw the cans after the departing students. They stopped, turned, and began to taunt me, and one fellow even threw them back a second time. *Calm down, Pastor Mike. Remember who you are!* I reined in my temper and the confrontation ended there.

The advantages of a home next door became obvious. I saved both time and gasoline by walking to my office each day. If I forgot an important paper, I could simply run home to retrieve it. There was no need to pack a lunch either. On their part, the congregation took care to give us privacy unless there was an emergency or a special gift was to be delivered. One day the doorbell rang, and we found Jim and Jan Pomerenk and some of their children standing on the porch with a coffee cake to celebrate my birthday.

When we arrived in Vancouver, Melanie was our only child. The next year that changed. Late in 1973, we learned that a second child was on the way. On the evening of July 23, while I was at the church council meeting, I got a phone call. I arrived home to find Bertha Burgstahler playing with Melanie. "I'm baby-sitting," she said, and you and Sue are going to the hospital – pretty soon!" Sue, I discovered, was in the bathroom shower, dutifully washing her hair. The contractions increased with startling rapidity and we sped to Vancouver Memorial Hospital. By the time I parked the car and put on my green hospital gown and foot coverings, Sue was being wheeled hastily into the delivery room – just in time! Less than an hour after our arrival, Christa was born. No Lamaze class review. No time for coaching at all. Just a sudden advent.

With the arrival of our children, Sue made a firm decision to be a stay-at-home mom. Both our home and our church were blessed by her decision, for daily life picked up speed. The evenings were especially wearing. Month by month there came meetings of Elders and Church Council, confirmation classes, Sunday School teachers, youth counselors, marriage preparation, home visits. The schedule at church often involved both of us. At times, it made for a circus-like atmosphere at home as we dressed the children and fed them, dressed ourselves, changed diapers, and raced off, usually a few minutes late, for that day's event.

I was conscientious about my church duties, but almost oblivious to my familial responsibilities to my wife and children, the same mistake I had made at seminary. As a consequence, things at home were not happy. I was at the office most evenings after being away all day. Sue was left to tend the children and clean the house by herself in the early years of parenting when the children's needs were most urgent.

Tension was an increasingly frequent visitor in our home. The crowded schedule often left us edgy. Angry confrontations erupted. I was having an 'affair' with my job and didn't fully realize what I was doing to Sue. I did not know that she left the house at times to stand and weep angry, lonely tears beside the bus barn in the dark. We were sliding from the disillusionment we had experienced at the seminary into a more serious kind of misery.

God sent us help in the person of Bob Kunz, who had been pastor at St. Matthew in Washougal and was now an area hospital chaplain. I don't know if Bob was aware of our struggles, but he invited us to join some other couples at his home for Sunday evenings together. He and his wife Eunice encouraged us to open up about marriage matters, first by playing recorded talks by marriage counselor Urban Steinmetz, then by facilitating the sharing of our feelings. It was a revelation to learn that other couples were facing some of the same disappointments we were feeling. We weren't alone! His gentle manner soothed our spirits and restored hope.

We made the decision to set aside one night a week as 'family night.' Other than the occasional wedding rehearsal, there was no scheduled church activity on Fridays, so each Friday we kept the television off, ate as a family, did dishes together, and had sit-down time with the children. We sat on the living room rug, with a lighted candle on a towel, for family devotion time. The first time we did it, Melanie, now age four, looked up with wonder and said, "We're having a worship service!" Prayers and songs and lessons with puppets kept things lively. After the devotion came popcorn or some other treat and a board game. 'Chutes and Ladders' was a mainstay.

There was no overnight cure for our trouble, but a start had been made. Friday night became the cornerstone on which marriage and family leaned. Not until several years later, at another church in another state, would we learn to put into practice more fully what it took to make a harmonious marriage.

Being a minister did not guarantee marital happiness. Nor did it solve the persistent problem of my pride, which surfaced again in a variety of ways. In conversations with members I found myself fishing for compliments. In conversations with Pastor Schroeder, I found that both of us turned judgmental about parishioners with distressing frequency.

God brought it home to me with particular clarity one night. I had just finished making a phone call to our youth counselors about a planned outing. A few minutes later I picked up the phone once more to speak to someone else, but instead of a dial tone, there was a strange silence, then some voices far away, as if I were hearing someone in a tunnel. "Hello?" I said. Then much louder, "HELLOOO!!" but it was obvious that the folks at the other end of the line could not hear me. I listened hard, trying to discover the problem, and then realized that the voices were those of Brad and Leah, the youth counselors I had just spoken with minutes before. They had not replaced the phone correctly on its cradle. Now I could hear everything they said. As I listened, I realized with horror that they were talking about me, and it was not at all complimentary! With a mounting sense of anger, I heard my faults being discussed, while I sat helpless to defend myself.

I finally hung up and sat, brooding darkly. Then, as if someone had turned on a light switch, I saw the dreadful truth. This was the very thing Pastor Schroeder and I had been doing – speaking unkind words about our parishioners. How might they have felt if THEY had been listening in on us? How long would it take me to control my tongue? God had much to correct in me, and much yet to teach me.

YOUTH PASTOR

Pastor Schroeder, experienced though he was, found the multiple tasks of the pastorate at Memorial an increasingly heavy burden. He was thankful to have someone share the weekly preaching and visitation load. Now 57 years old and feeling a growing gap between himself and adolescent youth, he was especially eager to divest himself of the youth confirmation class. Confirmation class was designed to prepare young people for full adult membership, especially for reception of Holy Communion. I agreed to do that. He told me later, "You saved my life!"

My first confirmation class numbered twelve. Initially, I taught a single year of Luther's SMALL CATECHISM. Within a year or two, however, because of concern about the biblical illiteracy of most of my students, I added two more years to the program, one in Old Testament, one in New Testament. I prepared memory charts for each year, requiring three separate recitations of each item to assure that these had been firmly fixed in their minds. The charts were posted on the wall as motivation. I had high hopes and high expectations.

Each year's class began with a trip to Camp Colton, 30 miles southeast of Portland, for confirmation camp in August. A half-dozen of us pastors brought our classes for both study and fun. The site itself was set amidst towering firs and cedars. At the center of camp was a long, sturdy dining hall. Although the kids' cabins were rustic, I determined to stay with them instead of in the pastors' cabin. It meant long hours and loss of sleep, but there was an irreplaceable bonding as we joked and sang and played pranks. I wanted the kids to see a real human, not a plaster pastor.

Meals were raucous affairs that began with a sung prayer like 'Johnny Appleseed':

Oh, the Lord is good to me, and so I thank the Lord
For giving me the things I need –
the sun and the rain and the appleseed...

Counselors led prayers, told jokes, conducted mail call, and handled announcements. Tables competed with chanted puns.

Did you ever see a horse fly, a horse fly, a horse fly?
Did you ever see a horse fly? Now you tell us one...

Our class table rose to the challenge ("Did you ever see a home run?" "Did you ever see a broad jump?").

Class time filled the morning hours, and I aimed at covering the Ten Commandments in that week. The afternoon was set aside for swimming, crafts, and other electives. I brought two chess boards and gave lessons to neophytes. Both boards were in constant use. The highlight of the week, for both pastors and kids, was a challenge volleyball match between the pastors and the college-age kids who served as counselors. We pastors, an arrogant lot, loved to demonstrate how old age and experience could overcome youthful bravado. The kids cheered wildly. The teaching of faith, the fun of volleyball and the energy of the kids, all bundled in a beautiful wooded setting, made the camp experience feel like heaven on earth. It was a high point in my years as a youth pastor.

For confirmation day itself, I opted to change the routine I had learned. Instead of a public examination before the congregation, with scripted questions and answers, I endeavored to have something more personal. I asked each of the young people to prepare a brief testimony of faith, written on paper and read to the congregation. We spent the final two weeks of class time preparing these, and a large portion of the confirmation service was taken up with their sharing. I did not at the time fully appreciate how frightening any kind of public speaking (or even reading!) could be. Yet somehow, all of them, even the most timid, pulled it off. For my part, there was also a lot of administrative work preparing certificates, each with a specially-chosen Bible verse such as I had once received from Pastor Albers, fitting robes for the big day, arranging for a class photo, and choreographing the confirmation rite.

Once confirmed, our kids moved into our high school youth group. There was fun in the form of scavenger hunts, roller skating parties, and even a free car wash, done as a way of witnessing the gift of God's grace in Jesus. Bible study was a staple in our spiritual diet. The Sunday morning class was conducted in the cramped 'upper room' in the old balcony of the parish hall. As youth pastor, I was, by default, the perpetual teacher. Things did not always go according to plan. One morning, our session was interrupted by a loud crash. We ran to the window and saw a car that had smashed into a tree. The young woman inside was slumped over the steering wheel, alive but bloodied. EMTs hurried her off to the hospital. I later visited her there and brought her a card signed by the class. On another morning, the students were completely unresponsive to the lesson. Frustrated, I walked out in the middle of class and did not return. My temper and immaturity were on display that day.

A more successful kind of gathering was our weekly 'Thursday Thing' at the parsonage. Six to ten youth came, Bibles in hand, for a time of study, snacks, and games. Only the most motivated kids came, and all were wide awake. As the kids met, our daughters hovered behind the banister on the stairway, listening. Afterward, Sue brought in the evening's snack from the kitchen. She was rarely alone as she prepared. Young people dropped in to talk, for they found her a ready and cheerful listener. The night concluded with a game time, which might take us downstairs for 'round the world' ping pong, outside for Frisbee golf, or right in the living room to play 'barnyard,' a wild affair in which participants were assigned animal identities, got down on hands and knees, and (with lights out) mooed and bleated and oinked to find their partners.

The most memorable times of all were the back-pack trips we took during summer months. The first was a five-day hike in the Mt. Jefferson Wilderness near Bagby Hot Springs. Our guide, Terry, instructed us in the proper carriage of our packs, the making of freeze-dried food, and the application of moleskin patches to blisters. Twelve youth, with Terry and me as adult chaperones, covered 35 miles of wilderness trails. The third day out we came upon a real-life forest fire, visible several miles away, and we watched in awe as forest service planes dropped orange fire retardant on the flames. The mosquitoes proved persistent, in spite of our abundant bug spray. We came to treasure the water in our bottles since the water in the streams, Terry advised, was too polluted to use.

A second trip took us down 125 miles of the Willamette River by canoe from Eugene to Portland. The water presented a greater hazard, so we were assigned two guides, who demonstrated how to load our belongings in a balanced way and lash them securely to the cross-braces so that, if the canoe tipped, nothing would float away. We all learned the J-stroke by which the rear occupant steered the canoe. Finally we launched our five canoes, each with a crew of three and a hefty pile of baggage.

The journey began peacefully in sunshine. The quiet of the river was like a slow, gentle narcotic to the soul. One felt, looking down, like the boat and the water were standing still and everything else – the shore and the rocks beneath the surface – were moving swiftly past. After a day or two, civilization (in the form of bridges, power poles, or irrigation pipes) felt like an intruder. Not all was quiet. We sang, stopped to swim, and conducted miniature sea battles, splashing with the flat of our paddles. The few rapids were tame ones, though two of our boys were toppled into the water when they passed under a low-hanging branch.

In the midst of our journey, the sunshine which had burned our legs yielded to dark clouds and then a rain which grew more and more intense. We were compelled to come ashore and seek shelter, but we saw no likely spots. "How about a farmhouse?" someone suggested. Several boys and I set out slogging through muddy fields. Nearly a mile away, we finally spied a house with lights on and knocked. Though we must have looked like apparitions from a nightmare, the middle-aged couple who answered the door took pity on us. The farmer drove with us in his pickup back to the river's edge to load our supplies and transport our water-logged campers back to their warm, dry garage, where we spent the night most comfortably. Our hosts, on hearing that we were a church group, identified themselves as Methodists and joined us for our devotion time that night.

The third trip was a beachcomber hike from Oswald West State Park to Fort Clatsop, where Lewis and Clark had left a salt cairn. It was the most public of our trips. Besides generous helpings of wind in the faces and sand in our shoes, we had frequent encounters with others who trekked the coast, people who proved to be curious and friendly. Once again we had a rainy night – this time on Tillamook Head. The rain drummed on our tents and soaked us as we stuffed gear into backpacks. Along the way I was struck by the wide variety of dead creatures – crabs and birds without number, a seal, a small shark, and even the rotting remnants of an observation post built during World War II to spot Japanese ships and planes. All this made a large impression on me, now in my thirties and beginning to feel my own mortality.

Young people grow into adulthood, and over the years we watched scores of youth make that passage, leave home, and head off to military life, college, and careers. There were occasional heartaches in the watching. Some abandoned the church. "I don't believe that any more," one boy, who came from a very faithful family, admitted. Another boy served time in jail, where I wrote to him and urged him to stay connected to God. Yet there were also causes for celebration as I watched young people mature into the gifted and productive servants God intended them to be. Pam Edwards realized her dream of going to medical school, and she later became a psychiatrist and teacher at Oregon Health Sciences University. Dave Nufer became a Lutheran teacher and wound up as a public school principal in Alaska.

Watching such stories unfold was very like becoming a father all over again. It was especially so with Steve Eaton, who entered Concordia College in Portland to train for the ministry. He had been aiming at architecture as a career, but God changed his mind, in part because of a prayer he heard me pray one Sunday for "more workers for the harvest."

"Has my mom been talking to you?" he asked after the service.

"No," I replied honestly.

"Well, I'd been thinking about the ministry. When you prayed that prayer, I felt like God was tapping me on the shoulder."

I knew about that sort of tap.

Sixteen years later, God put us together as a pastoral team in Sequim, Washington.

MISSOURI'S CIVIL WAR

The early years of ministry at Memorial were lived under a cloud that darkened our entire church body and had its effects on work and relationships in our congregation.

The tension at the St. Louis seminary finally exploded into an ecclesiastical civil war the year after I graduated. Newly-elected synod president J. A. O. 'Jack' Preus, a man with a bulldog face and a determination to match, had appointed a fact-finding committee to investigate the continued rumors of false teaching there. The professors cooperated, but groused that the fact-finding was really a fault-finding effort designed to purge them. The committee's report was issued in a blue-covered booklet with transcripts of interviews for all the church to read. Professors' identities were thinly masked by assigning them letters (Professor M and so on). The subjects were mostly biblical. What did they think about the historicity of Adam and Eve and Jonah? Did they accept the Virgin Birth? The Resurrection? Out in the hinterlands, some called the professors 'Bible doubters.'

The professors responded by publishing a document affirming their faithfulness to Scripture and explaining their use of the so-called historical-critical method of Bible interpretation. But the affirmations fell on deaf ears. The July 1973 convention of the synod in New Orleans condemned the position of the faculty majority as something "not to be tolerated in the church of God." They were branded heretics en masse. It only remained to pursue them and remove them one by one. Not everyone agreed, and supporters of the faculty made their way to the podium to record their dissent while singing the hymn *'The Church's one Foundation.'*

With the thunder of coming ecclesiastical discipline rumbling in the distance during the following school year, students at St. Louis made a momentous decision. In January 1974 they walked out of classes, demanding to know which of their professors were supposed to be false teachers. The professors joined the moratorium. The seminary's board of control responded with the demand that teachers and students return to class or the teachers would be fired. The teachers said no. The newspapers smelled a big story and sent reporters. A photographer from the *St. Louis Post-Dispatch* captured the image of students hoisting cafeteria tables against seminary doors and spray-painting a single word: EXILED. The now-fired professors and a large majority of students left the campus and created a 'seminary in exile' at nearby Eden Seminary and St. Louis University. Thus SEMINEX was born.

It didn't stop there. A support organization called Evangelical Lutherans in Mission (ELIM) was formed and began printing its own newspaper, *Missouri in Perspective*. Meetings were held around the country. People chose sides. District presidents were faced with the unenviable task of deciding what to do with seminary graduates.

President Emil Jaech of the Northwest District was one of eight presidents who welcomed and installed them. Many in our district, and some at Memorial, were angered by Jaech's decision. Pastoral conferences were divided, and some pastors refused to commune with others. For the first time, I felt ashamed of my church.

As a graduate of St. Louis, I felt a loyalty to the men there, whom I admired as kind and knowledgeable, and certainly not 'Bible doubters.' While I did not agree with them on every issue, I felt that they were not getting the due process which even secular courts afforded. I signed on with ELIM and attended local meetings. At our circuit conferences I carried on a running skirmish with Jim Rehley, a conservative pastor from Grace, Longview. At the state pastoral conference, an older pastor named George Reule quizzed me about my stance on evolution, a matter over which I felt personally conflicted.

As a new graduate of St. Louis, I was automatically suspect by some of Memorial's older folks. The group, which included my own secretary Ruth Pasewalk and her husband Paul, scrutinized and criticized me. My confirmation instruction, some said, wasn't substantive enough. "He doesn't require any memory work" and "He wants to lead us out of the synod," were whispered rumors that got back to me.

Pastor Schroeder invited some of the principal players in the district (from both sides) to come and explain the issues as they saw them. One was President Jaech, who had worked side by side with Schroeder for some years. In this way Schroeder deflected some of the criticism from me and by his diplomatic speech calmed an atmosphere that, had I been alone, might have provoked a more strident response or even a defection from me.

For my part, I wrote a letter to the congregation and read it at one of those gatherings as a way of explaining my position:

> *A number of you have asked, 'Where do our pastors stand?'*
> *You do have a right to know…*

I told them I had grown up in the Missouri Synod and felt a deep loyalty and love for her. My experience in Operation Live-In in Chicago showed me that we were not very good at translating doctrine into action. My experience at seminary, I went on, was faith-strengthening, and I saw genuine respect for the Bible. I allowed that the professors were human and were sometimes too critical of conservatives, but "never did I hear the Bible disparaged as 'myth' or belittled." I told them that I dissented from Preus's *Statement of Scriptural and Confessional Principles* and had expressed my formal dissent through channels provided. "I have a copy of my letter if you wish to read it," I added. I told them of my membership in ELIM and explained it as my way of protesting the lack of due process for the faculty. I concluded with a plea, "If you still have a question about my stand on a specific issue, how about asking me directly?"

Pastor Schroeder and I did not, in fact, lead the congregation out of the synod. It survived intact, and the furor gradually subsided, although several hundred congregations eventually left our church body. Though the synod's civil war finally wound down, my secretary was still heard to be grumbling behind my back, and there were times when Pastor Schroeder and I considered firing her. I made it a subject of prayer, asking God to give me insight about her and to help us forge a healthier relationship. A few weeks later we were in the copy room. She wore a look of consternation, and I asked, "Are you OK?" She began to cry, and the floodgates opened. She shared a burdensome unhappiness in her family and a worry about her son. I concluded that her unhappiness had sought an outlet, and that I had become a convenient target. My resentment of her melted away that day. Our relationship healed and a wholesome sort of peace descended on the office.

Years later, long after we had moved away from Vancouver, Sue and I came back to Memorial for a visit. Up to us came Paul and Ruth Pasewalk. They were visibly aged, but brighter-faced than I remembered. They welcomed us with broad smiles and we talked with genuine warmth. Time and grace had done their work.

LARRY GANTKA

Pastoral ministry is a two-way street. I expected to be shaping others by the sharing of God's Word. But I learned that I was also being shaped by those encounters. One of the most memorable of those took place when I met and ministered to a man named Larry Gantka.

Patrons at Diamond Jim's Bar looked on as the couple quarreled. Sherrie Gantka, a tall, slender blonde, worked as a barmaid there, and Larry, her husband, came in to talk. But as it did so often, their talking turned into shouting. Their marriage, the second for both, was coming apart. Larry rose from his seat, stormed out of the bar, and drove off in a rage. Little more than a mile away, his speeding car careened out of control and slammed into a tree. Firemen pried his battered body from the wreckage and rushed him to St. Joseph Community Hospital. He was alive, barely.

Larry's first wife, Dixie, was summoned, and the doctor spoke urgently to her. "He's terribly injured. I need you to help me decide whether or not to use heroic measures to keep him alive. His neck is broken, and if he lives at all, he will probably be quadriplegic." Dixie was stunned. "Oh, yes," added the doctor, "and if you have a pastor, you'd better call him."

Larry was a lumber salesman in his early forties. The father of two children by his first marriage, he was now a stepfather to two more in this second marriage. He had been a member of Memorial some years before my arrival, but because of an accumulation of personal problems aggravated by alcohol abuse, Larry's life started to unravel. He was a bitter man, alienated from God and angry with the church, and he had stopped attending worship several years earlier. When he was finally removed from membership before I came to Memorial, he concluded that the church had taken the action because his contributions had ceased.

Pastor Schroeder took Dixie's late-night call and headed for the hospital. Knowing Larry's history and the state of his broken relationships with God and his own family, Pastor Schroeder urged Dixie, "Don't let him die. He's not ready." He explained that this was Larry's opportunity, even in the midst of trauma, to experience urgently needed change in his life. By this time Sherrie had arrived at the hospital. The extended family huddled and agreed. They urged the doctor, "Take whatever measures necessary! Larry must be spared." As the medical team worked feverishly to stabilize his condition, the family prayed.

Larry's life was spared, but it seemed a dark victory. The doctor's prediction of paralysis came true. Larry was a C-4 quadriplegic – paralyzed from the neck down. A few days later, he and I met for the first time. Pastor Schroeder handed the responsibility to me. "Larry and I have too much baggage between us. Why don't you see what you can do?" A few days later, when Larry was conscious, I went. Our initial visit was brief. Larry had a tracheostomy, and he could speak little more than a whisper. I introduced myself, tried to listen, and prayed a brief prayer with him. How could I demonstrate the love of God to this man?

I began by making regular visits. During those first critical weeks, I went daily to St. Joseph Hospital. Together we marveled at his progression from critical to fair to stable condition. After several weeks, Larry was moved to Rehabilitation Institute of Oregon across the Columbia River in downtown Portland. Our meetings now happened once or twice a week. Some slight shoulder and arm movement returned, and therapists trained him to use an electric-powered wheelchair with a large joy-stick control knob. His life was jeopardized by recurring bouts of pneumonia and chronic bedsores which could become infected. "They have to put this thing under my fanny," he smiled, indicating a doughnut-shaped foam pad on his tray.

More significant changes were happening inside Larry. He spoke, hesitantly at first, about his pent-up anger at the church, about alcohol's pervasive power, and about his fear of death. I acknowledged that the church had not been the caring community it should have been toward him. "We're all sinners," I told him. "God tends us just as you are being tended here at RIO. You could say the church is a hospital for sinners, and we're all in rehab." He nodded agreement.

Larry and I spent many hours walking hallways, meeting staff and other patients, and learning together about his therapy regimen. We began to read the Bible together. The entire Gospel of Mark, chapter by chapter, was our first accomplishment. Larry was a perceptive man and not hesitant to ask hard questions. But I heard no bitterness or cynicism.

It wasn't all serious. We discovered that we shared an interest in chess, so I began to bring along my wooden box of Staunton-design pieces and a board. He exulted that he could still play this game simply by directing me to make his moves. He flashed a wide smile the day he finally beat me.

Eventually Larry returned home and continued therapy there, but his physical progress ceased. For a while Sherrie and the children stayed with him, but the enormous strain proved too much, and she divorced him. Yet things between them had changed. There had been a healing, and she continued to show care for him in the years afterward. Meanwhile, government aid allowed Larry to rent an apartment of his own and secure some daily help from hired aides.

It was a morning of sunshine and tears when, at last, Larry rejoined Memorial Lutheran Church. That bright Sunday morning the wheelchair van pulled up to the entrance, and Larry, assisted by his aide, came up the walk and through the front entrance, hair blown wild by the breeze and a wide smile on his face. He came all the way down the aisle to take his place on the outside of the front row. My voice trembled with emotion as I introduced him. It was a moment of indescribable sweetness, touched with his tears and mine. A lost sheep had come home.

His return was no flash in the pan. He continued coming, and his face became familiar to others. His wheelchair learned its niche at the end of that front row.

There came a day when I received and accepted the call to a church in Ohio, and I made a last visit to Larry before leaving. He took time to look back with me over three years of visits. "Pastor Mike," he said, "I guess you know what I've been through has been bad. I wouldn't wish this on anyone – this being paralyzed and living in a wheelchair and having aides help me do everything…" He was quiet, and so was I. "But for me, that accident was the grace of God. If it hadn't happened, I'd be dead from alcohol by now, and in hell too! But here I am, alive. I love God again. And one day he will give me a new body. I am thankful it turned out this way."

It was a miracle I had witnessed, as wondrous as any recorded in the Gospels. A dead man had come back to life before my eyes.

Each Christmas for years thereafter, a card from Larry found its way to our mailbox in Akron. It contained a brief, typed message, indicating that Larry was making steps along his new path:

"I have joined a home Bible study group."
"I'm still coming to church every week."
"This poor sinner received the gift of tongues."

At the bottom of each card was his name, written painstakingly in his own, unsteady hand.

His life became, for me, a living illustration of why Jesus came, and what even a frightful tragedy could accomplish in the hands of a gracious God.

PLAYFUL TIMES AND DEEP FRIENDSHIP

The Benedictine monks say that every day has enough time for work and prayer, for study and for play. My intensely driven nature assured that I would work hard. Pastor Schroeder's disciplined approach to ministry had laid on me the assignments of daily prayer and study. But I discovered that I also needed to take time away from the pressurized pastoral routine. The beautiful scenery of 'God's Country' in the Northwest invited us, finally, to come and play.

Stretching away east of the Portland metro area was a scenic wonderland within a day's easy drive. The Columbia River Gorge, carved and chiseled over aeons by water, wind, and volcanic fire, begged to be explored. A drive east along Highway 14 on the Washington side brought us to Beacon Rock, an 800-foot monolith that stood like an ancient sentinel by the river. During World War 1, workmen built a stairway up the face of the rock in a dizzying sequence of switchbacks that took climbers to the very top for a panoramic view in about half an hour. Our girls were old enough to attempt it now, and we made it one of the first stops in a day's vacation loop.

A few miles further, we crossed the river over the Bridge of the Gods, a man-made span built at a site where, according to legend, there was once a natural rock bridge across the river. Native Americans said the gods put it there.

Coming back along the Oregon side, we had our choice of stops. The Bonneville Dam offered a visitor center and a fish ladder for salmon returning to spawn. One could visit the fish counting room where volunteers kept track of how many chinook, coho, humpback, and shad swam past. Nearby was a state fish hatchery which housed a pond for giant sturgeon, one of them ten feet long. By this point in the day, we were ravenously hungry and spread our tablecloth over a table to enjoy a picnic lunch.

On the way back to Portland came a string of wondrous waterfalls – Wahkeena, Bridal Veil, Horsetail, and the towering Multnomah Falls, at 620 feet the seventh highest waterfall in North America. Now and then we would devote a whole day to hiking the trail into the Oneonta Gorge, a challenging two-hour loop that rewarded us by taking us behind the roaring water of Horsetail Falls. Along the way our children delighted when they saw a deer or spotted orange mushrooms or immense banana slugs. Overhead the towering firs and cedars made it feel that we were hiking through an outdoor cathedral.

To the west of the Portland area was the Pacific Ocean, just 90 miles away. Family outings to play in the waves and make sand castles at Ecola State Park or in Lincoln City were both thrilling and exhausting. Pastor Carl

Losser made his family cabin in Lincoln City available to area pastors for getaways, and Sue and I decided to make periodic retreats there with married couples from Memorial. The cabin offered ample space, so Sue and I took five couples at a time for marriage retreats. Each couple was assigned one meal to fix and clean up so that all the rest of us could be treated. We planned talk sessions, games, and couple quiet times for taking long walks on the beach. The retreats always ended with a worship hour in which all the couples played some role. These times away were a much-needed tonic for our relationship and for the others who accompanied us.

Of course, one needn't leave home to have fun. There were some playful people at Memorial. Two groups, dubbed the Memorialites and Koinonians, planned festive activities. The favorite was a progressive dinner, which might start with salad at the Shaver home, then a main course at the Reitzensteins, then dessert and a devotion at the LaValley home. One dinner was especially memorable because we had to drive through a thickening fog to each successive house, and at one the sheer number of electric skillets blew the circuit breakers. We wound up with skillets in every room.

For Sue, relaxation at home most often took the form of sewing clothes for the girls, and she produced a succession of pretty dresses, and even a set of Easter bonnets. For me, relaxation with the children meant sitting in the green rocker to read stories. First with Melanie, and then with Christa in her turn, we followed Bilbo the hobbit into Smaug's frightful lair in the Lonely Mountain. Then, more ambitiously, we embarked into *The Lord of the Rings*, a journey that took months and strained my voice as I tried to imitate Gollum and the orcs. When we finished, I fought to hold back tears as Frodo, Sam, and Gandalf parted company for the last time.

The soul needs relaxing too. We felt a need for something deeper and more sustaining. There remained for Sue and me an empty spot in our hearts, for we were far from our families in Indiana and craved something more than the persistent busyness and a full schedule of fun activities could offer. The people at Memorial were thoughtful and kind-hearted toward us. But without family nearby, we hungered for at least one intimate set of friends.

The generation before I graduated from seminary, prospective pastors were warned not to have close friends in the congregation. It was, the reasoning went, a potential source of trouble, for a pastor was not to be a 'respecter of persons' and must maintain a healthy distance between himself and the people he was to preach to and admonish. But we hadn't heard those lectures, and would likely not have heeded them anyway.

God's grace provided us the friendship we sorely needed in those years in the person of Chuck and Kathy Cusack. Kathy was the older sister of

Steve Eaton, the lone daughter in a rollicking family of boys. Kathy and Sue were both teachers, and both were endowed with lovely soprano voices. Her talent and looks had earned her the runner-up spot in the Miss Washington pageant not long before our arrival on vicarage. It didn't take long for Sue and Kathy to discover their shared interests and abilities, and a friendship was born.

During the vicarage year, Kathy was dating a man named Chuck Cusack, a ruggedly handsome, athletic fellow from California who was studying to be a lawyer. Chuck's church background was scant, and he harbored lots of questions. But she adored him, and his fun-loving nature and integrity captured her heart. They married while we were finishing seminary, on the very day Melanie was born.

Our return to Vancouver gave the friendship opportunity to form and flourish. Sue and Kathy made a wonderful music team at church, whether singing duets or working together with the children's choir Sue had organized. Kathy had become the adult choir director, and all of us practiced in the balcony. Chuck and I, meanwhile, enjoyed a shared interest in sports. We played basketball together on Memorial's church league team and volleyball on a city league team.

The friendship was more than mere fun together. We took serious time to reflect together on matters of marriage, faith, and the church. As the one newest to the faith, Chuck brought me questions that were often beyond my depth, especially on the subject of predestination, an issue that boggled both of us. The four of us shared a burden of concern about our church's civil war, unfolding in those years. We enjoyed a trip together to a cabin on the coast where we let our hair down (literally and figuratively) and discussed the things that placed stress on our marriages.

The arrival of children in both families changed the mix. Chuck and Kathy had three daughters. Shayna, the oldest, became our godchild, and for years afterward, Kathy playfully referred to us as Godfather Mike and Godmother Sue. A second child, Kelly, was born near the end of our Vancouver years, about the same time as our son Peter. A third daughter, Katie, arrived after our move to Akron.

The move to Akron put a vast distance between us, but we were determined that we would not let our friendship wither, so we took time to plan trips back and forth across the country as time and money allowed. The Cusacks came to Akron, visited Sea World in nearby Aurora with us, and splashed merrily in the plastic pool in our driveway. We journeyed back to Vancouver on Amtrak, and we re-visited many old haunts, like the Enchanted Forest and the Horsetail Falls trail. Still later, when we returned to the Northwest in our move to Sequim, Washington, we continued our visits, taking a vacation trip together to Victoria, B.C., via ferry boat across the Strait of Juan de Fuca.

But all was not well for our friends. They told us of growing discomfort between them, born out of serious differences between their personalities and aggravated by the pressures of parenthood. Our visits together were sometimes punctuated by tears and prayers for understanding. We feared for their future, even though the strong threads of faith and the shared task of parenting held them together.

Several years later came a dreadful piece of news. Kathy was diagnosed with brain cancer. "Likely terminal," said the doctor. It was a shocking blow to us, and we felt the pain of our geographic separation ever more sharply. It put the marital differences both of us couples had struggled with into perspective. Chuck stepped up and tended her faithfully. Perhaps, Sue and I thought, this was one of those 'severe mercies' C. S. Lewis had written about, for the troubles they had faced were eclipsed by this greater challenge.

Kathy was treated with steroids as her condition worsened, and her once-pretty face was bloated and grotesque. Late in the summer of 1994, Sue went down to Vancouver for a few days to help Kathy with household chores and the children's care. With time running out, Kathy recorded her favorite songs as a parting gift for her family and for Memorial. The album, '*Shine Through Me*,' was a memorial gift both beautiful and courageous.

She died on Thanksgiving Day, 1994. We sat together with Chuck and the girls in the crowded sanctuary for her service, and one last time we heard her lovely recorded voice sing, '*How Beautiful is the Body of Christ.*'

In our friendship, we had been privileged again to see God's grace at work over time. Even in trouble, even in death, we were blessed by the bond that connected us to our friends through the deep, deep love of Jesus.

A PROPHECY AND AN EXPLOSION

The year 1980 was a tumultuous one, changing forever the landscape of the Pacific Northwest and that of our own family. The tumult was not entirely unexpected. There were rumblings.

The first was a quiet, nagging rumble inside me. I was getting restless in my role as a co-pastor. I wanted to try my wings, do pastoral ministry on my own. Already in 1979 I had felt the stirrings. Pastor Schroeder was by then 64 years old, had weathered a bout with cancer, and was just a year or two away from retiring. His pastoral seismograph detected my tiny inner tremors, and he began to say things like "I hope you can stay on until I lay this thing down." On my own, I made an appointment to see District President Emil Jaech in Portland and tell him my feelings. I didn't believe in dictating to God, but I felt that God might be at work in my inclinations and in the wisdom of my superiors. I shared in detail and he listened. "I'll just leave all this with you," I concluded. Having spoken it aloud, I let it go. That rumbling died down.

The second rumble was inside Sue. "Honey," she said sweetly to me one day, "I've been thinking I'd like to have another baby." The ground didn't shake, but my stomach fluttered. I was not so inclined.

"We already have a lot of responsibility," I pointed out reasonably. "We have two children of our own to care for," and then, after a pause, "and a whole church full of people too!"

Sue pressed on. "Could you at least pray about it?"

How could I refuse to do that? "Okay," I agreed.

Weeks went by, and I did pray. Sue was praying too, likely for God to change my mind. And He did. My insistence on our self-imposed family limit eroded, and we agreed to let God do the deciding.

The third rumble was sharp, specific, and almost startling. Our worship service had ended one summer day in 1979, and Pastor Schroeder and I were greeting people at the doors, our usual custom. One of the last people out that morning was Pat Vinsonhaler, a red-headed woman in her early 50s who had recently returned to church after an extended absence. "Could I speak with you and Sue?" she asked unexpectedly.

"Sure," I agreed. I summoned Sue, and after the last worshippers exited, we sat down with Pat in one of the back pews. She had something significant on her mind, I could see.

"This morning in church," she began, "as I watched you both, three things came to me. I feel that I must tell you about them." We gaped, clueless. "The first thing," she said very softly, "is that Sue is expecting a baby." *Really?* We had been trying, but there was nothing yet to report.

"The second thing," she went on, "is that it will be a boy." A moment of silence. "And the third thing is that within a year, you will be gone from here." *A direct, personal prophecy to us? Does God do that?* Sue and I returned home, quietly stunned.

Within a month, her first word to us was confirmed. Sue was pregnant with our third child. But confirmation of the rest was months away, and as things unfolded that year, we forgot all about it.

During that time the newspaper and television were laced with stories of a literal rumbling at Mt. St. Helens, just 55 miles northeast of Vancouver. Seismologists recorded tremors of increasing frequency, and the earth on the north side of the mountain began to bulge noticeably. On occasion, little plumes of steam and ash were vented into the air. Harry Truman, a grizzled fellow with a presidential name who lived at the mountain's foot, was the subject of frequent interviews.

"Are you planning to move out of here?" reporters queried.

"Nope," he said, square-jawed. "The mountain is my friend."

The mountain itself settled back into restless sleep for weeks thereafter. We got on with life. Authorities established "safe zones" around the mountain and warnings were duly posted. Most of us didn't expect much to happen.

Meanwhile, Sue was about to have her own eruption. At 4:30 a.m. on February 6, she wakened me. "Honey, I think my water's broken." The bed was soaked, but we weren't distressed. It was a clear signal that a labor we had prayed about and planned for was finally underway. The doctor had hit his prediction right on the nose. We began, quickly and calmly, to gather our things for the short run to the Vancouver Memorial Hospital, where we were pre-registered.

By 6 a.m. we were at the hospital and Sue's contractions prompted me to start the coaching we had been practicing. The delivery took place in the birthing room, a place with a homey feel where husbands and wives could welcome a new baby. Our son arrived at 9:01 a.m. He weighed in at eight pounds, thirteen ounces, the largest of our three children. He was hungry! The nurse put him to Sue's breast and he began to nurse like a veteran. We both wept for joy.

Our little, joyful 'eruption' was followed just three months later, by an eruption both great and dreadful. It was Pentecost Sunday, May 18. We had sung about the Holy Spirit, prayed our prayers, and shared Holy Communion. The service was ended, but before we could exit the sanctuary, our congregation president, Paul Prigge, strode forward to the microphone with an altogether unfamiliar look on his face. "Brothers and sisters, this morning, just minutes ago, Mt. St. Helens blew up! When you go out, you will see the cloud of ash from our parking lot."

It was true. Once outside, we stood rooted to our spots, disbelieving. An enormous black column, as if from a coal-burning chimney, rose 80,000 feet into the air. Our family rushed home and turned on the television set, where on-the-scene cameras and breathless reporters brought the story of the gigantic explosion just an hour earlier. Fifty-seven people, including old Harry Truman, had been buried, burned, or otherwise blotted out by the blast, which had fanned out to the north and east, the opposite direction from us.

It was an unforgettable day, but not the end of an unforgettable year, which had already seen a birth and a volcanic explosion. The first two parts of Pat Vinsonhaler's prophecy had come true. But still we were not thinking about it.

Within a month, however, her words came rushing back at us when I received a call from Concordia Lutheran Church in Akron, Ohio.

Sue and I and baby Peter sat together on a jet streaking west toward Portland after a hurried visit to Akron. The call had come two weeks earlier as Washingtonians were still assessing the damage from the St. Helens eruption.

I made my report about the call at a special congregational meeting and solicited their advice and prayers. After the meeting concluded, Steve Eaton approached me. "I listened to what you said about that church," he began, hesitantly. "Sounds like they really need help. Even though I personally want you to stay here, I think you should go." It was a surprising word from someone so young. It confirmed what Sue and I had felt on the way back from Akron.

A few days later, after more prayers and more advice, I made the decision to accept the call and wrote a letter to the people of Memorial. I told them:

> *I want you to know that my acceptance of this call reflects no dissatisfaction with the work God has given me to do here. On the contrary, it has been a source of joy and thanks and personal growth since the beginning. Pastor Schroeder has been a faithful brother and teacher to me. The congregation has been generous and thoughtful of our needs. Opportunities to serve and grow have been abundant. In fact, if it were not for the strong push of God, I would never have chosen to leave on my own...*

The acceptance necessitated finding someone who could step into my role with the youth confirmation class. I chose Mike McCoy, one of our lay catechists. Mike, an army engineer whose quiet manner masked a fine mind and an intensity of purpose, agreed to take the kids to camp later in the summer and keep the new individualized program we had developed running smoothly. My choice of Mike was, apparently, another 'tap on the shoulder' from the Lord. The year after we moved to Akron, Mike made the decision to begin study for the pastoral ministry. A few years later he became a pastor in Emmett, Idaho.

Memorial bade us farewell on a Sunday afternoon. Dave Swan, our genial dentist who was also head elder, served as emcee. As our family sat in front in a row of chairs, Dave introduced a sequence of humorous vignettes reviewing our years in Vancouver. There came thoughtful gifts. The Children's Choir presented Sue a booklet of letters and memories to read on our trip east. The youth group gave us a quilt with squares on both sides, each fashioned by one of the group's members. Pam Edwards had spearheaded the project and stitched all the pieces together in record time. There was a beautiful banner on white felt with a family of five silhouetted in black, covered by a rainbow of pastel colors. There was a plaque presented by Terry Hannan expressing thanks and promising prayerful support for more years of fruitful ministry. There was music by the choir with Kathy Cusack directing. There were hugs and tears aplenty. The call to Vancouver had been all joyful anticipation. The call to Akron involved a wrenching goodbye from my mentor Win, from our friends Chuck and Kathy, and from a congregation that had shaped and loved us. The thrill of a new challenge was attended by the trepidation of starting over in a new place with an entirely new group of people.

Moving day came. Members Gil Jahn and Dave Eaton, both of whom worked for North American Van Lines, gave special care to our possessions as they helped us wrap, box, and store our belongings on the van. "I'll see you folks on the other end!" Gil said cheerfully as he drove away.

Pat Vinsonhaler's prophecy had come true in every detail. It was a reminder that God had a plan and a timetable for our lives. The ministry in Washington had been rich and marked with marital and spiritual growth. Now I would stretch my wings as a sole pastor. What awaited us, we wondered, in the grimy industrial city of Akron?

Condordia Lutheran Church

Akron, Ohio

(1980–1988)

SOMETHING LIKE A WEDDING

Akron, Ohio, was prettier than we feared. An old pamphlet called it a 'grimy industrial city,' but that description was now an anachronism. The sooty smoke from the big tire companies – Goodyear, Firestone, Goodrich, and Uniroyal – had dissipated long ago. Many of the old multi-storied brick structures remained, some remodeled and some vacant. Most of the actual tire-making had moved years earlier to single-story buildings down south where land and labor were cheaper.

Though it was a long way from 'God's Country' in the Pacific Northwest, Akron and its environs had their share of beauty. The countryside was rolling and green. Forty miles to the north was Lake Erie and Cleveland, where we watched the Indians and the Browns at massive old Cleveland Stadium. Not too many miles south by freeway sat Canton, with its Pro Football Hall of Fame. Further south our family liked to make excursions to Amish country with its farms, horse-drawn buggies, and family stores.

Our first look at the city came in the spring of 1980. Shortly after I received the call to Concordia Lutheran Church, Sue and I were invited to come for a visit. She and I and little Peter, who was still nursing, flew in to Akron-Canton Airport, where we were met by congregation chairman Bob Tofanelli. Bob was a trim, courteous, and very pleasant man who managed the downtown O'Neil's department store. He drove us to the home of Clarence and Mary Kelley, with whom we were to stay those few days. Their home was palatial. Clarence owned the Dixie-Ohio Express trucking firm, and he was a wealthy man.

The Kelleys housed us and gave us a daily breakfast of oatmeal out on their lovely back patio, but they left the tour guide work to younger folks. Gary and Susan Weiss and Bob and Chris McElcar took us to a luncheon at a club near Akron University. Since Sue didn't feel well afterward, we dropped her and Peter off at the Kelley home and I was given a city tour.

My hosts pointed proudly to landmark buildings as we passed. Akron University, a school well-known for its polymer science, occupied much of the city's south side. I was fascinated by Quaker Square, where a set of old grain silos once used by the Quaker Oats Company had been remodeled into a Hilton Hotel with rounded walls. Southeast of the city was the immense Goodyear Airdock, which once housed the giant airships Akron and Macon, and still provided quarters for their tiny descendants, the Goodyear blimps. Nearby one could see the Derby Downs, where generations of soap box derby cars raced each other downhill, and the Rubber Bowl, a football stadium where the Akron University Zips played.

Altogether, the city had quite a story to tell. But the only story that mattered to me at the moment was the one I was to hear about Concordia Church. There was an evening meeting in the downstairs classroom. There I met with the leaders of the congregation, including the men who had phoned me months earlier – Matt Battista, Bob McElcar, and Clarence Kelley. The men portrayed a congregation hungry for a pastor. Attendance was minimal. The interim pastor, Ed Ulseth, was tired. "We're ready to follow wherever you lead," offered President Tofanelli. It was heady stuff for me to be so needed. It appealed to my pride, which had taken a few licks but was still firmly entrenched. "Yes," said Pride, "you'll be important here."

On the plane heading home there came a moment when I took Sue's hand. We looked at one another tearfully and fearfully. "I think we may have to go." I told her. Early in June of 1980 the decision was made, and I phoned the news to Tofanelli.

On June 12, he wrote back on behalf of the people at Concordia:

Dear Pastor Kasting,

Words cannot express our feeling at Concordia for the news that you have accepted our call... The congregation is elated, and we all thank God that He has chosen you for the job.

Let me assure you that you have the full support of both the congregation and the Church Council, and we plan to work with you side by side to spread the Gospel according to Christ's Word.

Your congregation must be very sad at the idea of your leaving them, but from what you have told me, they will understand that your decision to leave is based on what God has indicated he wants you to do.

I hope you will express to them how we feel and that they will understand that we wish only the very best to them and that God will bless them as He has us.

Yours in Christ's name,
R. Tofanelli

The installation took place on August 3. A sequence of phone calls in the weeks before cemented the details. "The ladies want to know if they can put candles down the aisle," queried President Tofanelli, "something like they do at a wedding." Then he added, "I guess it is a kind of wedding, isn't it?"

I selected hymns and prepared an order of service. George Bornemann, the President of the English District, did the installing. An old seminary friend, Jeff Anderson, was the circuit counselor and did the preaching. Ed Ulseth, sporting a curly goatee, was the liturgist.

The church was crowded and hot. We entered to *'Holy God, We Praise Thy Name.'* Jeff's sermon, tailored to a congregation on the decline, employed the parable of the workers and made God's plea that there be "no unemployment in the vineyard." After Bornemann did the installing, members of the congregation made presentations. Tofanelli presented me a pulpit Bible, the Elders' Chairman held out the Communion chalice, and the Altar Guild President handed me the silver baptismal shell.

Downstairs the congregation welcomed us in a cordial reception, chaired by a handsome, genial emcee named Dave Wykoff. Teddy bears were presented to our children, jokes were told, pictures taken, and refreshments consumed.

It was, to be sure, something like a wedding. And what followed was very like the work every married couple needs to do when the festivities end and life in the real world begins.

GOTHIC IN GOOSETOWN

Concordia Lutheran Church was an impressive Gothic edifice, brick with stone trim, set down in an old German neighborhood that some still called Goosetown. The name preserved the memory of days when German immigrants kept geese in their yards, partly as a source of food, and partly as a living burglar alarm system. The geese could be depended on to honk noisily at intruders.

By the time we arrived in 1980, only a few of the original Germans were left, along with their German-American Club a few blocks south. In their place was a mixture of blacks, Appalachian whites, and Akron University students, few of whom had any meaningful connection with Concordia. Decades earlier, Pastor J. Franklin Yount had been able to walk through the neighborhood and make a score of brief visits in an afternoon. Now only Leroy Dietz, the Aberth family, and Gracemae Rudgers were within walking distance of the church.

The neighborhood itself had long ago been bisected by the expressway. Concordia's parking lot came to an end at a chain-link fence which overlooked the busy thoroughfare. High atop the education annex was a white plastic sign with bold blue letters: CONCORDIA LUTHERAN. A pedestrian bridge at the southeast corner of the property brought folks across the expressway to walk past our front door. Further west, there was a Greyhound bus station on the other side of the highway at the Grant Street exit, and from that station came forlorn beggars who would ring the church doorbell and ask us to provide money for bus tickets to Pittsburgh or Wheeling, West Virginia.

The church itself was still physically impressive. The nave was long and high, and worshippers walked to their seats on an elegant red carpet. The pulpit was elevated like the prow of a ship. All the pews, banisters, and woodwork in front were a fine, richly-finished oak. The right transept was the choir loft, and held the console for the Lyon & Healy organ that once accompanied silent movies in an Akron theater. Eileen Koski was Concordia's capable, very traditional organist. She proved to be a steady working partner during my years in Akron.

The left transept was actually an opening to the education wing. One could look up through an open balcony to the upper floor, where there was a ring of small classrooms. On the main level were a classroom to the left, a library behind a strange, blue window with white angels on it in the center, and a nicely-furnished sitting room to the right with imposing pictures of the two previous pastors. Several cautioned me that this room was the pride and joy of the ladies' group.

Nevertheless, it was obvious that the church's glory days were past. Pastor Paul Hoffmaster at Fairlawn Lutheran Church told me that Concordia was once a large, proud congregation, the mother to several daughter churches. Now she was in decline. The church building still sat like a fortress, surrounded by mostly dingy frame homes slowly decaying all around. Neighborhood urchins gathered on the church steps to smoke and occasionally leave graffiti on the stonework. In one front yard we passed as we drove in to church, there was a pit bulldog, whose owner took pleasure in having it hang suspended, mouth gripping a towel tied to a chain affixed to a tree branch.

I was to be just the third senior pastor in the church's 77 years. Founding pastor J. Franklin Yount had come as a newly-graduated seminary student in 1904 and stayed for 63 years until his death in 1967. His tenure was marked by hard work that often included as many as 2000 home visits in a single year. A succession of confirmation class pictures showed a man growing older, grayer, and more haggard. People at Concordia had called themselves 'Yount Christians,' and many a congregation home still had a copy of his book, *The Pastor Speaks*, on its bookshelf.

When Pastor Yount began to slow down, he was joined by a younger pastor named Ernest Eggers. Ernie assisted until Yount's retirement, then stayed on until 1979, when he left to take a call to Kentucky. The vacancy, which had stretched to 18 months, was the first for Concordia, and the people were anxious, especially after the first call was declined. "They're proud," said Paul Hoffmaster. "Can't believe someone would say 'no' to them." But I had said yes. The challenge of a church in decline, along with my own need to try my wings and show my mettle, had a strong pull.

Upon my arrival, I moved my books and files into the office in the old Ertl home next door to the church. My secretary was Miss Susan Weiss. She had a true heart, but her secretarial skills and social graces were minimal. In the home's upstairs apartment there lived a woman who was a television addict. I would sit dutifully at my typewriter trying to fashion a bulletin or sermon, while from somewhere above there came the voice of *The Family Feud* host Richard Dawson and the maddening ringing of a bell at each correct guess from the contestants. Once the water in the bathroom overflowed while she sat oblivious in the living room, and only when it began to drip down on us through the ceiling and we went upstairs to investigate did she realize she had left it running.

Concordia was a church with well-entrenched traditions. For years there had been a Washington's Birthday banquet. The congregation's snowy-haired patriarch, Walter Harnack, had, through sheer persistence, brought such big-name speakers as Wendell Wilkie and John Glenn. He personally sold tickets year after year to ensure the banquet's success. But his health was in decline, and within my first year, I conducted his funeral.

The banquet died with him. Not so with the annual Sauerkraut Supper, which lured hundreds of folks from around Akron downstairs for sauerkraut, pork, mashed potatoes and gravy, vegetables, and apple pie. The basement was filled for three separate settings. There was also a women's card party and a holiday bazaar. But there was no evangelism to speak of, and little outreach of any kind. Vacation Bible School had ceased a year or two earlier, probably because of the pastoral vacancy. I chafed at the congregation's propensity to major in minors and do so little to reach lives of people in the neighborhood.

The physical oddity of a Gothic church in Goosetown was more than matched by a string of bizarre events in my years at Concordia. Some of it went with being in an urban setting. We repeatedly found children on the roof. Someone spray-painted '666' on the stonework. A dead fish showed up on the doorstep one morning. On another occasion, I heard a sound outside the office and went out to see an adolescent boy defecating on the back entrance. I had him pull his pants up and marched him home to his mother, who was stunned to learn of his behavior and sent him back to the church with a bucket and sponge and orders to clean up the mess. A few years later there came a college-aged fellow to my door, asking if he might come in and "get the stuff I left here last night." Curious, I let him in, and he went straight to the bathroom, climbed up on the sink, and removed a ceiling tile. From the space above, he retrieved a knapsack with his belongings, jumped down, thanked me for the nice accommodations, and left!

Sometimes the whole congregation got to watch the human drama unfold. A woman dressed in army fatigues came to the parking lot one Sunday morning and hustled people for quarters as they went in. Later during the worship service, she came into the sanctuary, moved deliberately forward to the pulpit while I was in the midst of a sermon, looked up at me and endeavored to ask a question. "Not now," I whispered to her. "Just sit down and I will talk to you after the service." Her name, we learned, was Alice. Her relatives told us she was mentally ill. They had offered her lodging, but she chose to live as a bag lady on the street. "She's on her own now. She won't accept any help from us."

Another memorable character was named Jerry, who seemed to be a twin of Alice. He wore Salvation Army-style clothes, let his oily brown hair grow long and unkempt, and appeared at irregular intervals at church on Sundays. Arriving just after the service began, he would make his way downstairs to get a cup of coffee, then ascend to the sanctuary to find a front-row seat. In his left hand the cup of coffee twitched, sloshing coffee on the red carpet. His right hand swatted at invisible insects, and his mouth drooled. The odor of long-unwashed clothes and skin formed a pungent aura around him, and the women in the choir seated in the transept gagged at the sight. Some time later, I got word that Jerry had been struck by a car while jay-walking. I visited him in the hospital, but he said little. We never saw him again.

Even animals got into the act. One especially hot summer morning, the ushers had left the main doors open to allow a breeze through the stifling church. As I preached, a large, black Labrador retriever wandered in. He followed his nose up into the chancel and I found myself unable to concentrate on my message. Finally, an usher came forward to escort Rover outside. But that wasn't the end of our morning's adventure. As I sat back down with acolyte Philip Jandrokovic, we both noticed a score of bees scattered about on the carpet, some writhing, some still. Others, we then noticed, were dropping like miniature paratroopers from the rafters. "Wow, Pastor," observed Phil, "it's like Wild Kingdom in here!"

Indeed. God's wild kingdom in Goosetown.

AT HOME IN FIRESTONE PARK

We bought our first home without ever laying eyes on it. Concordia had no parsonage to offer as had Memorial, so we told Concordia's leaders to be on the lookout for something we could afford reasonably close in. Bob Tofanelli and Clarence Kelley went to work. Several weeks before we moved, Bob wrote that they had found a three-story home in Firestone Park two miles south of the church. "It's in a nice neighborhood," Bob volunteered. He knew firsthand because he drove around it, parked nearby, and watched the comings and goings. The price was right too. The owners were asking $62,500. Bob sent pictures of the nicely painted and carpeted interior – a spacious enough place. Outside there were big trees, something I personally liked. Clarence Kelley offered to secure the financing. Sue and I decided to trust their judgment, and we made an offer of $59,000, which was accepted. All that remained was to make the actual physical move.

Firestone Park turned out to be an ideal choice. The neighborhood, developed originally for families of Firestone Tire Company employees, was by now well-established. The homes looked solid and welcoming under the shade of maples and oaks. In the evenings, people sat on their porch swings, rocked and called back and forth. Our home, stately looking in its muted green siding and white brick, sat at the corner of Reed Avenue and Neptune Street atop a slight hill. Two blocks east of us ran Interstate 77, but the auto noise was muffled by a solid wall of trees. Reed Avenue would take our children straight to their school, Firestone Park Elementary.

Our children liked their new home, amply endowed with rooms to explore and stairs to climb. On the main floor was a modest living room with an oak-mantled fireplace, a dining room with plenty of shelves, and a wondrously big family room, an add-on to the original home. Peter and I later turned it into a miniature soccer field with our Nerf soccer ball. The living room and family room were connected by a narrow galley kitchen barely wide enough for two people to pass. It was the only bad feature in the house.

On the second level were the bedrooms and bathroom, and higher up was our 'penthouse' bedroom and study nook where my stamp collection took up residence. It was to that top floor the children would flee screaming when pursued by the leopard I pretended to be. The basement housed our daughters' 'Dolltown' and dress-up closet, a laundry room, and our two-car garage.

Most of our new neighbors were Roman Catholic. Among them were Mary and Leo Heisser, who lived across the street with Mary's ancient father, Mr. Gless. The old man, who was nearing age 100, kept an eye on

Peter and shouted over at us if Peter wandered out of his sight. Leo was a bibliophile who gave me reading suggestions. "Here's a good one," he said one day, handing me a volume about the Shroud of Turin. A few doors down were Ray and Mae Sullivan. Ray wanted to talk politics ("Did you know the Jews are trying to take over the world?"), while disabled Mae would smile sweetly and wave at us from her chair on the porch. The Signorinos were a simple, noisy Italian family. In traditional fashion, Ross went off to work while Annette stayed home to ride herd on the children – Vita Ann, Tony, Kay, and developmentally disabled Russell, who loved lightning bugs and 'lallowjackets.'

There were other neighbors too. Chuck and Frankie Lindermann kept busy with their yard, and their grand-daughter made our girls aware of wedge heels. Pipe-smoking Presbyterian pastor Moss Ruttan was down the street a few doors. Across the fence to the north lived Margaret, a middle-aged woman who had a cat and a young man friend who shared her house. Sue took courage after we'd been there a few years to invite the neighbor women to a Bible study, and half a dozen came with regularity.

Firestone Park School was within walking distance, and the children made their daily trek down the hill, past the friendly crossing guards, and into the old brick building. Across the street from the school was a pet store of dubious reputation called Tanks a Lot. We heard that it was a drug hangout, and the dark-visaged men inside seemed not to be doing much animal business when we walked through for a look. Beyond the school was a nice park with walkways and trees, a ball field, and space enough for a large throng that normally came down to watch the fireworks on the 4th of July.

When the snows came, rumor had it that Superintendent Conrad Ott took his dog out for a walk. If the snow impeded Conrad's dog, school was to be called off that day. We never did see Ott or his dog, but we got to know the children's teachers, and a colorful lot they were. Mrs. Dyak wore purple, but it was her challenge to her students to find '100 ways to make a dollar' that piqued Melanie's interest in math. Mrs. Becker was a reading fanatic who introduced our children to some 'junior great books.' Miss Gombar, whose breath was pungent with garlic, taught her students to count to 100 with two hands, a lesson that stuck. Mrs. Pokky gave students an opportunity to take part in a stage version of *Little House on the Prairie.*

The school also gave Sue an opportunity to dust off her classroom skills. One day the principal, Norman Wingate, phoned to ask Sue if she might help in the school's new computer lab as a volunteer. Though she knew little about computers, Sue loved working with children and readily agreed.

Because Sue had no computer experience, Mr. Wingate donated an old Apple II GS unit for her to take home. Our son Peter seemed genetically programmed to understand the machine, and, though only a pre-schooler, he helped his mother figure out how to load and operate the discs. In the school's lab, Sue helped teachers select discs that would reinforce math and language skills. Having learned to manipulate the discs herself, she demonstrated for the pupils. After that her chief task was to monitor behavior.

The move to Akron brought Sue and me across a threshold into a deeper marriage relationship. The memory of unhappy times in St. Louis and Vancouver was still vivid in our minds. Our communication was still roadblocked occasionally by the resentment of needs unmet and feelings buried. But the hope kindled in Chaplain Bob Kunz's marriage enrichment group had made a difference. Instead of resignation and withdrawal into our respective shells, there was a hunger to grow together.

That hunger was about to be satisfied. A couple of years into our stay in Akron, Dale and Nancy Meech presented us the gift of a weekend at Marriage Encounter. Sue found a friendship with Nancy already in our earliest days in Akron as the two sat in the church nursery. Now they offered to sit with our children while we spent a weekend with a dozen other couples at a motel in nearby Canton. Neither of us knew what to expect. Dale and Nancy smiled broadly. "You'll love it."

We arrived at the motel in a snowstorm. Temperatures plummeted to 26 below zero. It was the coldest weekend in Ohio's recorded history, but we were safe and warm on the inside. Group sessions with three presenter couples alternated with times alone in our room as a couple. We were given assignments built on 'Ten and Ten's' - ten minutes to write about a question the presenters posed, ten minutes to read what each other wrote and respond. "Write about times your mate does something unexpected. HDTMMF? (How does that make me feel?)" What sounded initially forbidding became a door opened between our hearts. The words and emotions flowed freely. We felt free for the first time to be completely transparent.

At the end Dale and Nancy came to congratulate us and share the joy we felt at making a new start at our communication. The house in Firestone Park became a place of greater care and sensitivity. Dale and Nancy's grace-filled gift kept on blessing us for years thereafter.

Every family develops traditions, and some of those are shaped by the opportunities offered in the neighborhood. Autumn in Firestone Park brought a magnificent array of colors, and tons of leaves to rake into piles for jumping. Winter brought more snow than I remembered from my Indiana childhood, and we enjoyed lovely, quiet walks in the snow and stopping to make snow angels. Summer evenings, after neighbors had turned in for the night, were times for Sue and me to rummage in waste cans on Neptune

Avenue looking for wrappers and packages that could be mailed to manufacturers for a refund. Hot afternoons afforded a chance to play in the plastic pool we set up on our concrete drive by the garage.

The years in Akron were a time to watch our children growing up. Melanie became a gentle, musical bookworm. Christa showed an early interest in writing and drama. Both took piano lessons from Florence Willey, a woman who liked to say that the piano keys were their '88 friends.' Baby Peter loved to gather, then scatter what he had gathered (dishes, toys, chess pieces). After church one Sunday evening, he gazed for a time into the bright, moonlit sky and shouted "Moon!" Then after some reflection, "Sun!" And finally, "Holy Spirit!" In spite of spending most of his time at church under the pews, he had apparently been listening to the liturgy.

Not far north was Mary's Garden Center. Each Good Friday we took the children there to look with delight at the 'Peeps and Ducklins' she advertised and to pet the velvety-soft fur of bunnies.

Family portrait from the early years in Akron – Melanie, Peter, and Christa

Summers brought me a reduced work load at church and time to take the family further afield. One of our first vacations was to Camp Pioneer in western New York on the shore of Lake Erie. The following year we traveled to Fife Lake, Michigan, where Pat Goolsby opened her cabin to us for a lovely week of swimming, boating, and relaxing. Still later an extended trip through the South brought us to tobacco farms in North Carolina, rides at Disney World in Orlando, and car trouble in the 'boonies' of Tennessee.

During our years in Akron, Peter was still young enough to enjoy coming in with Sue and snuggling beside her yellow robe while she had morning devotions. Meanwhile, the girls were blossoming into young ladies. Melanie landed a spot on the Kentones, a singing group at her junior high school. Christa, not to be outdone, had her time in the spotlight playing a piano piece called *Musical Jewel Box* from memory at a recital at Guzzetta Hall. Each began to regale us with tales of boys who were or weren't on their boyfriend radar.

Every Friday night came family night. That tradition, begun in Vancouver, grew more elaborate as the children grew older and more capable of participation. Now, besides fighting over who would light the candle, there came little fingers playing hymns for all to sing, little hands in puppets, acting out Bible stories, little mouths speaking prayers of surprising sensitivity and honesty. We taught prayers by modeling them. We went round the family circle, Sue and I saying a simple 'thank you' prayer, and each child following. Then an "I'm sorry" and finally a 'Please help so-and-so.' Prayers were followed by popcorn and a game of Clue. Such simple things made our house a home.

Not everything was pleasant there in Firestone Park. The Angel family beside us on the east would have an occasional Saturday night party which kept me awake. More than once I made a phone call after midnight to say, "Do you think you could be quieter? I need to sleep because I get up early for church tomorrow." Normally they toned it down. The neighborhood's tranquility was occasionally jarred by cursing, fighting, or screeching tires. One night a car driven by juveniles deliberately ran down a road sign beside our house. Sue, looking out the window in a rare display of temper, shouted at them the only thing her mind could muster at the moment: "You... BUZZARDS!"

We had settled in between the angels and the buzzards.

A COLLISION IN VALUES

I came to Concordia as a headstrong young man. At age 33, with a long history of personal pride and eight years of 'successful' ministry at a healthy church, I thought I knew what worked and what didn't. The blacks and whites were clear. I had little sense of how many times Pastor Schroeder had intercepted hard cases and handled them, and even less notion of how regularly his accumulated pastoral wisdom restrained or re-directed me and kept me from disaster. Now I was on my own in a congregation that had grown old and hardened doing things its way.

It was to be expected that a young, headstrong pastor and a congregation fixated on preserving its traditions would eventually have a collision. After an abbreviated honeymoon period, the opening salvoes of coming conflicts were fired. "You forgot to thank the choir," someone told me one Sunday. A public thanks from the lectern was good form, she continued, something previous pastors had done with clock-like reliability. I began to do what was asked. "Don't tell us about Memorial," another groused after I reminisced about the years there. Sue and I were homesick for old friends and happy times. Couldn't they understand that? We kept our memories more to ourselves from then on.

One of the more outspoken of the congregation's turf guardians was Karen Wallick, an angular, bespectacled woman who reminded me often of how things were done at Concordia. She meant well, but her reminders and suggestions made me bristle, even while I grudgingly admiring her hard work. Relationships at Concordia became the potting soil for growing patience and tact, two things I had in short supply!

Two issues in particular became major battles. One was the remarriage of divorced people. Requests for weddings came to me more frequently in Akron because I was the sole pastor now. Each wedding involved a significant investment of my time. At the very least, there were three counseling sessions with the couple, a rehearsal, and then the wedding and reception following. As a rule, the receptions were elaborate affairs with sit-down dinners in rented halls. I had been accustomed to easy informality in dress and use of the church for cake-and-punch receptions in the Northwest. But here in the Midwest tuxedoes and formals reigned, and stuffed cabbage rolls were served in huge banquet halls to hundreds of guests. There was another tradition, unwritten but expected: "The pastor will marry those who ask, as long as they have membership in the church!"

The Christian Church takes seriously the sanctity of marriage. "What God has joined together, man must not put asunder" was written into the wedding rite. God intended it to be permanent, I knew. Though our teaching allowed for exceptions (unfaithfulness and desertion), the general rule was 'no divorce.' But of the first six couples who requested marriage, four involved the remarriage of divorced people. What was to be my policy?

It was not a new problem for me, but facing it alone was new. I was determined to be obedient to God, and willing to let the chips fall where they might. My first opportunity came almost immediately. In my first session with the daughter of Arnold and June Rutherford, I learned that both bride-to-be and her fiancé were divorced. The reasons? "We grew apart," said she. "We didn't love each other anymore," said he. That was the summary of their two failed previous marriages. I swallowed hard and said I did not think I could perform the wedding, and the couple looked confused. Later I heard from mom Rutherford, a long-time member of Concordia and a leader of the ladies' group. Her tone was not confusion. It was sheer anger. "You marry them or we will leave the church." The heavy artillery had been rolled out.

I conceded, but only part of the way. "They can use the church, but I won't do the wedding," I countered. The Rutherfords side-stepped me by asking neighboring pastor Del Bertermann, my circuit counselor, to do the ceremony. He agreed, as long as it was "OK with Mike." I consented, but resentfully, upset with Del for agreeing to help my opponents, and upset with them for plowing ahead. After the wedding, the Rutherfords quit the church anyway.

On the heels of this unhappy event came another. Jim Norris, another long-time member, came in for a talk one day. He was not a young man, but had children and even a couple of grandchildren. "If I got a divorce, would you allow me to remarry?"

When I asked him why he intended to divorce his wife, he gave me an answer that floored me: "She's too fat."

I had no history with Jim or his wife, and I did not listen as long as I ought to have listened. "That's not a Scriptural reason," I argued.

Jim asked a second question. "If I got divorced and went ahead and remarried outside the church, would you kick me out?" This was totally unexplored territory.

"That's the wrong question," I said. "Shouldn't you be asking what God's will is for your life?" But he was not interested in exploring that with me. "I don't know what I will do," I said at last. "I would have to talk to the elders about this."

Jim didn't wait. He forged ahead with both the divorce and the remarriage. Neither the elders nor I approved, but we did not take action to remove him. Months later Jim told me he had been headstrong and expressed remorse over the selfishness of his decision.

The advent of these hard cases forced me into a long, salutary discussion with the board of Elders. The chairman of the group was a grandfatherly man named Vernon Zittle. He and the other men on the board, including Jim Scheck, Dick Weiss, Karen Wallick's husband Jim, and Joe Pohlod, proved to be both a sounding board for the working out of my pastoral theology and a much-needed shield in the coming battles. The elders endured long, often emotional narrations from me as each case came up. We ransacked the Bible for direction, and all of us became familiar with Matthew 19 (Jesus' prohibition against divorce) and 1 Corinthians 7 (Paul's advice to couples about marriage and divorce). I wrote to English District President George Bornemann. I asked fellow pastors to discuss the matter at circuit meetings. I brought the topic before the congregation in classes and meetings, and most people listened with interest. It was a topic long overdue for discussion.

Time and grace brought a change of heart to some. Phil and Marcia Cianchetti were married early in my years at Concordia, but only after a painful confrontation. After living together for a while, they had approached me to do a wedding. Another messy situation! "I don't know," I responded. In fact, I needed to consult with my elders for support and direction. "You are living together. I'll have to pray about it and wait for God's answer."

They were speechless, shocked that I might decline. Marcia recovered her voice first and gave vent to her anger, "What's He going to do – call you on the phone?"

A day or two later I called her back and said, "I'll do the wedding, but we need to sit together for some counseling." The counseling was done, and the wedding day came and went. In the process, Marcia and Phil were humbled and softened. They reflected on the direction of their lives. They made worship a priority, and they studied the Bible with a new-found seriousness. Everyone could see the change. A respect and even a friendship blossomed between me and this young couple. As God softened them, He was also softening me, making me more patient with couples in their situation.

It was a few years later that I approached Marcia with a request. "During the season of Lent this year, I've been hoping to invite some lay people to share the working of God in their lives. Would you be willing to share what's happened to you?" Marcia said yes. On a Wednesday evening, she walked to the lectern and told the story of their living together, the request for marriage, and my hesitation. "I was angry with pastor at first," she admitted, "but I came to realize that we had done wrong, and that God was at work in this to change our hearts." I trembled with gratitude to hear such humble words of affirmation for my ministry and obedience to the Word of God.

There was a collision on another front. What should be done with people who were missing from worship, especially if that delinquency stretched on for years? The congregation had found a convenient way to hide its missing members by placing them on an 'inactive' list and not reporting them to the district in its annual reports. The district, I discovered, assessed congregations on a per-communicant basis. It was financially shrewd to report the minimal figure. Shrewd, yes, but not ethical in my book.

When I began making home visits (my goal was to be in every home within two years), I kept hearing about relatives who were members at Concordia. Finally, I took a parish census. Using Concordia's directory and adding those who were widely understood to be members, I discovered that instead of the 457 communicants listed in the *The Lutheran Annual*, there were more than 600. More than 100 of them were inactive, some for years.

I strategized an approach. After an initial get-acquainted visit, I followed with a second, then a third visit, trying to confront the attitudes and habits that were strangling the spiritual life from these folks. A few responded and returned. Some made promises which were rarely kept. And some simply told me that they did not intend to do anything at all. The visits began to stir a reaction. One father took exception to my pursuit of his son, a grown man who had not been to church in years. He called one day, angry at me: "You leave my son alone!" he shouted. After a futile attempt to curb his wrath, I hung up on him.

His son and others I brought before the board of elders, explaining each situation in detail. In the case of some, I recommended removal by congregational vote after all efforts were made and all appeals ignored. The elders agreed, with some trepidation. The first time the action was taken, the congregation went along, albeit with some hesitance. Something like this had not been done in many years. I took a further step to make it clear to all what we were doing. I used the Agenda 'Announcement of Excommunication' on the Sunday following the action.

That brought an open reaction from some. "What right do you have to remove anyone?" was a question voiced to me. "We'll just lose members," was a common refrain. "We never used to do this!" said another.

In March of 1984, the opposition had mounted to the point where a second resolution to remove someone was narrowly defeated. In a pastoral letter to the congregation written shortly afterwards, I tried to explain my practice and answer the objections point-by-point. Among other things, the letter said:

> *The word 'discipline' is closely connected to the word 'disciple.' It is a good word, a loving word, a life-giving word! It is what fathers are to give their children.... in a family, discipline is vital to the*

correction and training of children. Where there is no discipline, something is lacking in the family's love... In the church, discipline is the whole process of loving confrontation, counsel, and admonition that seeks to awaken the sinning Christian to see his sin and be restored through repentance and pardon...

I quoted Scripture (Hebrews 10:23, Galatians 6:1, John 20:23). I cited Luther, who had been tough on church delinquency in his day:

Let it be understood that people who abstain from the sacrament over a long period of time are not to be considered Christians... When a person, with nothing to hinder him, lets a long period of time elapse without ever desiring this sacrament, I call that despising it. If you want such liberty, you may just as well take the further liberty not to be a Christian...

I pointed out that excommunication had been long practiced in the Lutheran Church, and that Concordia's constitution and bylaws mentioned it. For the erring person, it was a way to say, "Do you realize how far away you've drifted?" It was a 'tough love' measure that was done in the hopes of waking those drifting away from God and bringing them to see the wrong and say, "I'm sorry. I need to come back." I assured the people that the intention of the act was ultimately to regain people, not to lock the door and throw away the key.

Over the coming months, tempers calmed. The congregation, under the steady direction of the elders, came to agree that this practice had merit, though all of us found it a sad duty. Few were actually removed, but many took membership more seriously.

Not all of the conflicts we experienced were so serious. Some, in retrospect, were simply funny. The most memorable centered on a youth service with a 'death and resurrection' theme. Someone had the idea of getting a real casket from Dunn-Quigley mortuary and having one of the kids play dead.

On the morning of the service, worshippers were astonished to see an open casket in the narthex as they arrived. Later, with the service underway, two boys walked down the center aisle chatting, while two others followed, pushing the casket on its rolling stand (to symbolize death's nearness to each person). In the center of the aisle, one of the pushers tapped one of the unsuspecting boys in front, and he stopped and climbed into the casket. In dramatic terms, he had 'died.' That boy, Brad Schonover, remained in the casket for the duration of the service, much to his mother's chagrin. So long did he stay motionless that he actually went to sleep! Toward the end of the service, when 'Gabriel' Jeff Jones blew a blast on his trumpet from the balcony, Brad jerked awake with startling realism and climbed from the casket. For weeks afterward, the youth and I endured complaints about the poor taste of the skit and the offended sensibilities. But no one ever forgot that service.

Meanwhile, God was at work on me. The conflicts became what Charles Spurgeon called 'the furnace, the hammer, and the file.' They forced me to re-examine my pastoral practices and admit my often judgmental spirit. One Monday morning my phone rang. It was Ruth Zuelsdorf, a kindly older widow and former high school journalism teacher who had been helping me edit the church newsletter. "May I come see you?" she asked. I agreed to meet within the hour. When she arrived, she asked whether we might go somewhere in the church where we would not be overheard. *What can she want to talk about?* We made our way to the deserted sanctuary, and there began a conversation unlike any other I'd had.

"Pastor, yesterday at church, I overheard something you said to one of the men. You were talking about Robert Schwabe." She proceeded to detail what she'd heard me say about this man long missing from church. I had been critical, even caustic about Mr. Schwabe. "Did I hear you correctly?" she added.

I lowered my eyes, ashamed to hear my unkind words repeated. "Yes, Ruth."

She continued, "Our last pastor's ministry was ruined because he didn't know how to keep his mouth shut. You're new here. There's so much that needs doing! I don't want your ministry ruined..." Ruth trembled as she spoke. I realized how hard it must have been for her to confront her pastor this way.

"I was wrong," I confessed. "Would you pray for me? Would you help remind me to watch what I say?" She agreed. We prayed together, and she left without further talk. But her words stayed in my mind for a long time afterward. It was grace – a pain-filled grace – that had moved her to give me such a gift.

GETTING ORGANIZED

Concordia was well organized, I discovered. But around what? Miss Anne Hracky rang the bell each Sunday to announce the end of Sunday School hour. A faithful crew materialized every Lent to don aprons and make soup suppers. The Ladies' Aid conducted a card party and a holiday bazaar. Custodian Harold Clayton sweated in his red bandanna as he dusted and swept. But to what end? How did these things contribute to the larger mission of the church? What impact were we making with the Gospel of Jesus on people's lives? I was uncomfortable with what I saw because Concordia seemed to be 'majoring in minors,' but what would I propose as an improvement?

Part of the answer was provided by a pastor named Donald Abdon, whose mother was my grade school teacher in Indianapolis. Years earlier, I pegged him as a model pastor when he led a teen class at Calvary. Now shepherding a growing church in Peru, Indiana, Abdon had written some parish planning materials called *Organizing Around the Great Commission.* The Great Commission (Matthew 28:19-20) was the command of Jesus to make disciples of all nations. How could we make that central?

My parents alerted me to a Parish Leadership Seminar that Abdon was to conduct in Indianapolis the year after my arrival in Akron. I decided that he offered what we needed, and I recruited Bob Tofanelli and Carol Pohlod to accompany me there for the sessions.

In the summer of 1981, we made the trip and listened to Pastor Abdon for several days. We went out to eat with him, and I enjoyed watching his prominent Adam's apple bobbing as he talked. He was humorous, but also insightful, and I was challenged to think about my whole approach to ministry. Too many congregations, he asserted, settled for a 'maintenance' ministry that aimed only at securing a reasonable attendance and enough money to pay the bills. Instead, he urged, we have a charter from Jesus Christ to make disciples (as opposed to church members).

Abdon showed us how to organize everything in the church to serve the Great Commission - the constitution, the budget process, elections, and more. He also made available the tapes of his adult class called *Life With God*, a title borrowed from the book by Herman Theiss.

The seminar focused my vision. Bob and Carol and I returned from Indianapolis eager to put flesh on the ideas we had heard. In the fall I offered the first installment of *Life With God* and was pleased to have several dozen people participate in the sessions in the basement, where we had ample room. We also put together a committee of people to study and implement the seminar's ideas. The next year, we sent 14 people to a Parish Leadership Seminar in nearby Willard, Ohio.

Their work eventually led to the re-writing of our constitution and bylaws, and the total reorganization of Concordia congregation in 1984. One change was holding elections for every position at the same time and not allowing for staggered terms. The staggering of terms, Abdon insisted, served not so much to provide continuity as to insulate a church against serious change. A 'fruit basket upset' approach would allow us to clean out non-functioning boards all at once when we needed to.

There were other program changes initiated in those early years that served a more mission-minded approach to ministry. The Vacation Bible School, which had been left to die a year before our arrival, was revived. Sue led music downstairs with a rowboat as a very visible prop. Susan Weiss and the Pohlods were a big help, and there was a fair turnout of youngsters from the neighborhood in addition to our congregation's own children.

Sue had a hand in helping start another ministry. She assisted stalwart Ruth Zuelsdorf in organizing a prayer chain among the women. One of the noteworthy features of the chain was the practice of passing along a Scripture reference with each request. The chain kept very busy, and the prayers seemed to knit our fellowship together.

A few years later, the congregation agreed to sponsor individual mission projects through the synod's Together in Mission (TIM) program. One was a preschool in Puerto Ordaz, Venezuela. A second was former classmate Larry Bergman, a missionary in Nigeria. The Bergmans actually came for a visit to Concordia dressed in Nigerian clothing and displaying cultural artifacts to make more tangible the work we were supporting. Our daughter Melanie was especially interested in Larry's handsome son, Dane.

Form follows function. As Concordia began to function in a more outreaching way, it became obvious that we needed a building that could accommodate an expanding ministry and feel more welcoming to people. Our present quarters were cramped! The offices in the old Ertl home next door were detached and too small. None of the church classrooms held more than 20 people, unless we were to use the basement or the sanctuary. In addition, most people entered the church through the narrow rear entrance, which was dark and dank.

Just as we began considering the matter, Mr. Clarence Drake died. One of a multitude of shut-in members at Concordia, Clarence was a widower who was childless. Years before, Pastor Eggers had talked with him about remembering Concordia in his estate, and now that seed, planted years before, sprouted into a sizable gift for the congregation. The estate executor wrote to us, advising that we were to receive $55,000 in a lump sum settlement after the sale of Mr. Drake's house.

That gift was the catalyst for action. A building committee was formed, and Dave Wykoff donated his architectural expertise to designing an addition that would provide new office space for both pastor and secretary, a new multi-purpose room that could hold 75 students, a covered, well-lit entry area, and even two new bathrooms. Our euphoria was such that we went even further and included a set of new vandal-proof windows for the entire existing facility and some needed roof repairs. The total expense was $180,000.

The building program energized our slumping congregation. The committee chose a theme (Build for Christ), designed a tri-fold to invite participation, and set to work contacting large donors. One gray Sunday afternoon in March, 1982, the congregation gathered for a historic groundbreaking ceremony. Shortly thereafter the sound of an enormous bulldozer roused the neighborhood children as it crumpled the old Ertl home.

The construction team made quick work of the building, and in short order there stood a handsome new addition. The pitch of the roof and the colors of the brick and stone masonry were a close match to the old building. The *Akron Beacon-Journal* included a little write-up of our accomplishment, and the people smiled broadly the day we dedicated the new addition. For an old church to add a new wing after so many years of inaction was something like watching an old man in a nursing home get up, don a baseball cap, and go outside for a walk in the sunshine!

That new building opened up a world of possibilities. One of the spacious closets in the classroom served as a new food pantry, a necessary service in an urban neighborhood like ours. Soon I was hearing the (almost weekly) ringing of the doorbell by someone wanting groceries, and I was able to supply the needs with bags of tuna fish, peanut butter, soup, and crackers from that pantry.

The new classroom allowed for large Sunday morning classes, such as the study of Revelation that brought nearly 100 students for three months. It also became the site for a new, exciting adult study called Crossways.

No one at Concordia could remember any systematic teaching of the Bible at the church outside of the regular Sunday adult classes. In the mid-eighties, Sue and I went again to Indianapolis to sit at the feet of Harry Wendt, who had developed a two-year survey of the entire Bible. I remembered how The Bethel Series blessed Memorial in Vancouver, and I hoped this new course would do the same at Concordia. I ordered the overhead transparencies that illustrated the lessons, recruited students, and launched the class. Many committed themselves to the two-year study, and as the class unfolded they made excited testimonies of the power of the Word of God to shape their lives.

My assistant teacher was a lanky young man named Terry Terwilliger, who had been on the 'delinquent list' for a few years but had come back to church after some visitation and prompting by me. Terry was a computer man, bright, and hungry to learn. I played chess with his Sargon program on one of my first visits, and we found in one another a kind of kindred spirit. He soaked up Crossways the first time through, and by the next time was willing and eager to help with the lectures.

At the end of our second class, we had a celebration night in that new classroom. We played 'Crossways Baseball' with questions that reviewed our two years. We sang 'Onward, Crossways Scholars,' presented certificates of accomplishment to the graduates, ate cake and posed for a class picture. We all basked in a sense of delighted accomplishment.

Sue also had a hand in organizing Concordia's children around the Gospel mission. The move to Akron was hard on her because she had left behind our familiar home and good friends. My vacuum was filled immediately with pastoral duties and new relationships. She, on the other hand, began life in Ohio as a very lonely homemaker. Her dear friend Kathy Cusack was 2500 miles away. Her children's choir was a memory in a book of pictures. The girls went off to school. And I was often unavailable to her because I had plunged into my work with an intensity that left her on the outside, looking in. Baby Peter was her sole companion in those early, empty days.

No less than I, she was trained for a career - as a teacher. But while the children were young, she made the commitment to be a stay-at-home mom. What could she do that would employ her teaching skills?

She decided to resume her ministry as a children's choir director. When she made the announcement that a new choir would be formed, there was an enthusiastic response. "I'll bring my twins," promised Bob Tofanelli. Other families brought children too. Our two girls helped form an experienced nucleus. Neighbor boy Chaka Clemens was the first black child to take a spot in Sue's choir.

Sue directed, but who could accompany? Eileen Koski, the regular organist, had her plate full as the accompanist of the adult choir. Could someone else volunteer? There stepped forward an unlikely prospect – an 80-year-old man named Paul Kares. He was bent and wrinkled like a human prune. He had a tiny, clipped moustache and wore baggy pants. His wife Helen had been teaching Sunday School for decades, but Paul was not much involved. In his younger days he played the piano with energy, mostly by ear, but now his gnarled hands weren't so steady. His playing was sluggish, and he often improvised his own tempo and accompaniment by chording instead of reading the music, causing some moments of anxiety for Sue. Nevertheless, he had a sincere love for kids and was willing to stay with the task, which he did for two years. Later, Pat Goolsby, a pleasant woman with musical skills and a servant's heart, filled the role and served beside Sue for the rest of our years in Akron.

Practices began in the annex, and Sue arrayed her chairs in the familiar alignment of semi-circular rows, with wood blocks, bells, and other simple instruments placed under chairs for kids to use.

There were challenges to overcome. When Sue asked some children to play their instruments before the annual Christmas program, she butted heads with Anne Hracky, who was the turf guardian of Sunday School spaces and program routines. But gradually things smoothed out, and in later years Anne smiled with others to hear the children play.

One memorable Christmas musical was *Mary Had a Little Lamb*, a delightful portrayal of Jesus' role as the Lamb of God. Jessica Hill was 'Tiny,' a small spotted lamb who learned the meaning of God's plan to send a lamb for sin. Lisa Liddle was a diminutive girl who brought a giant-sized heart and voice for her solo:

Messiah is coming and his blood's gonna wash every sin away
Messiah is coming and the earth will be singing for joy that day.
Prophets have foretold that He'll be born in Bethlehem
Shepherd of the fold of men and yet Himself a Lamb –
He'll be the Mighty King; salvation He will bring
Messiah is coming and it's gonna be a brighter day!

Another musical entitled *'Kids' Praise'* revolved around a living book of Psalms, which taught children to sing their prayers to God. Bruce Emerick played the role of 'Psalty,' and he dressed the part, coming onstage as a large book.

The final musical was performed just a week before our departure in 1988. *We Like Sheep* portrayed the relationship between Jesus, the Good Shepherd, and the sheep of His flock. All the children dressed as sheep, each boy bearing a black-lettered 'Ram' on his chest, each girl sporting a large red heart with a cursive 'Ewe.' Each also wore a headband, from which dangled floppy white lambs' ears. By this time, our girls had outgrown the Children's Choir, and a new group of children rose up to be leaders.

Bruce Emerick was involved once more, this time as the shepherd who had to seek the sheep and count them each night before putting them to bed. The drama in the musical was paralleled by the real-life drama of the Ernst children – Colleen, Brock, and Ryan – who came from a troubled home. Each week Sue picked them up for rehearsal, then took them home again. The youngest, Ryan, was a real lost sheep of a child who played the role of the recalcitrant 'Grimy' in the program. When the time for the performance came, illness struck. Sue was sick, and she leaned on the words of 2 Corinthians 12:9, trusting God to make His strength perfect in her weakness.

One of the main characters also had to stay at home, and Sue pressed eight-year-old Peter into duty. He knew all the parts by heart, and he seemed to be a natural stand-in. It was a memorable day, and the words stayed long in the hearts of the children:

No matter how baaad we are, the Shepherd loves us,
No matter how faaar we stray, still He carries us home
No matter how baaad we are, the Shepherd loves us,
Yes, He loves us and he calls us His own.

In such ways both adults and children were organized to grow in grace and to serve the Lord as best we could in our Goosetown neighborhood. That the church did not grow numerically continued to trouble me over the years there. By now, I knew that was a matter of my old sinful pride. But many individuals grew in faith and in service, and ministry in Akron became increasingly a thing of joy.

Confirmation class at Concordia, Akron (1985)

JOURNEY TO ISRAEL

"Pastor, have you ever thought about taking a trip to Israel?" The question came at the end of one of our Crossways sessions in the fall of 1985. Marlene Norris, Jim's new wife, posed it, and I answered it academically. "Oh, it would be nice, I suppose, but I've never considered it that much – probably too expensive." I continued gathering my teaching notes.

"If someone invited you, would you go?" she persisted. I looked up. This wasn't an academic question.

"Are you inviting us?" I asked, raising my eyebrows.

Jim jumped in. "Our business has done well," he explained. "We have been wondering what to do with the extra money. The other night Marlene had a dream. God appeared to her and said, 'Take your priest and Jim's pastor to Israel.' So, if you'd like to go – you and Sue – we're inviting you." A shocked silence followed.

"Well," I laughed, "how can I argue with God?"

That's how it began. Jim turned over the planning of the tour to me and told me not to worry about expenses. By January of 1986 we were ready. Passports with new photos were in hand. I had a 35mm camera on loan from Dave Wykoff. Our parents agreed to come to Akron in shifts to babysit the children. Sue prepared 18 pages of notes for them.

It was a very compact tour group. Father Jim Klein, Marlene's priest at St. Paul's parish, joined us in a limousine for the ride to Cleveland-Hopkins Airport on a snowy Monday morning.

DIARY NOTES

Monday, January 13

The first short hop on TWA takes us to JFK Airport in New York. A sign in the terminal warns against pickpockets and baggage thieves. We see two Orthodox Jews with black hats and ringlets in front of their ears, priests in collars, Indian women with scarlet dots on their foreheads, and a man in a flowing Arab robe and white cap.

Our international flight is to be aboard ALIA Royal Jordanian Airlines. Our cream-colored 747 bears the name 'Prince Ali.' Announcements are in Arabic (very fast), then in English. Sue's thinking about the kids. "We've never been away from them for such a long time," she muses anxiously.

Tuesday, January 14

'Prince Ali' descends for a landing at Vienna. We pass low over red-roofed houses and high church spires. The surprisingly small airport bears the sign FLUGHAFEN WIEN. Terrorists, I remember reading, struck here recently. After a two-hour stop, we take off again.

About dusk we make the approach to Amman, Jordan, from the east across sandy desert. Why are people fighting over this? I wonder as I scan the lunar landscape. A cavernous airport, dimly-lit. Signs all in Arabic, and almost all the people I see are dark-skinned, the men with moustaches.

We are met by a man named Waddah, who guides us through customs and onto a waiting bus with a group from Minnesota. On the 25-mile ride into Amman, we receive a lecture on the Palestinian plight. How different to hear about the West Bank situation from a Jordanian: "Israel has occupied our land!"

We arrive at the Tyche Hotel under a brilliant starry sky. We meet our travel guide, Adnan Shaweesh, a man of gracious manners who has spent time (in 1967) in Utah, living with a Mormon family, studying the Book of Mormon. Unconvinced, he remains Muslim.

In the room, we find apples and oranges from the management. I settle into bed, but Sue stays up a while to read a book about Israel borrowed from Father Klein. She comes to bed feeling cold and lonesome for the familiar. Our children are far away, and we are 'strangers in a strange land.'

Wednesday, January 15

Morning brings a cold rain and leaden skies. Our party gathers at 7 a.m. to meet Kahlil, a 24-year-old man with a winsome smile ("my name means 'friend'"). We set out on a 165-mile trip to Petra, a trip Kahlil makes twice a week. The desert is surprisingly busy with trucks shuttling to the gulf port of Aqaba. We see small Turkish-made forts, a phosphate mine, a prison under construction, a Palestinian refugee camp, and a roadside meat market with a freshly-killed sheep hanging by its feet. At a roadside panorama – biblical Moab – I buy a Jordanian khoufieh (cloth headpiece) for $5.50 American.

Petra is a city in stone constructed by Nabatean Arabs in the centuries just before Christ. The dwellings and tombs are carved into beautiful rose-colored rocks. Some of the columns and designs are up to 80 feet high. All this is accessed by horseback. Each horse has its own handler, who walks the horse down the narrow defile among towering rocks.

Once there, our tiny tour group reads from Psalm 90 – I feel like a brief minute on eternity's clock among these ancient ruins. On foot we explore a Roman prison and an Arab amphitheater. The ground is littered with candy wrappers and pop cans – a jarring anachronism in this place. After the ride back we tip our horse handlers $2.00 each (they wanted more) and practice sales resistance against the constant pestering of peripatetic Arab salesmen hawking statues, coins, and jewelry.

Thursday, January 16

After breakfast, Adnan drives us to the Jerusalem Hotel, where we converge with two other groups who will cross the Jordan River today. On the bus he gives the large group a lecture about Jordan's history, and the growth of Amman – from 5000 people to 1.5 million in a span of 40 years – due to influx of Palestinians. As we near the Jordan, he recites the story of Moses for us, and points out Mount Nebo. All is more rugged than I expected.

Our first view of Israel is of sunlit mountains rising from the Jordan valley toward Jerusalem – the view Moses had. The valley is like Florida, with citrus trees, banana palms, and tilled fields with cucumbers and tomatoes. But we are disappointed with the Jordan River itself and the famed Allenby Bridge – astonishingly small. I can understand Naaman's complaint when Elisha told him to go bathe there! A disturbing addition to the scene is a pair of military checkpoints – Jordanian soldiers sandbagged in on one side, Israelis on the other.

We bid farewell to Adnan and hello to our Israeli guide, Yehuda Guy – a British Jew who emigrated to Israel 30 years ago. He's tall and thin with dark glasses. Not, we learn, an observant Jew. Our bus driver, Ismayil, a stocky 35-year-old, is both Arab and a practicing Christian. A tiny tour bus is all ours.

First stop is a fruit market in Jericho, very close by. Yehuda gets us a pomelo, a sort of over-sized grapefruit with thick rind – very sweet. I buy dates, figs, and tangerines. Then we stop at Kathleen Kenyon's archeological dig. In the trench below us are the remains of an ancient tower from 7000 BC. Jericho is the oldest known city site in the world.

On our drive north we pass Mt. Gilboa, where Saul and sons were slain and Gideon recruited his tiny army. On one height are the remains of a Crusader fort. Date palms line the road. "Most of these trees," explains Yehuda, "were planted in your lifetime. Last century, Mark Twain visited and complained how barren everything was."

Our first view of the Sea of Galilee reminds me of Grand Traverse Bay in Michigan. The hills of Galilee are rocky, but pretty with trees. We see the Horns of Hattin, where Saladin defeated the Crusaders, and Mt. Tabor, where Deborah defeated Sisera. At Nazareth we exit the bus for a walking tour. The Roman Catholic Church of the Annunciation is architecturally awesome. Somewhere near here Jesus preached his inaugural sermon. The larger impression is of traffic and Coca-Cola signs and the realization that this isn't holy ground for the people who dwell here now.

Back at Tiberias we settle in to the Ron Beach Hotel on Galilee's shore. Day closes with a devotion on the veranda as we gaze out. Here Jesus called fishermen, walked on water, and stilled a storm! The lake is quiet tonight.

<u>Friday, January 17</u>

The day dawns clear for our trip across the Sea of Galilee. We occupy the lower section of a large pontoon boat – a group from Germany has laid claim to the upper deck. We take pictures of Tiberias in our wake and Capernaum up ahead, and we toss bread pieces to hungry seagulls. We imagine Jesus with his men crossing the lake as sunlight sparkled on the water.

Finally ashore at Capernaum, we visit a ruined synagogue, where we see an engraved stone ark. At a nearby monastery there are brilliant pink and red bougainvillea plants. A place not spoiled by modernity! We make leisurely stops also at Tabgha, site of the breakfast story in John 21, and the site of the Feeding of the 5000. We five take leave of our guide for a bit and ascend to a higher spot overlooking the lake where we take turns reading portions of the Sermon on the Mount. Father Klein adds meditative comments.

We are to lunch at a kibbutz. On the way our bus passes Tel Hazor, largest tel (mound of ruins) in Israel. Here Joshua conquered a city by that name. I'm amazed that this and other sites are so small. We lunch at Kafar Blum, within sight of Mount Hermon, a snow-covered peak. Yehuda tells us that 3% of Israelis live in kibbutzes and produce 40% of the country's food supply.

<u>Saturday, January 18</u>

We are sad to leave Lake Galilee, but comforted by one more lovely drive past Mount Tabor. Not far away is Megiddo, a large tel with 26 layers of occupation. Solomon's is the fourth from the top. Yehuda points out stables for his horses. From the wall of the ruins we can see from one end of Israel to the other – Carmel on the west shore, Gilead on the east. Israel's no larger than Vermont!

As we drive west toward the coast, Yehuda asks us "What's the leading money-producing industry in Israel?" We guess. Fishing? Grain? He answers his own question: "Diamonds!" Actually the cutting of diamonds flown in from South Africa and elsewhere. In the port city of Haifa we see a large Baha'i temple (world headquarters). Not far away is Caesarea, where we see ruins of the Roman theater where Paul likely went on trial before governor Felix. We also observe a beautiful aqueduct, mosaic pavements, statues, and a sarcophagus. The strong sea breeze reminds us of the Oregon coast.

The ride to Jerusalem takes us first through Tel Aviv – a very American-looking city with a freeway. On the way up to Jerusalem, we drive through country surprisingly green. Entering Jerusalem, we see Orthodox Jews with fur hats, beards, and ringlets in their hair.

Sue and I phone home. Our kids' voices sound far away and not too excited. The girls tell us that our 100-year-old neighbor died the day we left. At evening prayers we give our loneliness to God and pray also for the spiritual welfare of guide Yehuda.

Sunday, January 19

We awake to rain and cold. We attend worship at the Lutheran Church of the Redeemer in the walled city. The service in the main sanctuary is in Arabic, so we attend English service in the smaller Crusader Chapel. About 50 worshippers join in using the LBW (halfway around the world and we are using the Lutheran liturgy!). Good organist, good singing, and a friendly pastor.

Today we drive to Bethlehem, just 10 minutes away. Yehuda points out the Valley of Hinnom (literally gehenna, the word for 'hell') and the Kidron Valley on the way. Bethlehem is more hilly than I imagined. We go to shepherd's field and see a cave with smoke-blackened roof used over many centuries. Was Jesus, perhaps, born in a cave like this rather than what is pictured on Christmas cards? We read the story in Luke 2 together. We stop at Three Arches store to get mementoes, and the salesman, an Arab Christian, tells us most of the Arabs in Bethlehem are Christians too. Surprising!

The afternoon is spent in the Old City. As at Megiddo, there is a water shaft down to Gihon Spring first dug by Jebusites 4000 years ago, then added to by Hezekiah. At David's Tomb we are accosted by a drunken man who singles out Jim for verbal abuse and shouts "I am a Jew!" Yehuda steps in and speaks fast Hebrew to him, quieting him.

At supper the head waiter tells us he likes American tourists best of all groups. Why? They say "thank you" and are friendly, he tells us. This day, like most others, is punctuated by the Muslim call to prayer over nearby loudspeakers.

Monday, January 20

We begin the day's travels on the Mount of Olives. On the way there we pass a BYU extension that has caused a furor here. Orthodox Jews don't like the idea that the Mormons will be proselytizing. At the crown of the hill, we get a panoramic view of Jerusalem, but are bothered by a swarm of hawkers. I finally give a camel-handler a dollar to allow Sue to get hoisted up on his beast for a picture.

Down to Gethsemane just below. A lovely spot with a well-maintained grove of olive trees. Impossible to measure age, but some accounts say a few trees from Jesus' day are still growing. Nearby Church of All Nations is beautiful, but we feel we are swimming in mosaics, inscriptions, candles, paintings, and frescoes.

Back inside Jerusalem, we are told about the four quarters into which the Romans usually divided cities, with major arterials bisecting the sides. The Old City has Jewish, Christian, Muslim, and Armenian sections. In the Jewish Quarter, we are fascinated by archeological digs going on underneath while construction projects proceed above.

By late morning we are at the Wailing Wall where a considerable throng has gathered (men to left side, women to right). Some men pray while chanting softly, rocking, and sticking tiny pieces of paper in the wall's cracks. Nearby a boy is carried on a relative's shoulders for his Bar Mitzvah. Another man carries Torah scrolls in a portable ark. From across the divider between the men and women, female relatives toss wrapped candies while the men sing, and all clap. It's easily the most joyful moment I witnessed in Israel.

The holiest moment of the trip is at the Garden Tomb. On the wall is a poster announcing "Jesus Christ is alive today!" An elderly British man leads us out to see Gordon's Calvary site, just behind a nearby bus station, and then to the tomb. Our guide speaks reverently of "Our Lord." When at last he ushers us into the tomb itself, he asks, "Have you ever been here before?" I answer, "Many times…in my heart!" This place (or something very near) was the hinge on which all history turned. Very humbling.

We come to the Temple Mount, the world's most politically explosive real estate. Guards search us for bombs, and then we must remove shoes before we enter the mosque. It seems every square inch outside is covered with fine design work. Inside under the dome is the rock from which Muhammad was supposed to have ascended to heaven in a vision. The carpeted floor insures quietness. Downstairs, three Muslim women are at prayers.

Down to the Via Dolorosa. Not just Good Friday, but every day, groups process down this narrow street. Stations of cross are marked with plaques. We pass shops, and the aromas of fish, bread, meats, and heaps of spices mix with the sights of olive wood carvings and other sale items.

We arrive at Church of the Holy Sepulchre – actually a conglomerate of six churches run by different groups! A group of Japanese priests and nuns arrives, along with some Franciscans in brown habits chanting the Sanctus in Latin. This place inspires none of the simple joy we felt at the Garden Tomb.

Tuesday, January 21

Today we go to Masada. We take the road from Jerusalem down to Jericho (really 'down' – a 4000-foot drop in 15 miles). We are caught in a time warp, with Bedouin tents on one side of the road, and modern apartments on the other. Spread before us is the Dead Sea, deceptively beautiful but bitterly salty (each quart contains one-half pound of salt, says Yehuda). Because irrigation siphons off water from Jordan, the Dead Sea is dropping 10 inches a year and has already shrunk into two smaller lakes.

Masada looms before us. We wait in the gift shop for our ascent by cable car. T-shirts for sale proclaim "Masada shall not fall again!" and Israeli jets roar overhead as if on cue. Herod the Great built palaces up here, and our guide shows us plasterwork with painting still visible. In the surrounding desert we see remains of Roman walls, guard towers, and camps that housed 30,000 soldiers during the siege. The huge ramp from the west constructed by the Romans still remains, as well as the smaller one constructed for the TV re-enactment.

On the drive back toward Qumran we see acacia trees (from which Ark of Covenant was made). We stop beside the Dead Sea, touch the water, and feel its stinging, oily residue. Qumran itself is a smallish ruin – the caves nearby are where Dead Sea Scrolls were discovered.

Wednesday, January 22

Our last full day is a free day. Sue and I go on shopping jaunt to West Jerusalem. A walk of nearly two hours yields little – only two small mezuzahs (Scripture boxes affixed to doorposts) for friends and a Jewish doll for Christa. We decide we'll do better in the Old City, so we return there in a light rain, and in a short time are bartering with merchants. Sue gets a cross for Kathy Cusack. She wants a black blouse with fine handwork for herself, and persists until the price is lowered from $40 to $23. We buy a ceramic jar from a boy named Faisal.

After lunch we head to Yad Vashem, a monument to Holocaust victims in West Jerusalem. Yad Vashem is park-like and reverent. Part is an art museum with works on display made by some of the victims. Outside is famous sculpture of tangled barbed wire and corpses – beautiful and hideous. Another building gives one a graphic tour of the Nazi death camps, and I reflect how sheltered we Americans have been from harm.

Thursday, January 23

After breakfast, Jim leaves tips for our helpers. His generosity astonishes me. We bid farewell to Ismayil, our driver. On the way to the airport, we see three sheep being dragged, struggling against their handler.

"They are going to be killed," the driver explains. I think of Jesus being led to slaughter "like a lamb."

Waddah meets us at the airport, guides us through customs, and we are on our way home...from one world into another. Our memories are stored in our hearts and our photos.

IN RETROSPECT

The journey to Israel has been a vivid reminder that we are part of something larger, older, and deeper than we normally stop to realize. It was an experience both faith-strengthening and challenging. It was faith-strengthening to see the stage on which the drama unfolded. I was forcefully reminded that the Bible presents not a fantasy story in some neverland, but a historical narrative that may be retraced, examined, and to some degree experienced. "Right here is where it happened!" I found myself saying repeatedly. The Bible became more three-dimensional during our time there.

It was also faith-strengthening to see the impact of Jesus' life in people of cultures other than my own – in our Arab driver Ismayil and some Japanese nuns we watched in procession in Jerusalem, for example.

There were challenges, too. The flip side of seeing the real places was the discovery that they were often visually unimpressive – they had no special aura about them. The Jordan River was small. Nazareth had a city dump! Even the 'Holy Land' has weeds and mongrel dogs and human debris. The holiness of the place felt more elusive after encountering such things. Was it that way for the people who met Jesus? Might they have said to themselves, "How can this man be our Messiah? He looks so ordinary."

Meeting people from alien cultures opened the door to being challenged by people who do not accept things as we do. How is it that Yehuda, in spite of his knowledge of biblical history, remains a decidedly secular Jew who cannot even remember what day is the Sabbath? How are we to answer Adnan Shaweesh, a committed Muslim, who was not hesitant to address uncomfortable questions to us about the ease of divorce among Christians and our often unexamined support for Israel against the Palestinians?

I know this: I will never be able to teach another Bible class or preach another sermon without the memory of this journey in my mind's eye. I will not be able to use the words 'Arab,' 'Jew' or 'Muslim' without seeing the faces of people who remain in my heart.

A PROCESSION OF VICARS

The work load at Concordia was nearly unmanageable. There were 18 people on the shut-in list, and I tried to take Communion to each one every other month. There were hospital patients at four area hospitals, and I tried to see each every 2-3 days. I planned and led all services, taught four times a week, attended all the expected meetings, and put out congregational fires that flamed up unexpectedly.

I had still not learned how to empower lay people, and the lay people had not learned to do their part. That was a lesson that still lay in the future. For now, the congregation and I wrestled with getting additional help. An assistant pastor? The budget was not sufficient. A deaconess? She would not be able to help with the worship load. We decided on requesting a vicar, partly out of financial considerations, and partly because the vicarage experience had been a positive one for me.

Early in 1985, we notified the English District of our need and filled in the required application. In a surprisingly short time, we heard that we were to receive our first vicar. It was something like learning that one's wife is expecting a baby. Preparations needed to be made. Budgetary allowances had already been seen to. Office space was cleared in the sacristy. Late in August I preached on 'How to Treat a Vicar,' urging the congregation to do two things:

> *First, respect him!*
> *It is true that the vicar isn't yet 'officially' a pastor...yet he is not merely an employee on the church payroll. This is no mere business arrangement to secure cheap help for the pastor! No. He is assisting me in the duties of the pastoral office...and he deserves the respect proper to that office...*
>
> *Ah, but what about his faults?*
> *Yes, I'm afraid he has some of those...How do we treat a vicar when he does wrong? In response, let me ask: HOW HAS GOD TREATED YOU? ...He has loved you! Loved us all!*
>
> *So I preach to myself as well as to you today.*
> *Let the pastor, the vicar, and the congregation pledge*
> *these three things:*
> *Let us pray for one another earnestly, daily.*
> *Let us not accuse one to the other, but gently admonish and forgive the sinner when it's needed.*

And, week by week, let us stand at the foot of the cross, trusting Jesus Christ to grant us peace with one another.

What a joyful moment! What exciting days lie ahead...

There was nothing more to do but await the arrival. The three vicars who came to help me in Akron proved to be as different as the children that showed up in our family.

Dale and Elaine Pritchard drove up to our home in Firestone Park late that summer. He was of medium height with dark hair and a boyish face, slightly rosy-cheeked. His wife, Elaine, was flaxen-haired, pale in complexion, and more shy than he. While he talked, she smiled but stayed slightly back like a timid deer, laughing awkwardly now and then. It was a moment of utmost satisfaction for me, like the passing from childhood into adulthood. Once I had been a vicar. Now I was to have a vicar! Dale later told the congregation that he felt like my new puppy.

As Pastor Schroeder had done with me fifteen years earlier, I now did with Dale and with each succeeding vicar. We met to get acquainted, and then took each area one by one – preaching, administration, teaching, visiting, meetings, and the like. As I had been assigned once, so I made the assignment that he have a time of devotion each day. Dale was to preach every third Sunday or so, help with confirmation class, make visits (initially together, then on his own), and go to all the required conferences.

Dale took to it with enthusiasm, if not with skill. His background, I discovered, was very shallow. At one of our initial meetings with the confirmation class, we sat with the students in a circle in our family room. I had just handed out the memory charts for the first part of class, which included the books of the Bible. "OK, everybody," I directed, "you'll be asked to learn the books in order and recite them twice to check them off the sheet." I turned to Dale, wanting to involve him and give him the chance to impress the kids. "Vicar Pritchard," I invited, "why don't you recite the books for them?" His eyes opened wide in a look of helpless terror. He shook his head. "Pastor, I can't do it. I haven't learned them!" That misstep taught me not to assume too much about my vicars, but rather to communicate with them before we embarked on teaching, visiting or leading worship. I didn't quiz Dale again.

That afternoon's uncomfortable moment was the first signal to me that Dale brought some unexplored issues with him. He had experienced some unpleasantness in his childhood that he was unwilling to unpack. He carried with him a disturbingly low self-image that emerged in a sermon in which he told the people that he had learned that his name meant 'pile of dirt' (in fact, a 'dale' is a valley!). He wrote his own youthful struggles into the form of a play called *The Puzzles of Life* and had the youth group perform the play. It was a therapeutic exercise for him, and it was evident that some of our youth could identify with the characters they played.

The year went by quickly, and we gathered in the basement to have a farewell dinner. Emcee Dave Wykoff addressed a packed hall, "Well, Dale and Elaine must have made a lot of friends!" There were lots of gifts, and lots of laughs at the gentle roasting we administered and at the cacophonous rendition of 'Happy Birthday' by our adult choir. Brad Schonover spoke for the youth: "You made our faith grow." I reflected that Dale had grown in confidence. And Dale called the day one of the best of his life – "my wedding day was the happiest, but this was close!"

In the summer of 1986 there arrived a couple of irrepressible Texans named Keith and Johanna Gravesmill. At our very first meeting, they bounced from their car like twin jack-in-the-boxes from a confining box. "Howdy, y'all!" they gushed, and ran to us with arms out wide for a hug.

Johanna was dark-haired and snappy-eyed, the daughter of Pastor Richard Wagner of Houston. She had a career goal of counseling, but was also determined to have a happy family of her own and to help her husband succeed as a pastor. Keith was a short, sandy-haired, aw-shucks sort of fellow, inclined to cover nervousness with laughter. He told me that he had worked at Frito-Lay's big plant in Texas. The family also had one small child, a boy named Seth, and a blond cocker spaniel named Caleb (the Hebrew word for 'dog,' Keith explained).

Keith took readily to the assignments I gave him and especially enjoyed going with me on calls where I attempted to model the pastor's role. But neither Keith nor his predecessor Dale seemed to have the appetite for work that I had. I would sometimes find Keith in his office quaffing down his daily Diet Coke, a drink to which he admitted being 'addicted,' and listening to the radio. Keith's relaxed style was something like a mirror held up before me, and I began to see myself as something of a workaholic, an insight parishioners had been trying to impress upon me.

The Gravesmills proved to be the warmest of my vicarage couples. They valued relationships above all things, and we visited one another and kicked back to talk frequently. Keith and Johanna conspired to plan a fortieth birthday party for me shortly before they were finished with the vicarage year, a party that left indelible memories.

The evening of the party began with a grand deception. Sue persuaded me that we needed to go to a children's program somewhere, and I reluctantly agreed to go. But she must stop first at church to get something. When we drove into the lot and I saw it filled with cars, I knew something was up. Down in the basement a large crowd awaited. Black balloons dangled, and signs announced, 'Lordy, Lordy, Pastor's Forty!' and 'Over the Hill.'

A large birthday cake topped with forty flaming candles was brought from the kitchen. At the other end of the hall there awaited some surprises. I was invited to be the honored guest of 'This is Your Life,' and from somewhere came the voices, in sequence, of my sister Natalie ("Mike, you get in here and dry these dishes!") and brother-in-law Kenny, Sue's parents and mine. Couple by couple, they emerged from behind the curtain to greet me. "Boy, am I surprised!" I said. The good folks of Concordia exulted in having pulled it off.

But the biggest laugh was to come when the curtain was drawn to reveal an enormous black-and-white cardboard cake. While the congregation sang 'Happy Birthday,' Sue was to pop out from the top. But something was slightly off-kilter inside the cake, and just as she emerged through the top, the cake collapsed, accompanied by a surprised scream from the assembled throng. In a moment, plucky Sue crawled out, still holding a 'happy birthday' poster, and Johanna led the relieved laughter.

There were more gifts. My dad brought out a new white chasuble (festal liturgical vestment) adorned with a red Chi Rho and a green vine on each side. The congregation oohed and ahhed as he removed it from the plastic protector and put it on me for the first time. Then from the congregation came a large and thoughtful gift. Dale Meech made the presentation of a vacation trip to Niagara Falls. Like a herald, he unrolled a scroll ordering us to do this very thing, and directing us to leave the children with duly-appointed baby-sitters from the church.

There was even a tiny theatrical vignette, in which Terry Terwilliger played the role of Pastor Mike, studying to prepare his sermon, and kneeling in prayer for the congregation. It was a simple, yet very touching tribute, and I realized that night how fully we had come past the heartache years and into a loving relationship as pastor and people. The Gravesmills had orchestrated it all for me, and Karen Wallick had done much to help.

The third of my vicars was the most competent and experienced, and the least satisfying to supervise for that reason. Bob Raedeke and his wife Chloe were markedly different from the two previous couples. The Pritchards had been friendly in a very shy way, and the Gravesmills had been friendly in an effusive way, but the Raedekes were cool and slightly distant. Where Dale and Keith had been both awkward and inexperienced, Bob seemed polished and professional. The son of a pastor himself, Bob was knowledgeable to the point that I could tell him little that he didn't already know.

Bob was tall and thin, an accomplished musician who could play fine Irish music on his guitar. Chloe was in a separate world, like someone observed through a store window. She had a job as a sex education teacher in schools. She was mother to a year-old daughter, Tessa, and seemed very competent, like Bob. Rarely, however, did we manage to enter her world and learn how she felt.

Nevertheless, Bob seemed to come to Concordia at the right time. During his year in Akron, the centennial of C. F. W. Walther's death was observed, and I determined to have Walther come to life. Bob proved to be a skillful actor, and with a bit of makeup, he became Walther come back from the dead and paying a visit to our church one Sunday morning. Later, when I accepted the call to go to Sequim, Bob filled in the breach in an admirable way.

The presence of that succession of vicars freed me to pursue some things that I might not have taken time for otherwise. I took a canoe trip down the Cuyahoga River with the youth group. I did some extra writing, including a book review and a couple of contributions to the local newspaper. In addition, it prepared me for team ministries that I was later to enjoy in subsequent congregations.

Just as parents continue to be concerned about their children long after they leave the nest, so I felt a fatherly interest in each of the young men who had been my charge. Dale and Elaine Pritchard had a baby daughter within a couple of years, and he pastored a church for a while in the St. Louis area and continued to try his hand at writing. Later I was saddened to learn that their marriage had ended, and Dale's name disappeared from the clergy roster. Then the saddest news of all from Elaine: Dale finally took his own life. I felt a pain akin to a punch in the stomach.

Bob and Chloe Raedeke had three more children. He served congregations in Alsip, Illinois (a Chicago suburb), and Spooner, Wisconsin, before taking on a dual parish at Junction City and Dancy, Wisconsin. A scholarly man, he has added both a master's and a doctorate in theology.

Keith Gravesmill invited me to preach at his installation in a little church in Illinois, and I did so. Learning that the area had been hit by a prolonged dry spell, we took a moment in the service to pray for rain. During the reception afterward, there came a sizable downpour. "I hope, Keith, that all your prayers are answered in such a dramatic way!" I told him. He and Johanna had two more children and eventually he took a call to a church in Austin, Texas.

ROSES AND THORNS

My first sermon to the people of Concordia had been 'Treasure in a Pot,' a reminder to them and to me that I was a frail human being, sinful and breakable. The intensive work load of those years in Akron made it clear that I was no Superman. My workaholic tendencies, coupled with the demands of the schedule, resulted in recurring tension headaches and bouts of depression. I wondered how long I could sustain the pace.

My congregation was showing its frailty too. Some of our young people dropped out. Several of our couples divorced, including our president Bob Tofanelli. Every divorce, especially his, brought heartache beyond telling. Our aging congregation experienced a disproportionate number of funerals. One year alone I had 22 funerals to plan. Six of those came in the already-busy season of lent. Ruth Zuelsdorf, who had mustered her courage and love to admonish me, withered away with cancer. We said a tearful good-bye to Carole Gungle, whose return to the faith and re-marriage to her ex-husband Mike had encouraged many, and to Paul Kares, the children's choir accompanist.

Early in May of 1987, Dick Yount, nephew of old Pastor Yount, dropped dead of a sudden heart attack. He failed to show up on a Sunday morning to teach his class, and his lady friend Pat Bair hurried to the house and discovered him there. I conducted his funeral, using as my theme "To Die is Gain" from Philippians 1.

It was autumn when Pat approached me with an unexpected offer. "Have you ever thought of publishing a book of your sermons?" she asked. "Oh, I guess most pastors fantasize about doing that," I laughed. But she was serious when she answered, "Dick always liked your sermons so well. I'd like to give you some money to do that, as a memorial gift. Do you think $5000 would be enough?" I was humbled, astonished. I agreed, and Pat smiled her shy smile.

The first task was to select the sermons. Over the years I had kept all the manuscripts of my sermons in file folders organized by texts in the sequence of the Bible books. I also had a typed summary of the texts and titles in order. I went through those and picked what I thought would be a representative sample. Remembering Mark Bertermann's installation sermon, I chose *Treasure in a Pot* as the title. Things were busy, however, and progress on the book was slow.

Late in 1987 there came a phone call from a man named Dean Hart in faraway Washington State that would change the timetable for the book and everything else. I was one of two candidates remaining on the list for the pastorate at Faith Lutheran Church in a place called Sequim. Where was that? We would soon find out, for the congregation there was calling to invite Sue and me to visit for an interview.

On December 17 we flew to Seattle, then on to Sequim, a small town on the Olympic Peninsula, for a one-day meeting. It was a stark contrast to our urban setting in Akron. The airport was a glorified landing strip. A sign said the town had a population of 4080. There were no freeways in sight, only mountains, water, and fir forests. The modern, angled frame church was from a different architectural world than Concordia's gothic edifice.

We gathered for an evening meeting in Faith's fellowship hall. The other pastor on the call list, a man from Minnesota, had been there two weeks earlier. Nearly a hundred people jammed the hall, and Sue and I were invited to stand and share about ourselves, then field questions.

The gatherings were cordial and the people very positive, but the town of Sequim was a 'retirementville.' Slow. Lots of senior citizens. Just not like us, we concluded. As Sue and I took off in the little plane to retrace our steps through Seattle back home, I told Sue I was doubtful we would ever see those folks again.

The Sunday after Christmas the issue was thrust into the middle of our agenda, for the folks at Faith had made up their minds and issued us a call. Though we had planned to take the next week and head for Indiana to see the relatives, it became essential for me to stay in Akron to announce the reception of the call.

I phoned Dave Wykoff and Dale Meech. I made the announcement. "I hadn't anticipated being here with you this morning, but those plans changed last Sunday evening, when I received a phone call from Faith Lutheran Church in Sequim, Washington..." I assured them that receiving a call did not automatically mean that a pastor would go, and that most calls are declined. I invited them, if they felt moved to do so, to call or write me with their wisdom.

Things grew more complex when, shortly thereafter, I received still another call, this one from Trinity Lutheran Church in Hillsboro, Oregon. Sue felt, more strongly than I, that two calls this close together meant God was softening me up for a move as navy ships' guns soften up a beach before a military landing. I tried to gain time, sending a letter to the congregation that a decision would be delayed because of this new twist. "Please watch and pray with me some more."

All of this was having an impact on our children, especially Melanie, who for the first time was old enough to realize what a change another move would bring. I pointedly asked the children to join their prayers to ours.

Dave Wykoff and John Lovich invited me to lunch and labored to persuade me to stay. "We just got a new hymnal," they pointed out. "And we're just about to send 40 people to the Great Commission convocation. We're on the verge of some changes that we need you to help us see through." Meanwhile, there were letters from Sequim, beseeching me to come, with reasons why I was needed there. I swayed in the wind. In His mysterious way, the Holy Spirit began to nudge me. Gradually my mind changed from 'no way' to 'maybe' to the conviction that I was to move.

On February 3, I wrote the congregation a letter announcing the decision to decline the call to Hillsboro, but accept the call from Sequim. "After many weeks of waiting, praying, and listening for the Lord's leading, I have reached a decision...I am accepting the call...This has been a painful, difficult decision..." I explained the reasons, and I tried to encourage the people by noting that our congregation's spiritual life was healthy and that there was a core of capable leaders in place. Terry Terwilliger would handle Crossways class, and Vicar Raedeke would be at his post on Sundays.

Among the matters needing attention was that book of sermons I had put on hold. The sermons were already selected months earlier. I still had to find a publisher. I tried several and settled on the Crawford Company in downtown Akron. Then began a feverish round of preparations that yielded a finished book only two weeks before we were to depart on April 10. I decided to give each household a copy of the book with a hand-written inscription in the front cover. The book would be my parting gift.

The farewell gathering took place on a sunny Sunday afternoon. The congregation rented Todaro's Party Center, and the room was completely full. Among the guests were fellow pastors and wives, former vicar Keith Gravesmill, and Sue's brother Phil and wife Linda.

We sat with the Wykoffs on a raised head table. Above us was a finely-crafted banner by Jim Liddle: FAREWELL, KASTINGS. Dave was a gracious emcee, and his jokes were appreciatively received. The choir sang, speeches were made, and wonderful, generous gifts were given. The spirit of the people that farewell day was more joyful than sad, and I was washed by a wave of thanksgiving that God had brought such a harmony between me and a congregation that had fought with me in earlier days. Karen Wallick, one of my early critics, was smiling, appreciative. Sue and I had come to love her and see beneath her stubbornness a fierce loyalty to Christ. Our early resentment of this old traditional bunch had long since evaporated. We could, we felt, 'depart in peace.'

"I was getting some things ready for a garage sale," I shared, "and I came across a book with the title *Roses and Thorns*. That's a good title to describe what the ministry is like. Anyone who wants to grow roses has to endure the thorns." I recalled some thorny times like our first newsletter, red-penciled to pieces and covered with caustic remarks, and the thorny issues of re-marriage and church discipline.

"But there were roses too! So many I couldn't begin to number them all. Some delinquents who came back (one man who came up to me just this morning and thanked me for pursuing him). This gathering today, and seeing all of you here! That birthday party last year and the trip you gave us to Niagara Falls.

"Knowing you as I do, I guessed that you might want to give us some things today. I thought to myself that I'd like to have something to give you, to turn the tables on you in a way. So I have a gift for you – a little book of sermons from my years here with you. I just got them back from the printer last week, and I am still in the process of putting a personal greeting in each for you. They'll be there for you at church next Sunday. I've asked Vicar Raedeke to help make sure that each one gets a copy."

The emotions began to take over, and I struggled on. "I'll just finish by thanking God," I said, "for my wife ... for this congregation ... and for the privilege of being your pastor."

It's the roses I remember best, not the thorns.

Faith Lutheran Church

Sequim, Washington

(1988–1999)

NOT QUITE THE END OF THE WORLD

It was nearing sunset on April 18, 1988. Our purple Olds station wagon crested the rise east of Sequim and we descended into the valley like a plane coming in for a landing. Barry Manilow was singing via cassette tape into our ears, "I am music, and I write the songs." We had driven from the crowded heartland of America to its lonely fringe. "It's not quite the end of the world," a brother pastor would tell me later, "but you can see it from there."

Many had made the move west to Sequim before us. In the year 1937 twelve Lutheran families from drought-ravaged North Dakota left their homesteads on the barren plains and moved west to Washington. To them, who had lost their livelihood in the dry Dakota dust, the Sequim-Dungeness Valley must have looked like an Eden. An ingenious network of irrigation ditches assured a year-round supply of water for farmers. Dairy cattle grazed contentedly in quiet pastures. Great trees in nearby forests promised work for those who had sworn off farming. Fish in nearby waters were abundant. The climate was mild.

The immigrants from Dakota were determined to guard their 'spiritual treasures,' said leader Carl Kettel. Aware that there was no Missouri Synod Lutheran church in the area, they had made contact with Pastor Eichmann of Mt. Vernon before heading west. He was there to meet the group when they arrived, and he helped them arrange for public worship. The first service was conducted in July of 1937. Less than a year later the baby church was named St. Matthew. By early 1939, Ray Rimbach was installed as the first pastor.

The growth of the congregation and the distance between Port Angeles and Sequim necessitated the cell division of the congregation into twin groups – one in Port Angeles and one in Sequim. Under the leadership of the second pastor, Ralph Wegener, a small church building was finally erected in Sequim in the late 1950s. By 1964 the twins were separated, and Faith Lutheran Church got its own name and its own pastor, Dan Parshall. The church's growth was slow and steady. Names like Brueckner, Jones, Kettel, Schuman, and Wilber remained from the days of the migration from North Dakota.

The 1970s were boom years in the valley. Sequim was discovered by more and more people as an ideal spot to retire. Magazines listed it as one of the top ten retirement destinations in America. Pastures were subdivided and homes built. Real estate values climbed, reflecting the increased desire of many to make the journey to Sequim.

Pastor Walt Huth, my immediate predecessor, brought his family from South Dakota in 1973. During his long tenure, the congregation grew to 300 souls and built a larger, modern sanctuary with an altar made of a single enormous spruce log. But after 14 years of ministry, Pastor Huth's health eroded and his limited availability led to some dissatisfaction. His reluctant resignation in 1987 left a pastoral vacancy and a somewhat divided and dispirited congregation. Pastor Al Beck handled things as interim pastor while the congregation began the search for a new shepherd.

We pulled into the church parking lot and found an unexpected greeting committee. Five of Faith's older ladies were, at that very hour, returning from a day-long 'Joy Shop.' They included Agnes Wilbur, Ione and Meta Brueckner, Edith Jones, and Val Kalnins, a tiny Latvian lady who had sent us a note a few months earlier with wise advice: "Just love us, and you will do wonders." As we emerged from the car, they greeted us with a basket of smiles.

Our temporary residence was the old Huth parsonage on Hendrickson Road, just a few minutes west of the church. The next day the moving van appeared promptly to disgorge our household belongings. A housewarming of sorts took place a day later. The choir, tipped off to my April 20 birthday, dropped by unannounced to sing and share ice cream. We were off to a good start.

Our new hometown was practically the definition of quaint. The name itself – Sequim – was tricky to pronounce. "Not See-kwim!" we'd say. "It's pronounced 'Skwim' – the 'e' is silent." With a population of 4000, half of whom were retirees, the pace of life in Sequim was noticeably slow. Older couples ambled about arm-in-arm. Businesses closed by six in the evening, most restaurants by nine. The tallest structure in town was a three-story grain elevator that had been converted to a Mexican restaurant. Close by was a loafing shed for cattle that attracted the attention of artists. The town newspaper, published weekly, was dubbed the *Jimmy-Come-Lately Gazette*. The most important civic event all year was the annual Irrigation Festival. It commemorated 'Crazy' Callan's ingenious network of ditches and pipes that spread Dungeness River waters around the formerly arid valley. Hundreds of people converged on the town for a 'shepherd's festival,' a logging skills show, a bonsai display, a festival run, and a lengthy parade down Washington Street.

"This is a lovely place," remarked Doris Minner, our realtor, as she parked at the house on Hogback Road. We had visited half a dozen other places already, none of them quite satisfying. One reeked of cigarette smoke from the previous owners. We dubbed it the 'Smithfield Smoker.' But this one appealed to us from the start.

It was a red ranch-style home on two acres with a slight elevation that provided a pleasing panoramic look at the Sequim Valley to the southeast. A buffer of long grass provided some elbow room at the edge of the yard, and nearby pasture land made it feel 'country,' definitely a plus for Sue.

Bob and Win Bloxom, a retired Christian couple, had used the home to provide some rest and relaxation for missionaries on furlough, and they hoped they might find a Christian family to buy it. They greeted us with warmth at the door. "Come in, come in!" said Bob, who was dressed like a square dancer in his checked shirt and bolo tie.

With pardonable pride he led us through the house, stopping to comment about the wood stove in the living room and the view out the kitchen window. We gazed with wonder. Right out the big kitchen window we could see the Olympics, with Hurricane Ridge to the right and Bell Hill in the hazy distance to the left. An open, bright kitchen was a dramatic change from our constricted hallway kitchen with a sink in Akron. The west end of the house was an add-on entered by going down three steps.

There were appealing features outside too. Lovely flowers caught the sun in front of the south-facing porch. A large concrete patio brought us nearly to the trout pond, surrounded by a sturdy fence. "Do you actually have trout in there?" I asked. Bob laughed and said, "Let me show you something." He got a small plastic bucket full of feed pellets and tossed a handful into the pond. The water boiled with activity as a dozen rainbow-striped fish splashed furiously to get their lunch. The pond was fed by a running stream that descended through the yard through plastic pipe, and then through a small, open gully the last few yards. "You'll have to tend that pipe up there," he said, pointing through the trees, "where it exits the ditch. It gets plugged with leaves now and then." The water of the Dungeness River ran practically to our door!

There would be plenty of space for a garden here. Rich, dark soil had been tilled and tended, and the Bloxoms had a patch of Jerusalem artichokes and some fava beans ready to harvest. A quartet of sizable apple trees – two Gravensteins, a Golden Delicious, and an early transparent – along with a winter pear tree and a prune tree, gave us a miniature orchard too. "Lots of grass to cut," Bob added, "but there's a mower we can leave," and he showed us a gray Sears riding mower.

There was no more looking. We made an offer of $82,500, and it was accepted. For the next eleven years, we would be at home on Hogback Road.

Our little road was aptly named. Walking west from our home one came out of the woods and saw that the land fell away on either side, so that you were perched as if on the back of a hog. To the right the land sloped down to a cow pasture with about twenty head of the peaceful animals. To the left was a marsh with a small drive and a sign that indicated a future housing development. Hogback Road ended at a diagonal intersection with Lotzgesell Road. Walking east from our house, one descended two hundred yards, past the Blake Sand & Gravel Company, to where Hogback ended at Cays Road. Altogether, it was a little more than half a mile long.

The lonely country roads were an ideal place to go jogging, and it wasn't long before I donned my sweat clothes and set out to explore the quiet countryside. I eventually settled into running three loops. Sue would take her turn too, not to run but to walk and pray as she went. It was a perfect place for communing with God away from the jangle of the phone. But it was not always uninterrupted. Frequently a car would pull up beside us as we jogged or walked along. "Say, do you know the way to…?" We would point the way and hope they didn't get lost.

Though we were in the country five miles from Sequim, there was plenty going on. Cement mixers roared nearby at Blake Sand & Gravel. Riders on bikes and volksmarch participants with walking sticks made their way past our back door. Hot air balloonists could be spotted overhead on sunny summer afternoons. To the south across the pasture we could see golf carts on the fourteenth fairway at the Dungeness Golf Club. In the field across Cays to the east a model airplane club conducted Saturday gatherings with takeoffs, landings, and dogfights.

Further east was the Olympic Game Farm, a kind of poor man's zoo that was a local tourist attraction. We heard the cry of the peacocks from almost a mile away. The carcasses of deer that had been struck on the roads around Sequim were regularly taken there to feed the bears and the big cats. But the most memorable encounters people had there were with a large bison that begged for bread and licked both cars and passengers when he could. An ad campaign could have invited people to 'get slimed by a buffalo.'

We soon discovered the joys and possible dangers of living in a more rural setting. In early July we spotted smoke drifting across the pasture from behind the woods, and Christa and I drove down Hogback Road to investigate. I found a small fire burning in the field, and some boys trying unsuccessfully to put it out. The wind was pushing it east toward the trees that bordered our property. Back to the house I raced for a shovel, a blanket and some helpers, and we made a call to 911. Back at the scene, the fire began to get away from us – a frightening feeling! Firemen arrived in the nick of time and doused the flames with a powerful spray. The boys admitted they started the fire while setting off fireworks.

The joys became evident too, often conveyed through animal neighbors. We were getting our first taste of real wildlife. A large blue heron came fishing for our trout. Eagles cried from high perches in the fir trees. Owls hooted on ghostly moonlit nights. Black-tailed deer passed through our property frequently, stopping to chew our roses or rear up to claim apples off the trees. I sometimes gave chase, but they bounded away easily and bounced over the fence with a flourish of their tails. We rarely saw coyotes, but often heard their excited communal barking.

There was occasional drama that sprang from the encounter between animals and people. One morning we found the partially-eaten carcass of a deer that had likely been wounded by a hunter. The coyotes had finished what the hunter started. On another morning, Sue and I awakened to the sound of a gunshot very near. I dressed hurriedly and crossed the fence to the wooded pasture where there was an old ruined shack and outhouse. I saw drag marks into the outhouse, and there found the carcass of a doe that had been shot illegally. I learned later that the hunter was a delinquent member of my own church!

We had other adventures next door. The shack itself was sagging into ruin and overgrown now with blackberry bushes. Every September we crossed the fence to enjoy a harvest. One afternoon, while picking berries there, Sue and I realized we had company. Several of the cattle from the pasture had wandered close. A young bull had found a full pail of berries and was nose-deep in them before I shouted him away.

A more endearing encounter happened a few years later. It was a glorious, sunny morning, and the herd of cows was congregated perhaps 100 yards away in the middle of the pasture. I noted that the calves were all still stretched on the grass asleep. I love watching calves. On impulse, I climbed the fence and made my way slowly toward them, hoping to get a closer look. So slowly did I approach, that the adults did not bolt. There wasn't even a nervous 'moo.' I continued until I was standing right beside the nearest calf. It slept peacefully, its pink tongue protruding from a mouth slightly ajar. I knelt down. Gently I petted its side. The skin shivered reflexively. It was a heavenly moment. Then the calf opened its eyes and contemplated me, but without fear. "Who are you?" it seemed to ask sleepily. Then it rose, stretched, and ambled off with its fellows. A perfect Sequim moment.

MINISTRY SNAPSHOTS

My installation at Faith Lutheran Church took place 1988. Howard Peterson, the interim pastor at neighborii Port Angeles, agreed to preach. A fine crowd turned oι ..υιιιϲ us. There was abundant laughter and the shaking of many hands. Not many of the local pastors came, seeing as how we were almost (but not quite) at the end of the world. One pastor who did appear was Win Schroeder, who came forward among the others, attired modestly in a suit for the laying-on of hands. "If I may call you my Timothy," he began quietly, remembering our nine years together in Vancouver. Then he gave his blessing, in words recalling the advice given to another Timothy long ago. Altogether it was a lower-key affair than installation day in Akron had been…and a good deal cooler! The ministry in Sequim had been launched.

I inherited a confirmation class of one. Robb Young was there to finish his year with me, and he was confirmed alone on Pentecost Sunday, my smallest class ever. Instead of 'class,' we shared one-on-one talks – a totally different dynamic than I had experienced before. There would be 55 more youth and 85 adults confirmed during my eleven years there. The Clinton children – Heath, Jeff, and Amanda – were among my first baptisms. During those Sequim years, there would be 161 baptisms, 34 of which were adults. It was a rich harvest for the Lord, notwithstanding the remoteness of the location.

My honeymoon with the congregation lasted longer than usual. If anything, Faith congregation was too nice for its own good. The people loved their pastor, enjoyed the fellowship, and were pretty much content with the way things were. That pleasant status quo could suck the life from any significant outreach effort. Looking for a way to ignite some mission zeal, I took a group of 13 leaders to St. Luke in Federal Way (pastored by Vic Hippe, my predecessor in the Vancouver vicarage). There Ken Callahan, a Methodist pastor and noted church ministry planner, was to speak.

Callahan's book, *Twelve Keys to an Effective Church*, provided the substance for the seminar. "The day of the parish church is over," he told us. "The day of the missionary pastor and people has come." While he shared six 'relational' and six 'functional' characteristics, our minds were engaged and ideas were hatched for ministry back in Sequim. Among those were or starting a mission church, adding a staff person, and expanding our ational offerings. Seeds had been planted. Over the years there were ascinating and diverse ministry ventures that touched us. Some originated in our little congregation at the end of the world, while others from outside pulled us into the wider arena of the Spirit's mysterious activity.

Sue and I met Dan Doran in his office at Washington Mutual Bank. He was a loan officer there, and he secured our home mortgage loan. Only later did we learn that Dan had long harbored a special dream of being in the pastoral ministry.

He had the wisdom and a heart for people. That was obvious to me both in how he treated us as customers and, later, how he came at his ministry tasks at church. He was a Sunday school teacher. He volunteered to help with VBS in Alaska. Dan was an elder too. In that role he didn't say much, but when he did, it mattered. One evening I came to a meeting steamed like a pressure cooker. Dan told me I needed to find a way to ventilate. He was right. I made a habit of sitting on pent-up emotion which led me to times of depression or rage at home.

Dan knew about human weakness because he had long ago come to terms with his own. A recovering alcoholic, he offered to start an alcohol support group at Faith, and though the group was small (only three men), he demonstrated a pastoral heart for his brothers in the group.

Halfway through my time in Sequim, Dan heard about the Lay Assistant Program (LAP) that was run by our district to give theological education to laymen and equip them for ministry work alongside pastors. He asked me to be his mentor and I agreed. For the next two years, Dan worked diligently on his studies. What he lacked in intellectual acumen, he made up for with a blue-collar work ethic and a blue-ribbon wisdom about human nature. He had wonderful pastoral instincts.

We met several times each month so that he could present the papers he had written and discuss them in depth. I routinely quizzed him on his work and met in him a healthy humility that was the opposite of the ego-centrism I often demonstrated in my student years. I taught him academically, and he taught me attitudinally!

Dan was finally licensed as a Lay Assistant and expressed a desire to serve among the Makah Indian tribe in Neah Bay, where he had helped with Bible Schools. Neah Bay was tucked into the northwest corner of the Olympic Peninsula, right on the coast. Dan and Carol, district mission man Dave Hoover, and I made the 'carsick caravan' ride on 80 miles of winding road out to the Makah Lutheran Church one day. Native American pastor Don Johnson had since gone to work with a missionary group in Canada, and the congregation was without pastoral care. We met with some of the people of the church and offered Dan's ministry service to them. They gladly accepted and we ate a meal in celebration.

So it was that Dan and Carol began several years of faithful ministry there. The Northwest District allowed 'word and sacrament ministry' by Lay Assistants as long as they were under the supervision of a local pastor. Bernie and Mollie Christianson were faithful partners who made many trips there to provide extra support. The congregation allowed Dan and Carol to use the trailer home Pastor Johnson's family had long used.

After I left Sequim, Dan received another assignment to Faith Lutheran Church in Juneau, Alaska, a larger congregation that had been vacant a while. There Dan served for four more years while completing his studies through the DELTO (Distance Education Leading to Ordination) Program so that he might, at long last, become an ordained pastor.

On a return visit to Sequim in 2004 when the two of us were sharing a supper meal, Dan honored me with a special request. "Pastor Mike, would you preach for my ordination?" I gave him a grateful yes, and in December of 2006, seven years after we had moved away to Oregon City, I returned for the joyful occasion. Dan was by then 69 years old. That day he became the oldest man ever ordained as a Lutheran pastor in the Northwest District.

Promise Keepers was a national movement started by Bill McCartney, the head football coach at the University of Colorado. It sought to renew Christian men in their relationships with God, their families, their churches, and their communities by teaching 'seven promises of a promise-keeper.' Men around the country found it faith and life-renewing. One such gathering, we heard, would be held at the Kingdome in Seattle in summer of 1996.

In a congregation dominated by women's groups, there was a crying need to rally our men to make the trip across Puget Sound and get energized. Several of the men, including Roy Swanson, persuaded me to get on board. Sixteen of us eventually made our way to the gathering. We stayed for the two evenings at Hope Lutheran Church in West Seattle.

The Kingdome, normally the Seattle Mariners' field of baseball dreams, had become for that weekend a venue for Jesus Christ to summon men to a more virile discipleship. It was rocking with nearly 50,000 men by the time we all arrived. The delegation from Sequim sat open-mouthed, taking it in. It was an electrifying experience to see such a crowd of boys and men, many wearing Jesus shirts, shouting and singing their faith unashamed. Someone was orchestrating cheers, as at a school pep rally:

We love Jesus, yes we do!
We love Jesus, how 'bout you?

A gigantic Styrofoam plane was sailed from the upper deck and soared all the way to the playing field level as we awaited the first speaker. A gigantic stage had been set up at floor level with Jumbotron TV screens that would allow us to see the speakers and the bands perform.

Though there were men from a wide array of denominations, the speakers and music had a decidedly evangelical, even Pentecostal flavor. One memorable speaker was a black pastor from Indiana who worked us as only a black preacher knew how. Lively singing rocked the mammoth dome. The speakers urged us to continue at home by forming small accountability groups.

Toward the end of the gathering came a heavenly moment. "We want all of you pastors who are here to come down onto the field," said our leader. Hundreds of us began making our way to field level as the crowd of 50,000 rose to recognize us. We passed downward like leaves in a virtual waterfall of faces smiling, speaking words of appreciation, "Thank you, pastors! Bless you!" Hands were raised to high-five us, while others clapped with a sound that grew and cascaded onto the playing field. The crowd began to cheer a long, swelling roar of thanks, and suddenly I was overcome. I wondered, "Is this what heaven will be like?" The standing ovation lasted a full ten minutes, and we pastors stood surrounded, humbled, overjoyed by the sound. The lift I felt that day lasted a long time.

The congregation's ministry reached even across the Atlantic Ocean with the arrival of an exchange student named Sabina Lobbes from East Germany. Deloris Ashmon provided both a home and a powerful daily witness to her pretty blond guest. Sabina's parents were communists, and Sabina herself was not a believer, but the example of Deloris and the congregation made an impact on the teen.

As the year progressed, it became increasingly apparent that Sabina wanted to know more about the Christian faith. She came to worship and to class, listening intently. At last she expressed a desire to be baptized. Since Sabina would be returning to Germany, our time was limited. As I prepared to instruct her prior to the sacrament, she asked if her younger sister, still in Germany and unable to speak English, could be baptized too. The whole family, including the parents, was to assemble in Sequim for the event!

I appealed to Pastor Erv Wichner, who spoke German with a native's fluency, to assist me in the pre-baptismal instruction. He was glad to do it, and for several hours one Saturday, he and I sat with the two girls. Irv also suggested that we conduct the baptism in German and English so that both Sabina's family and our Faith family could participate with full understanding. He brought me a copy of the German baptismal liturgy, and we prepared an interspersed English text.

When the day came, my assistant read the English and I repeated the same portions in German. The family nodded understanding, and the congregation looked on, captivated at this miniature Pentecost, in which the Holy Spirit overcame the barrier of language and enfolded those two girls into the Kingdom.

God had planted in my heart a dream that we might start a mission church. The question was where to launch this effort. To the north was the Strait of Juan de Fuca. To the west was Port Angeles and our sister church, St. Matthew. To the south was Quilcene, a small town with a too-thin population base and an uncertain future. The most realistic option lay to the east, in the area of Port Hadlock and Irondale.

I wanted to begin a mission from scratch, but our church planting team had heard there was a struggling Lutheran Church in the area already. In a meeting, the group decided to offer pastoral care to the group, which bore the name Hope Lutheran Church. They were without a pastor and seemed to have only minimal prospects. Yes, they would appreciate our help. So on Sunday afternoons, Sue and I took our turn driving out a couple of times a month to lead worship in the VFW hall they were renting. The planting team also met with Hope's leaders to assess their needs and formulate outreach strategies.

It was an enjoyable small church experience, and the leaders were grateful for help. But it was not long before things ran aground. We learned too late that the group was affiliated with the ELS (Evangelical Lutheran Synod), a rigidly conservative group that did not approve of women having any role in worship whatever – neither as lay readers nor as choir members (both involved women 'speaking' in church, they said, contrary to Paul's directive in 1 Corinthians 14). The more we learned about each other, the more we realized that this 'marriage' would not work. With a feeling of disappointment, we parted company. The team's bubble of excitement had burst, and they did not meet again. So ended our stab at church planting.

John and Vim Devine were a pair of trim, energetic retirees from California who had joined Faith early in my years there and plugged in to help with good cheer. I nicknamed them "Vim and Vigor" because they went right to work by our side. Vim helped in the church kitchen. John donated his time as a volunteer at the local Community Aid food pantry and offered his building skills to the remodeling effort in our fellowship hall. John became friends with a younger man named Greg Balzer, whom the church had hired to do carpentry work on the project.

The two men discovered that they had a shared love for the outdoors. Greg was a hunter and John an experienced hiker. Early in September of 1997, they drove up into the mountains for a weekend of camping. Balzer intended to go bow hunting for deer, and Devine planned to hike to the ridge of scenic, steep-sided Mount Baldy, a 6800-foot peak in the nearby Olympic Mountains. They set up camp and embarked on their separate quests after breakfast.

That afternoon, John disappeared. Hunters spotted him descending the mountain about 2 p.m., but that was the last glimpse of him. Greg returned to the camp in late afternoon and wondered where his friend was. After some frantic searching, he headed down the mountain and contacted the sheriff's office.

A larger search was soon underway, with sheriff's deputies, forest service workers, and volunteers combing the slopes of Mt. Baldy and the nearby Buckhorn Wilderness. I visited Vim to pray and share words of encouragement. We put John on the prayer chain that night.

Helicopters joined the search. The days passed with a mounting sense of dread, and news crews were dispatched from Seattle to report the story. "You talk to the reporters," Vim instructed me. "I don't want to do that." So it was that I stood outside the church, answering questions from a KOMO news reporter: "John was a quiet man who loved the mountains...Vim has asked me to speak for the family...she is holding on to hope...our people are praying, hoping for a miracle..."

But there was no miracle, only more tragedy. On Friday, September 12, pilot Kevin Johnston decided to lift off his rescue helicopter into overcast skies from Port Angeles. Unfamiliar with the terrain, he needed help from another copter pilot to find a hole in the clouds. He set down in a landing zone and picked up seven rescue workers, some of whom were anxious about flying into such clouds. Minutes later the helicopter crashed into Mt. Baldy. Three people, including the pilot, were killed, and the other five were injured. After ten days, the search was called off, and hopes for John's rescue were extinguished.

On October 9, more than a month after John disappeared, I conducted a memorial service at the church. In attendance were John's family, rescue team members, park personnel, and friends from the church and the neighborhood. From the pulpit I surveyed a room of somber faces...

> *"We are met here today because we shared a common hope, and now we feel a common grief... We have come to remember that fine man lost on a mountaintop..."*

I invited them to consider another man who met his Maker on a mountain – Moses. I told them that Moses had an appointment with God up there – not only to see the land, but to die. The next time Moses appeared to human eyes was on another mountain, at Christ's transfiguration. I reminded them that it was on another mountain named Calvary that Jesus died in the midst of a rescue mission, and that if we have been to the mountaintop with him, we need never be afraid again.

John had been to Mt. Calvary, and he knew a blessed peace.

Art and Lucille Thyrring were coming up on a fiftieth anniversary celebration. They were in their seventies and had survived trials sore enough to break up many other couples. Art had only very recently come to admit that he was an alcoholic. It was during a hospital visit that I heard him admit at long last that he was up against something he could no longer hide nor control. Lucille wept tears of thanks after bearing up under years of Art's self-deception and family feuding. Relationships with the children had been fractured, perhaps past mending. But Art agreed to join the alcohol support group that began at Faith led by Dan Doran.

"Would you come with us on a cruise?" Lucille asked us. It was an unexpected invitation, followed by an even more unexpected petition. "And could you also be our family chaplain?" she continued. "We'd like you to repeat our vows aboard the ship…and maybe help the family find some unity after all these years of hostility."

We agreed to go along, though I had doubts about my ability to mend a family so long broken. The Thyrrings graciously paid for all our travel expenses, as they were paying for the entire clan's cruise. It was a large investment in a venture of family repair.

We flew with them to Los Angeles, where we boarded an immense Viking cruise ship with several thousand fellow passengers. The cruise would be a brief one, lasting three days. The destination was Ensenada, Mexico, a small port in Baja, California, about 175 miles south.

The cruise seemed a sequence of sumptuous meals, separated by walks on the deck, naps in the cabin, and quiet talks seated in deck chairs. We did our best to encourage the family members to talk to us and each other, and there was an air of civility, if not warmth, between the children, grandchildren, and in-laws. At the appointed time, I led a renewal of marriage vows, along with a brief sermon, and Sue helped us sing together. Art and Lucille were greatly pleased, and when the cruise was ended, they expressed satisfaction that some progress had been made in thawing the family's long cold war.

Another shipboard ministry opportunity came from Russ and Ursula Wyatt, who operated a fishing boat in the Alaska fleet. Would I offer a blessing of the fleet? It was an annual ritual that was regarded with more than politeness. The fleet faced significant dangers from storms in the Gulf of Alaska, and lives were regularly lost in the fierce seas.

I agreed to do the blessing, and I was grateful to learn that I did not have to make a trip to the gulf, nor even leave the dock! "All you have to do," explained Ursula, "is to get up in the prow of our boat and have a small service. We will all be standing facing you on the dock." So I arranged a service with Scriptures of Jesus calling the fishermen to be 'fishers of men' and the story of Jesus stilling the storm. A scattering of fishing families came, along with a camera crew from Northwest Cable News in Port Angeles to film the blessing for the evening news.

Sequim was not quite the end of the world. But from that tiny outpost, we were furnished a multitude of opportunities to touch lives and share the Gospel in unexpected ways from Ensenada, Mexico, to the Gulf of Alaska to East Germany. Increasingly we saw ourselves as distributors of grace. It was a holy privilege.

HELPERS IN THE VINEYARD

An unexpected delight of our eleven years in Sequim was that Sue and I became co-workers. There was no secretary on staff, and in short order, Sue volunteered for the post. For Sue, an introvert, the post provided an automatic entrée into the social life of the congregation and many opportunities daily to get to know the people.

Our work styles differed dramatically. I left my office in a shambles, while she kept hers tidy. I was quick and sometimes careless. Sue was slower and more meticulous, good at catching the mistakes born of my hastiness. We liked to say that in terms of speed, I was a cheetah, and she a cape hunting dog. On a few occasions, when we raised our voices to one another in our adjoining offices, someone in the hallway would get an unexpected earful. Now and then, we heard criticism that "there's too much power in their hands." But teaming up that way gave us a deeper appreciation of each other's strengths and showed us how each supplied what the other lacked.

Though she found satisfaction in her secretarial work, Sue longed for something more vocationally fulfilling. Trained as a teacher, she wanted to get a music endorsement on her teaching certificate and return to the classroom as a music teacher. She enrolled in classes in music history and music theory at Peninsula College in Port Angeles. Her teacher, Dr. Crabb, took a liking to her, and she became a star pupil. But it generated a clash between us. For though she aspired to resume a teaching career, she was loath to relinquish her other responsibilities – the math tutoring at the junior high, the music ministry at church, the direction of the Sequim Community Children's Christmas Choir, and her secretarial work. "Too much!" I complained at her. My concern for her work load was legitimate, but instead of helping her search out a happy medium, I put it to her as an either-or. Unhappily, she let go of a dream, and in the years that followed I regretted that I had not been more encouraging and creative in allowing her to follow her heart's desire.

One of our weekly work partners was Jannie Bacon, our custodian, who lived alone in a lovely home with a spectacular view not far from us on Holgerson Road. Jannie had been born in the Netherlands and carried deep emotional scars from World War II. Remembering what the Nazis had done, she was uneasy about the government's ability to keep track of private citizens. She had also experienced a large measure of family distress. But she proved to be a loyal friend and a hard worker. She made her rounds sweeping floors, emptying wastebaskets, and cleaning windows, much as she did in her other job for residents at Dominion Terrace. On Fridays, she lent a hand folding bulletins and enduring my corny jokes. She in her turn liked to describe her almost weekly encounters with the deer that frequented her yard. Many were the tales of does and fawns that came to her door awaiting food. In 1993, we helped her celebrate her fifteenth anniversary working for the church, just before she retired.

As had been the case in my first two churches, I was blessed again to have a capable organist in Pat Marcy. Pat, wife to Spencer and mother of three grown children, fairly lived and breathed her music. She was a piano teacher to many, including our son Peter. She was an active participant in the annual community Christmas concert put on by the churches in Sequim. At Faith, she served as the minister of music who both directed and accompanied the adult choir, often using a pronounced bobbing of her head to bring the singers in at the right time. She encouraged congregation members to play their instruments and add them to the music mix for worship. In Peter's case, she encouraged him to compose music on the computer and perform it at one of her frequent recitals.

The choir cemented its fellowship ties with frequent gatherings, usually at the Marcy home, where food and music ran together, wrapped in laughter. Especially memorable was the choir's visit to the Clallam County Jail in Port Angeles, where we sang for several dozen orange-clad prisoners and I preached a message about Zacchaeus entitled, 'The Crook Went Straight.'

Pat oversaw the addition of a new electronic organ in 1992, an instrument fabricated by Associated Organ Builders of Auburn, Washington. The dedicatory concert was played by Austin Lovelace, a composer whose music the choir had sung. In time, we surprised Pat with a twentieth anniversary celebration, complete with a set of bouncy antennae to wear on her head that would accentuate her directorial nods.

After a few years of working alone, I resumed the role of vicar supervisor in 1990. My first Sequim vicar was a decided change from the young fellows I supervised in Akron. Alan Hubbard was older than I, a veteran of the U. S. Navy who had decided to change careers. He brought a wife, Carol, and school-age daughters Rachel and Sarah. He wore a big smile and practiced his trumpet in the bathroom. Ours was a mixture of vastly different personalities, but Al thrived and he eventually became a pastor in Auburn, California.

The Hubbards were followed by Joel and Pam Kaiser, relatives of our members Paul and Traci. Joel was a trim, handsome man with a ready smile, and he and Pam gave free expression to their affection for each other. Afflicted with macular degeneration, Joel was legally blind, but this impediment did not seem to slow him appreciably. He had enough vision to ride a bike and a cheerful, personable spirit that enabled him to tackle his assignments without fear. Upon completion of his seminary work, Joel split time as an assistant pastor at St. Lorenz Church in Frankenmuth, Michigan, and as a chaplain at the Lutheran home there.

The third man, Wes Hafner, was a rescue project. He had begun his vicarage at our 'twin' church – St. Matthew in Port Angeles. But something had gone dreadfully wrong there, and Wes had pondered leaving his ministerial studies altogether. The district president suggested that perhaps we could provide a partial-year placement. We agreed to that, and Wes and wife Cami plugged in at Faith. Wes had grown up on a farm. He had a simple faith and an appetite for work, and Cami was a loyal partner. In a few months' time, the Hafners' spirits rose, and by the end of the vicarage year, there was a renewed confidence and commitment to pastoral ministry. The Hafners made their way back to rural America when Wes took a placement in a dual parish in South Dakota.

The work load at Faith had grown enough that by 1993 the congregation decided to make the switch to having a full-time assistant pastor. One night during the months of the congregation's deliberation, I had a vivid dream. Steve Eaton, once my student in Vancouver, now a pastor in Alberta, was at the center of it. In the dream he and I were teamed as partner pastors, and a very pleasing arrangement it was. I awoke from the dream and thought about it for days.

Steve and I already had a long history together. He was in my first confirmation class in 1973. He was a mainstay in Memorial's youth group, a friendly opponent in chess, and a partner on several backpack trips. His comments had been part of God's direction as I considered the call to Akron. Later I had traveled back to Vancouver to perform the wedding for Steve and his bride Becky (niece to Pastor Schroeder). I had a high regard for this young couple, and I felt convinced the dream was from God.

I liked Steve, but would we be a good ministry team? Was the dream a sign from God, or merely a product of my nocturnal imagination? There was a way to find out. When the congregation assembled its call list, I quietly inserted Steve's name and asked President Erhard Bauer to provide biographical information for all the men. The list and the info came back, and we proceeded with discussions. I did no special lobbying for Steve. At the call meeting, he was elected on the first ballot.

To my surprise (and disappointment), Steve declined the call. "I don't know," he explained to me, "if we are different enough to make a healthy team. The things you like are the things I like!" It was true. I reluctantly let go of the dream and accepted the fact that God must have another plan.

Not long afterward, the district notified us that a man named Ron Blumhorst, then residing in Sand Point, Idaho, was desirous of re-entering the ministry after sitting out for a year due to depression issues. Would we consider calling him?

In surprisingly short order, the congregation agreed to place the call, but before it was accepted I got an unexpected (and disturbing) phone call from Ron, who told me "there is more you need to know about me." He proceeded to reveal to me that intertwined with his depression issues was a history of pornography addiction. He had left the ministry to deal with this matter. After nearly a year of treatment, District President Erhard Bauer regarded his progress as sufficient to warrant a new beginning. "If you don't want to deal with this baggage, let me know and I will decline the call," he offered. "We'll need to talk on this end about this," I responded. "We'll get back to you."

It was not the kind of thing I could place before the whole congregation. Neither could I hide it from our leaders. In the end, I met with two leading elders, Marty van Dyken and Frank Jones. Yes, we were a healing fellowship, but were we ready for something like this? The two men felt that we were. The consensus was that Faith, in light of our success at renewing Wes Hafner in his vocation, was a place of healing. My pride told me that I could be just the partner this troubled young pastor needed. We made the fateful decision to give Ron a green light, but agreed to monitor him closely.

Very soon Ron and Wanda, along with their three small children – Teddy, Marie, and Carissa – arrived in Sequim and were introduced to the folks at Faith. Things went well initially. Ron had a kind of TV-anchor personality, articulate and wearing a perpetual smile. Wanda, short and somewhat shy, was energetic and musical, and soon she was volunteering to play her French horn and help with our preschool. The family took up residence in the house next door, which the congregation had earlier purchased and converted into a vicarage and preschool.

Though the initial months went well, I was struck by Ron's procrastination. Often on Saturday nights he would still be at work on the next day's sermon, though the sermons themselves did not exhibit symptoms of hasty composition. Our weekly reviews of life and ministry were frank and productive. But within six months, it was obvious that something was going very wrong. Ron's depression was pronounced, and he was often in tears. Finally, he revealed to me that the pornography addiction had returned with a vengeance. Wanda felt betrayed, as if he'd resumed an old affair.

The elders and I took such steps as we could. We directed Ron to participate in Sexaholics Anonymous meetings in Tacoma, and both the Joneses and the van Dykens took time with Ron to listen and pray. He did as he was directed, but his meetings with me turned into weekly confessions of failure. It became obvious to the congregation at large that the Blumhorsts were unhappy in their marriage.

In the end, I put it plainly to Ron. "I think you need to resign." I told him that unless he explained to the congregation the circumstances behind it, some might guess that we had clashed and I wanted him out. Such things could divide churches, I observed. He agreed, and so one Sunday morning shortly thereafter, we asked the congregation to remain after worship for an urgent announcement. Ron stood before the assembly and laid it out honestly. I admired his courage. Many of the people were stunned, but most seemed to appreciate being told the straight story.

The Blumhorsts' marriage broke up. Wanda eventually married Ben Alfredo, our education chairman, who had befriended her during the separation, and they moved to California. Ron also moved south to remain close to the children. The rest of us grieved at this unhappy turn. Not even a healthy, loving congregation could heal all its wounded.

What would we do now? The elders met to consider a replacement pastor. "What about that man Steve Eaton we called before?" mused Marty van Dyken. "Could we call him again?" Not eager to repeat a lengthy calling process, the congregation jumped at the idea and extended a second call to Pastor Eaton.

This time he said yes. In 1995, within a year of his sister Kathy Cusack's death, Steve and his family moved to Sequim. It was two years after the fact, but my dream had come true. The young man who had been a confirmation student in my first class had come back into my life to work as a co-pastor.

Steve and I meshed harmoniously into a solid partnership that took us through my last four years in Sequim. He was gifted with a special sensitivity to people and a gentle sense of humor. He was able to lighten my workload and provide fine insights about people that I often missed. It was a blessing for him as well. With the extra time available because of our shared ministry, he was able to realize his own dream of becoming a military chaplain.

Steve's custom of extra reading and prayer time during Lent rubbed off on me. He liked to read *The Hammer of God* by Bo Giertz, the story of a young pastor learning ministry by painful example. I think he saw himself in that book. He also took time to pray for as many congregation members individually as he could during the six weeks of the season. Because of his example, I read Giertz's book and attempted for the first time the challenge of praying through our membership directory, name by name, as Lent progressed. It was a prayer discipline that became a permanent part of the season for me.

Two unusual moments we shared are etched deeply in my memory. One was a skit we did as cheerleaders during an evening meal for Faith's youth – complete with skirts and wigs! The playful child inside me rejoiced to be turned loose that night. The other was a not-so-pleasant late night trip to the hospital in Port Angeles – I with my foot on the accelerator and Steve doubled up with the pain of kidney stones. In those and other ways, we shared agonies and ecstasies that adorn the ordinary times and made our partnership memorable.

Pastor Win Schroeder and Pastor Steve Eaton share a laugh with me at the 25th anniversary celebration of my ordination

THE LOGOS PROGRAM

When Sue and I arrived in Sequim, we discovered that Sunday School came to an end when school let out. That wouldn't do! Church kept going. Why not Sunday School? We urged Pam Priest, the superintendent, to offer classes through the summer months, even if they had to be combined. Parents and kids cooperated sufficiently to make it work.

Faith had a steady track record with Vacation Bible School, owing partly to the presence of Ruth Tinsley, a tall, gravelly-voiced woman with mischievous eyes and a spirit that was equal parts hard work and fun. Ruth and I collaborated to plan the first summer's VBS, and we shared the openings in our alter egos as puppets 'Judah Lion' and 'Lucy Lamb.' More than 100 children watched with rapt attention as the puppets had their daily appearance. Sue jumped in to lead the music, and our girls filled teaching and helping roles.

The following year, Melanie took a turn as 'Honky the Clown,' communicating like Harpo Marx with only a bicycle horn. Christa was now one of the teachers, and if there had been a prize for most creative room décor, she'd have won. It was a special feeling for me to see my little girls, who had always been faces in the crowd of children, now suddenly grown women who partnered with me and the other adults to provide this experience for many little ones.

But what else might we offer to enrich the faith life of our young people? Sunday school and confirmation study seemed one-dimensional. We taught the faith, rooted in solid Bible study, and we began taking confirmation students on a single retreat to Camp Lutherwood in Bellingham each fall, but there was little else we did to touch young hearts and integrate the faith with daily life.

Then we discovered something promising. In 1992 the Northwest District notified its pastors and churches about a special youth ministry program called LOGOS. This fully-orbed approach had been pioneered by a Presbyterian pastor named Dale Milligan who, as a boy, found that almost no one in his church knew him by name. Then came a new pastor who took time to be interested in him personally. When that pastor called him by name, he was drawn back in to his church and his faith. Dale grew up, became a pastor himself, and determined that he would offer something to kids that would allow their young faith to work on all cylinders. The LOGOS program was born.

Sue and I needed a place to team up in our ministry together. LOGOS became that place. We went to a training workshop at Concordia University in Portland and came back convinced that this approach offered the kind of variety we had hoped for. We recruited several dozen helpers, led by Millie Molenda, who became the LOGOS supervisor.

The once-a-week programs lasted for three hours. Kids arrived after school and took part in four programmatic elements. There was basic Bible Study. To that was added Worship Skills, Sue's forte, which included music, art, and drama that could be plugged into the worship experience Sundays and Wednesdays. Kids set to work making banners, learning portions of the liturgy, and preparing small dialogues. Sue ordered a set of finely-crafted Orff instruments, which arrived in 1995, to the delight of the young players. Other adult volunteers led Play Time, which allowed kids to enjoy non-competitive recreation – 'having fun at the expense of no one.'

The program day ended with everyone coming to the fellowship hall for Family Time – a meal eaten all together in family groups. Each table had volunteer table parents and an intentional mixture of 5-6 children from different grade levels. Those groupings stayed the same through a semester to give them a kind of family identity. A kitchen crew under the direction of Pat Wickert and Betty Kettel fixed a hearty meal, and the tables each sent a server to carry the food back to the family groups. Manners were the order of the evening, with 'please pass' and 'thank you' expected. The table parents made sure that all the children at the table got to speak and took turns listening too.

I served as the Dinner Dean who called the assembly to order, led the prayer, made announcements, and introduced the theme for the evening. Week by week, the themes changed. One night was 'The Great Potato Race,' when all would have a baked potato for supper, followed by a spirited rolling of potatoes on a race course marked with masking tape. Another was 'Wilbur and Orville Wright Night,' during which we sang 'Up in the Air, Junior Bird-Man' and made paper airplanes afterward to sail around the dining hall. On 'Journey to Israel' night, I donned the khoufieh I had bought in Jordan and blew a real ram's horn.

The LOGOS program at its height involved nearly 50 children and youth, along with an adult staff of nearly three dozen willing helpers. The adults enjoyed the gatherings as much as the children.

Sue's involvement with children's music extended beyond the weekly LOGOS program. Every summer's VBS music was prepared and matched to the theme for that year. Every Christmas there was a Sunday School Christmas program. The most memorable of those was "*At Bethlehem's Inn,*" on an evening in which the congregation sat in the dining hall as if guests at the inn which had no room for the Holy Family. Don and Cindy Moore played the innkeeper and wife. Paul Honore designed Hollywood-quality backdrops. We all felt, by the end, that we could say, "We were there!"

Most years Sue also took on the direction of the children's portion of the Community Christmas Concert at the Sequim Presbyterian Church. Sue directed. Peter played bells (the token male in an all-woman ensemble!). We all joined in on the *Hallelujah Chorus* that ended each concert.

But the most ambitious commitments she made were to the occasional musicals prepared for the congregation. During the Sequim years there were four of these:

We Like Sheep – a repeat of the final musical in Akron

The Greatest Show in Heaven and Earth – a circus-themed musical based on the story of Daniel

Barbeque for Ben – the story of the Prodigal Son and his Elder Brother

The Don't Be Afraid Brigade – the Christmas Story told from the angels' perspective.

Each required some set decorations, costumes, props, microphones, scripts, prompters, and more. Sue's indispensable helper in these musicals, as she was for VBS and the Christmas programs, was Janet Reindl. Janet was a stocky, rosy-cheeked dynamo, whose husband Phil worked as a logger. Janet's appetite for hard work was matched by her attention to detail. Sue and Janet made an unbeatable pair.

Sue's great reward was the joy she found in relating to the children and, in after years, finding them eager to return and talk to her. She had found her perfect niche, one that combined her love for music and her skill in teaching children.

OUR DARKEST HOUR

The year 1993 began in bright sunshine. The ministry at Faith Church was going well. We basked in the glow of a successful church and a healthy family. Though we did not admit it, Sue and I felt a kind of pharisaic satisfaction: *Have a look at us, God. We're a good family who've worked hard. Our parishioners love us. Our children shine like stars.* We sometimes looked at other families, including the assistant pastor's family, with the sort of disdain the elder brother in the parable felt toward his wayward sibling. Why did they all have such trouble? The sun shone on our little meadow.

Late that summer, dark clouds rolled in with startling suddenness. One afternoon Ron Blumhorst took me aside in the hallway and spoke quiet, deadly words. Peter was playing with his daughters back in some corner of the church, he said. He touched those girls on their private parts. The girls went home and told their mother. She had told him. Now he must tell me.

I stared at him like a dumb animal. "Yes, I see," I told him, though I did not see where this was bound to take us. Something in me flashed anger. How can he, who has had such troubles of his own, tell me of this? What is this next to the horrific, years-long addiction he has exhibited – a behavior that has taken up so many hours and wrung my emotions as it has? It did not occur to me that it might not be true, for I remembered doing such a thing as a boy – playing doctor with my smaller cousin, pulling her pants down to look at her while she lay still as the patient. I looked at Peter's behavior indulgently, remembering my own 'normal' childhood.

Sue did not believe it initially. And Peter denied it with a resolute look in his eyes: "NO!" Had Wanda Blumhorst created this situation, probing her daughters daily to see if anyone had tried to molest them? Such preoccupation with possible dangers might simply have planted the thought, and the girls' imaginations probably did the rest.

I knew, however, that we could not simply sit and do nothing. Perhaps if we showed ourselves proactively open and honest, the cloud would pass. I phoned the Sequim police to report my son. Yes, we could bring him by for questioning. All right, we'll bring him then. A routine matter. Paperwork to fill in. This would pass.

We took Peter to the police station. It was night – cool and dark. Sue and I sat in the outer hallway on a bench while, somewhere inside, an officer probed him with questions. Sue felt her heart solid, heavy as a stone. Her mind raced. How can this be happening to us? To OUR son? We tried to grasp at the comfort of the familiar promise of Jesus, *"I am with you always,"* but we felt neither any presence nor any comfort. Peter finally came out, looking vacant, and the tone of the officer felt ominous. We would hear something soon. But not something good, I sensed. Thunder rumbled in the clouds.

It dawned on us that we would need a lawyer. I remembered Gary Stone, a blond, raw-boned man who had sat with me on several occasions for personal counsel. Gary was a bright man with a haunted look about him. A weak Episcopalian, he struggled to know the Lord. But he seemed a capable lawyer, and he had a decent reputation in the community. I called him and we spoke. His reaction to our description sobered me even more. I began to fear that serious consequences would follow. He recommended that we take Peter to speak with Brooke Carnahan, a counselor who dealt with sex offenders. It was the first mention of those dread words.

Days later, just after Vacation Bible School ended, there came a knock at the door. A policeman delivered into our hands a summons to Superior Court, Juvenile Division. Had anyone seen this policeman come to our door? We hoped not. Sue imagined a big red mark painted on our house, like Hester Prynne's scarlet letter. Life had to go on at church. There were services to prepare. Visits to make. Sue was robotic at her desk, her face masked. I tried to keep an emotional distance from our son's dilemma so that I could function. Our awful secret, our black cloud, hung heavy over us through the months of autumn.

The trial took place on December 7. In a special plea arrangement, Peter's charge was reduced from 'molestation' to 'indecent liberties' in exchange for his participation in a special program called SSODA - the Special Sex Offenders' Disposition Alternative. The sentencing included some minimum detention time (reduced from 30 days to four), forty hours of community service, and reports to a probation officer. SSODA also meant that Peter would undergo a year or more of court-ordered counseling with other juvenile offenders at Ms. Carnahan's office in Port Angeles. A cold rain fell on our souls. Our son was a criminal!

The shock of the verdict was followed by the sadness and shame of his incarceration. It unfolded like a slow-motion nightmare. The drive to the juvenile detention facility. The clank of steel doors. The sterile grey cement walls and floors. The buzzing of the intercom and the radio voices from some unseen room. Peter was frisked, and all was taken away from him, even his pencil. He disappeared, distressed, into the labyrinth, and we stood helpless outside. Of all the tearful separations from our children over the years, this was the hardest.

Very shortly after his release, the weekly counseling sessions began. Because of my pastoral commitments, Sue did most of the driving, the waiting, and the listening. Peter's account of these included wrenching details of what he and the other boys had to share about the most private thoughts, the most intimate sexual acts and fantasies.

Sue and I reacted very differently. What I felt, initially, Why should my son, who had done what I still regarded as such offense, be lumped together with other boys who sounded more truly delinquents and budding criminals? He would be exposed to them, sullied them! Why should we have to be inconvenienced like this week after week? And what right did this counselor have to go snooping into their lives in such an embarrassing way? After a time I let myself grow increasingly detached, immersed in my work. From Sue's perspective, I seemed to care very little.

She, on the contrary, was more involved and felt the burden daily. She identified with the Psalmist *("Every night I flood my bed with tears; I drench my couch with weeping")*. She heard the details about thinking errors and the deviancy cycle. The realization grew that Peter was not so very different from the other offenders as we had thought.

Then came a lie detector test. Peter failed it. It came out that he had not only lied to us initially, but that instead of one offense, there had been three, with other children! A new fear rose. What if these other families learned what had happened? What if a lawsuit followed? One day when I took a turn driving to Port Angeles, my pent-up emotions erupted. "Do you understand what you have done to us?" I shouted at him in the car while he cringed. "We could get sued! I could LOSE MY JOB!" I was more concerned with my reputation than with my son's future.

The cloud enveloped, suffocated us with a sort of cold darkness. But there came strengthening in the cloud. There were no angel wings, no audible voices. But the grandparents sent Bible verses and love in their letters. Sue continued her daily readings and found this in Oswald Chambers:

> *God does not get you into a cloud to teach you a lesson, but to get you alone with Him...to strip us down so that there is finally nothing in the cloud but me and Jesus.*

God had us alone in the cloud, and He stripped us to let us see our spiritual pride. Meanwhile, we were learning from God what Paul had discovered: *"My grace is sufficient..."* There was a sense of an umbrella of prayers over us in the midst of the storm. No one at church confronted us, no one left the fellowship, no idle talk reached our ears. Jacquie Dawley, who had welcomed us to the school so warmly, somehow knew what was happening. Her take on it? "This is a scheme of the Devil to bring down the ministry here at Faith." We began to understand the battle better and see the support God was supplying.

The passing of time brought wider ramifications. Every time Peter left the county, he was required to inform the authorities. When his high school Knowledge Bowl team went to Wenatchee, and later to New Orleans, this was a hurdle to clear. He would also, we learned, have to register as a sex

ult years. What would that do to his college possibilities?

readful revelation. Peter was close to finishing his riff informed us that he intended to 'poster' Peter in elephone poles and other public places. At nearly the that Kathy Grimes, a reporter for the Gazette, was article about our situation. I felt a sense of panic set in. Kathy I asked why it might be in the public's interest to know this, ly in the light of the damage it could do to our congregation and my position there. She decided not to write the story.

The prospect of the postering remained. There arose in our minds a sense of unfairness. Why should sex offenders be singled out this way? Why not murderers? Why not the kid who bashes everyone's mailboxes, or the dope pusher, or the home-wrecker, or the burglar? Suddenly we were seeing stories everywhere on the newscasts and in the papers about sex offenders, who had obviously become society's modern-day 'lepers.' The underlying fear, of course, was that our family's personal heartache would become known to everyone, and we would be despised by everyone. In the end, however, Peter was never postered. All the other boys in his group were, but by some clerical error we never understood, Peter was passed by.

One more hurdle rose before us as Peter's graduation approached in the spring of 1997. Though he had not been postered, word of his offenses had somehow leaked into the school community, through parents who had heard about this to their children, then other students. Though Peter was the class valedictorian and a National Merit Scholar, several parents approached Principal Mike Wilson with a threat. If Peter were to be allowed to deliver a valedictory speech, they and their children would boycott the graduation. Wilson called me in to tell me about what he was facing. I asked if I might write a letter to the parents which he would deliver to them, and he consented. I wrote the letter, in summary using the argument that our son posed no threat to anyone. I delivered the letter and waited. There was no response from anyone.

A few weeks later, Wilson spoke to Peter about the dilemma. He was worried that the graduation ceremony would be derailed to uphold one student's privilege. Peter decided not to speak. I struggled again with anger and spoke again to Principal Wilson. There was another option, he offered. "There's a baccalaureate for the class. It's not required but most students and families go to that. Perhaps Peter could speak there."

That is what we finally chose to do. Peter prepared a speech, and Sue and I sat among the throng in the Seventh-Day Adventist Church for the ceremony. Sue held my hand in a vise-like grip as Peter made his way to the podium. He spoke honestly to his classmates as they sat riveted to his words, a testimony of his spiritual journey. He was, he admitted, an egotist who knew God existed, but didn't have much personal need for His help...

But near the end of my freshman year I got jolted. Some policemen wanted to talk to me. They said I was a sex offender. They were right, too.

There it was, right out in front of everybody. The truth we had feared everyone would hear, the truth Peter had first denied. Now he was telling everyone that he had offended not once, but several times. He admitted to being upset that God had not removed the consequences of his actions. He told the story of his going to a Christian music festival called Jesus Northwest, and the beginning of change there. Then a back-sliding. Then a year later another, deeper experience at the next Jesus Northwest. A story of genuine repentance, heartfelt prayer, and a commitment to live a new way. He ended with a plea to his classmates:

I don't know where any of you are in your walk with God, or if some of you even know God at all, but let me speak from experience: if He can work with me, He can work with anyone. God doesn't give up... He answers when you call...even if you've made a habit of ignoring Him. God is the only reason I'm standing in front of you today...the only reason I have a loving family that has stood with me all these years. I pray if you haven't accepted Him yet, do so now. It'll make an incredible difference. He's more important than brains or brawn. Please pray for me that I continue in my walk with him. I'll be praying for you.

    I listened in a welter of conflicting emotions. Pride. Gratitude. And shame. I felt like an absentee father being introduced to his own son for the first time. I had been so busy with other people that I didn't know the drama in my own children's lives! But the shame I felt was washed away by a rising tide of grace that had given my son courage to tell the truth about Himself and His Savior. I was no longer afraid of what the people at Faith knew, what anyone in town knew. The clouds rolled away and the sun came out. God had forgiven him, and us.
    Neither then nor later was there ever a word of condemnation from the people at Faith, but only hugs and words of support. Peter went off to school, as his sisters had. At Harvey Mudd College in Claremont, he became active in InterVarsity, a Christian movement on campus. He married Caroline King, a girl he'd met at Sequim High School. He graduated from college and got steady work. Years later, his requirement to register with the

state came to an end. By our petition, his criminal record was sealed. The grace of God, over time, set us free.

LETTING GO

Once more she felt it. Those tiny inner rumblings that told Sue that were soon to go through some great change. "I think we're going to be moving," she confided in me. There came some more certain signs of it. I began to get feelers from a variety of places – Louisiana, Minnesota, Oregon, Texas, California. The inquiry from Minnesota was accompanied by a request from the Minnesota South District for any 'criminal history' and the requirement of a background check! The many clergy scandals had added a new, unpleasant layer to the call process.

The appearance of all these inquiries was likely the aftermath of our traumatic times with Peter. District President Erhart Bauer had earlier offered to move me, but I had demurred. Now, it seemed certain, he had made my name available to be called.

Among the inquiries was one from Trinity Lutheran Church in Oregon City, Oregon, a suburb of Portland. I received a questionnaire from them in 1998, filled it in and returned it, then heard nothing more. I went on with my work in Sequim.

Already years before that inquiry from Oregon City, our family life began to undergo some very systemic changes. We let go of our children one by one as they left the family nest and headed off to school. After her graduation in 1989, Melanie began studies at Pacific Lutheran University. Four years later, with a math degree in hand, she spent a year at Lutheran Bible Institute in Issaquah, Washington, obeying a growing impulse toward possible mission work. After exploring some possible mission agencies, she decided to spend a year in Kenya. There in Kijabe, Africa Inland mission operated a school for expatriate missionary children, and Melanie was accepted on the teaching staff. It was a day of joy for her and tears for all of us when she stood before the altar for her sending service. A year overseas!

Christa's graduation came in 1992. Her sights were set on teaching, and toward that end she enrolled at Concordia University in Portland, majoring in elementary education, as Sue had done so many years before. She was dating Jeffrey Zellar, a wiry young man from Anderson, Alaska, her classmate at school. They faced the same struggle for chastity Sue and I had endured. In obedience to Paul's counsel, "It is better to marry than to burn," they opted to marry in 1995, before either had graduated. Jeff elected to suspend his schooling and go to work while Christa finished her education degree. The little girl who fabricated Dolltown in our basement in Akron was making her home for real now.

Peter graduated from Sequim High in 1997 and charted a course in computer science – no surprise to us. He entered Harvey Mudd College in

, where, he told us, "We really have to work.
 rt!" He also discovered that life in college had no
morally, he was on his own. It was a good and
n to make, but hard for us as parents to let go of our

 ͻ adapt to our increasingly empty nest.

Back in Indiana, my father was in failing health. He was diagnosed with esophageal cancer, likely the by-product of his years as a smoker, even though he had long ago given up the habit. A surgery to remove a tumor appeared hopeful, but now, months afterward, his cancer was back with a vengeance. "If you want to see Dad," my sister Natalie urged me in a phone call, "you'd better come soon." I booked a flight alone in October and made the visit to see him. On the plane I sat beside a younger man who asked me about my trip. When I told him I was going to see my father, he vented his own feelings of anger about his father's death. It was clear he had no peace. I told him quietly that I did not feel that way. "My dad," I explained, "is at peace with God. He knows where he's going, and so I am not angry, though I will miss him when he dies."

Dad was waiting for me at the airport. I saw him before he saw me. He was sitting in the baggage claim on a bench, a physically wilted man. I hardly recognized him. Our visit was for only a few days. In spite of the illness, Dad was cheerful and at peace. I was moved with gratitude as I sat beside him on the couch just before my departure, thinking of how much I owed him. "I want to thank you, Dad," I said, "for three things. You gave me a faith to live by. You lived it for me to see. You loved mom faithfully. I'm trying to imitate you in the way I treat Sue. And now you are showing me how to die. Someday I'll face such a time, and I hope I can do it as you are doing, with faith and good cheer." I wept as I embraced him.

My father died in February, with Mom by his side. The service bore his stamp. Dad picked out the readings and hymns for the service. Pastor Wehrmeister, recalling Dad's love for God's house and his faithfulness in worship, entitled his message, "It's Sunday!"

Sue's father died later that same year. He had fallen on the ice a few years earlier, bashing his head on the concrete and suffering a sudden onset of Alzheimer's in consequence. He moved to a special locked unit at the Methodist Home where he and Sue's mom lived in Franklin. Our visits were attended by the pain of watching him grow more demented. He continued to be able to play the piano, even though he could not clearly remember us. The 'long goodbye' ended eight months after my own father died.

Sue and I grieved together at the loss of our fathers. By the grace of God, we were able to let them go into His arms and find a shared peace.

A few months later came a phone call from Oregon City. "We have called you to be our pastor," said head elder Ray Clack. The papers were to follow. "If you'd like to visit us, we'd welcome that." Sue and I made plans to travel the 240 miles south to Oregon City and check things out.

As we drove into town, I remembered driving here with Win and Lois Schroeder almost 30 years earlier. Win had described his experience as a student pastor at Trinity. He had showed us the municipal elevator at the side of the bluff and told us, with gratitude, that Oregon City had given him a wife. Now we drove up Twelfth Street to the stone church with its copper steeple. The staff shared lunch with us, a merry meeting over sub sandwiches and potato chips. I asked questions and so did they. At the end little Henrietta Bjerke came up to us to say, "I wish you'd come, but I don't think you will." An evening meeting at the home of Ted and Yvonne Phillips was well attended, and I was struck by the confident, almost audacious view of the future. There was a certainty among all that Trinity was on the verge of growing to two thousand souls or more in ten years! I was quietly skeptical of this, given the history of slow decline in our church body. Even my healthiest congregation in Vancouver had not experienced anything close to that.

Back home I assembled a sheet of summary thoughts about the congregation and the desired role of the pastor. The congregation, in my view, was busy, friendly, harmonious ... and proud. Haughty, to be more precise. The role of the pastor in Oregon City, I wrote, was to be "An equipper. Preach and teach. Train small group leaders. Visit. Assimilate. Coordinate things." This was on the heels of former Pastor Mark Halvorson, who was a dreamer and idea man, but not a visitor nor an administrator.

I pondered the advice of others. Paul Schmidt, the interim pastor, told me "You have what it takes, but you will have to change your style some." Lee Wendland, an advisor to the district president, told me, "They need a listener. They need infrastructure. You provide what they're missing." That was certainly me, I thought. But district staffer Denny Langston offered a more sobering word: "You would do well there. They would like you. But I don't know how well you would like them!" That opinion haunted me.

Sue and I were torn about the decision, she feeling much more hesitant than I. In our uncertainty, we decided to invite our inner circle of Sequim parishioners to sit with us and listen to their wisdom. One evening, we hosted the Van Dykens, the Joneses, and the Marcys for dessert and talk. We told them what we'd heard, and what we liked and didn't like. They listened with care, and an objectivity that amazed me. Afterward, they surprised us with their verdict. They believed that we were called to go to Oregon City.

Coming from those who loved us best, it was a powerful word, and made up our minds. We would accept the call.

I prepared a farewell letter and mailed it out as my parting message in the monthly newsletter:

> *Dear brothers and sisters in Christ,*
>
> *One last time, now, I sit down to prepare a pastor's page greeting to all of you. It won't be long before an Allied moving van pulls up to our home on Hogback Road to take our worldly possessions aboard for the trip south to Oregon City.*
>
> *When I address you as brothers and sisters, I mean it. That's what Jesus has made us, in spite of our differences in age and experience. We share one Lord, one faith, one baptism, one God and Father of us all. We have enjoyed years of blessings together. You aren't like family – you are family!*
>
> *What lovely pictures we have stored in the family album of our memory. I stand in the sanctuary and recall: here Peter was confirmed, here Melanie was commissioned to Kenya (amid my tears), here Christa walked down the aisle with me for her wedding (more tears!). Here Sue and I sat together as Pastor Eaton sprang that unexpected 25th anniversary service. More images come. Do you remember the Sunday we baptized Sabina Lobbes and her sister in German? The day the Sequim police stood at attention in their uniforms as we prayed for them? The children dressed in white, singing their hearts out, in the "We Like Sheep" musical?*
>
> *Not all the memories are cheerful ones. Like any real family, we have had heartaches. I can remember sitting with more than one of you as you struggled with anger and depression. I recall the sad day I conducted Pastor Huth's funeral after his sudden death at a New York airport. I can still see Pastor Blumhorst making his burdened resignation speech as he stood here before us. I can still feel my own bitter moments of disappointment and defeat, sitting here alone, head in hands. But afterward, there always came that great Comforter, the Holy Spirit, with his inexpressible mercy...*
>
> *I confess a mix of feelings as I say goodbye. I wonder what God has in store for us both, but not fearfully, for I know that because of His incredible love for us, we can always say "The best is yet to be." I marvel at how much some of you have grown in faith in the years I have known you. I marvel at others of you who once seemed so strong and are now, it appears, drifting away from both*

your church and your Lord. Whether your faith is weak or strong, God is taking me away to another place, and I can only say what Paul said as he met for the last time with his beloved Ephesians on the beach at Miletus: "Now I commend you to God..." For that is what good-bye really means – "God be with you." That's the good part of our good-byes – the goodness and constancy of God, even when we fail or grow fearful and faint.

While we are busy plunging into the new mission He has assigned us in Oregon City, you will be discovering the good things He has in store for this congregation... Pastor Eaton rising to a new challenge, new willing voices and hands of people saying, "I can help!", and the excitement of a long-range planning process that will propel Faith Lutheran Church into some unexplored territory.

For my part, besides the prayers, I hope to stay in touch by writing an occasional letter to you all and making an occasional trip with Sue to come and see you. Some of you, I know, are planning similar trips south to see us.

Thanks be to God for eleven great years. Thanks to all of you, so generous and so tender in your love for us. Now, I commend you to God.

Before we knew it, the farewell day came. There was a last worship service and a gathering at Carrie Blake Park for a meal. There were good wishes and tears, satirical skits about my ancient typewriter and Sue's habit of holding cards up for her children's choir, a barbershop quartet, a farewell book and some jokes from emcee Ed Sievert. But the moment in the day that lingers longest was a simple song by 11-year-old Andrea Perlwitz, sung near the end of the worship service:

Pastor Mike, you must go.
We will always love you so.
By God's grace you led us
Gently as our pastor
LOGOS time was really keen
You were Dinner Dean.
Children's sermons we did learn
Sitting by your knee.
Pastor Mike, you must go.
We will always love you so.
By God's grace you led us
Gently as our pastor.

Trinity Lutheran Church

Oregon City, Oregon

(1999–2010)

ON THE OREGON TRAIL

We arrived in Oregon City in June of 1999, only the latest in a lengthy string of immigrant families. More than 160 years earlier, a couple named Marcus and Narcissa Whitman journeyed by wagon train west from Missouri with a small band of missionaries. Their aim was to settle and start mission work in the Oregon Territory. It was the beginning of a great westward migration along the Oregon Trail. Nearly half a million people eventually made the trip, which ended at Oregon City, the town proposed as the capital of the new territory.

Oregon City was the oldest city to incorporate west of St. Louis. City officials liked to remind visitors that their town, begun in 1843, was even older than San Francisco. At the Oregon Trail Interpretive Center at the north end of town, three gigantic covered wagons drew tourists to come in and re-live the historic migration. A walking trail along the bluff above town gave walkers a nice view of the Willamette River with its wide, misty waterfall and the paper mill and other old buildings nestled by the water.

We settled in temporarily at the Pioneer Ridge Apartments on the south side of town while realtor Jonathan Heins, a member of Trinity, helped us look for a permanent dwelling. Before long, we made an offer on a modest ranch-style home on a small lot on Highland Drive. "You'll like this place," promised Jonathan. "Not much grass to cut!" Nostalgic for the tiny orchard we had left in Sequim, we planted four small trees at the corner of the back yard – two apple, one cherry, and one prune tree.

Trinity Lutheran Church was started in 1921, the direct result of a sidewalk conversation between two men. One asked if he could find a good place to study the Bible in town. The other notified Lutheran Church officials of the opportunity. A few months later, the district extended a call to Pastor Rudolph Messerli of South Dakota to begin a mission. Shortly thereafter, he and his family drove into town in their Model A Ford, and the new church plant was begun.

The congregation was a stable one, having been served by only three senior pastors (Messerli, Lornell Ruthenbeck, and Mark Halvorson) in its 78-year history. Other men had helped in various roles, including my own former vicarage supervisor Win Schroeder, who had served for a year as a student pastor and made more than 1000 canvassing calls.

One of our older folks remembered Schroeder fondly. "He made quite an impact," volunteered Leah Messerli, Pastor Rudy's daughter, a pleasant octogenarian who still lived in the house next door and gave music lessons.

"He made quite an impact on me, too," I told her.

The church had also operated a parochial school for more than forty years. Pastor Messerli taught all the grades and even some high school students before finally getting some assistance. What a man he must have been, I thought. Always the congregation demonstrated an interest in missions, and always there was good music, played on the pipe organ in the balcony and sung by a sizable choir.

I arrived in my office and found it occupied by a man sporting a pony tail and hard at work on the floor, fixing something for my arrival. He was Paul Brockmann, long-time member, former teacher at the school, and former part-time organist. He proved to be a model of helpfulness and a wellspring of information about the church. I was greatly encouraged.

Installation day was June 20, 1999, a lovely summer day. My friend, Pastor Mark Bertermann, was to preach. As we were getting ready for the service, there came an unexpected request from the youth. Would I like to come and play in the softball game at the park afterward? I pondered what this might mean about priorities, but decided not to be stuffy. "Sure," I told them. "I'll change clothes and come as soon as I can." Mark preached a memorable message, using my 'Treasure in a Pot' theme, holding aloft a flower pot with 'MDK' on one side and 'TLC' on the other. It was a meaningful touch for me. Nevertheless, I remember the game that day even better than the service because, for the last time in my life, I managed to hit a home run.

Ours was a move within a move. Even as we settled in on Highland Drive and I organized my books and files in the office at church, the congregation was getting ready to do its own moving. "What are your thoughts about being senior pastor in a relocation?" the Call Committee wrote earlier.

I wrote back:

I'd think people would want reassurance that some things don't change. God doesn't. The Gospel doesn't... So maybe it is a pastor's task to help us 'fix our eyes on Jesus' at all times, but especially when change comes... How could I assist? By being enthusiastic, seeing the good in the move and not complaining at the necessary inconveniences... Hey, I could also move some boxes like everybody else!

The coming move was more than wishful thinking. The plans were already set in motion. A building committee was well into its work. A fourteen-acre tract of land six miles southeast of town had been purchased from the Allen family. "It's right in the projected path of the city's growth!" the committee told me. It would, at the very least, give needed parking space and room to grow after decades of increasing strangulation at the corner of 12th and J. Q. Adams Streets. Long walks from distant parking spaces on hillsides in winter time were treacherous. On the inside, multiple stairways and too-small bathrooms presented more obstacles. The consensus was that we couldn't move soon enough.

Funding would come from three sources: a special initial offering, the sale of the old building, and a long-term mortgage loan from the church's extension fund. The congregation began the offering with an excited spirit. The chief task remaining in our path was to sell our church building, no easy task. The location was not a convenient one for a merchant. Nor would a school want our facility, since we already sat between two nearby schools. The months passed and we prayed for a buyer.

God's answer came a year or so later. Reformation Covenant Church, a younger and smaller congregation looking for a permanent home, contacted us. They had rented several venues, including a dance studio with mirrored walls, a grange building, and a gymnasium at a Seventh-Day Adventist campground. They were as eager to move in as we were to move out. We were eager, but not quite ready, for we had yet to build our new church facility.

Out of necessity, we decided to share our building. What followed, wrote reporter Vince Kohler of *The Oregonian* newspaper, was a lesson in togetherness, "an arrangement occasionally stressful, always good-natured, and everlastingly rewarding." RCC bought our building for $660,000 and agreed to rent the facility back to us.

Pastor Dennis Tuuri, the rotund, bearded pastor of RCC, proved a cheerful and resourceful friend. He and his lay leaders assisted in setting up a master calendar of events and color-coded bulletin boards – blue for Trinity and yellow for RCC. The Sunday shuffle began with our own schedule of two worship services and Sunday School abbreviated to end at 11:00 a.m. Our people had 15 minutes to clear the building and drive off, allowing RCC's folks to arrive, set up, and begin their single service at 11:30. It was followed by their weekly fellowship dinner that lasted through the afternoon. For nearly a year we joked about 'The Church of the Bruised Hip' as we passed one another on the sidewalk. Transition teams from the congregations kept open a steady communication and a bond of friendship.

In September of 2000 came the ground-breaking ceremony at the site on Henrici Road. Out to the middle of a large field tramped 100 or so people. Along with our officers, I donned a green hard hat and took a shovel. We sang *"Christ is our cornerstone, on Him alone we build!"* and then nearly broke our shovels trying to turn the weedy, stone-hard earth. The old church's cornerstone was opened and Paul Brockmann shared the old documents that hadn't seen the light of day for more than 50 years. We prayed God's hand on things as construction began. Then we went on our way, rejoicing to be underway at last.

Within a few weeks, the earthmovers began growling their way around the field, scraping and pushing the soil, leveling the site. Teams of workers began preparing the foundation and work progressed rapidly. Back at the old building, I developed working relationships with secretary Brenda Bruce, bookkeeper and financial manager Dick Brooks, youth director Larry Deyoe, and Susanne Walters, the preschool teacher.

Meanwhile, I began as I had always begun my pastoral work in a new congregation. I made a host of phone calls and home visits, learning names and faces, the key players, the faithful and some who were missing in action. I made it a goal to get to one home a day. During most of the visits I asked a question that sounded light-hearted, but had a serious intent: "If God appeared to you in a dream tonight and said, 'I'll grant three wishes you make for this congregation,' what would you wish for?"

I listened hard to the answers. What were the obvious and hidden agendas? What would they really expect of me now that I was in place? And what was God already busy doing inside them? I began to develop a lengthy 'wish list.'

Trinity was a big, busy congregation. Had I bitten off more than I could chew? One veteran pastor's advice was pointed: "You'll have to work smarter, not harder." I prayed repeatedly for wisdom. The work here would be a challenge.

SHADOWS ON THE WALL

The ministry in Oregon City began with two shadows on the wall. The first was the considerable shadow of my predecessor, Mark Halvorson. Mark, a man several years younger than I, served Trinity for eleven years. Those were good years, years of growth, most agreed. Many people remembered Mark by the mantra he had drummed into their ears: "Bible study, Bible study, Bible study!" Simple as it sounded, it was effective. Trinity's people seemed to have taken the lesson to heart. The Bible classes were healthy and well-attended.

More important, Mark was remembered as a 'visionary' pastor. The vision of a new and larger building in a new, spacious location was attributed to him. He had not, admitted his lay assistant Sharon Sides, taken much time for visitation and soul care, and even less for administrative detail. The congregation's records were a mess. "But you are good at those things," she added helpfully.

It was soon apparent that some were not happy with having an older man in place of a younger one, a man with adequate administrative and pastoral skills but (they suspected) lacking in vision. None of this came from Mark himself, now relocated in a new post in Minnesota. The only thing people did NOT seem to remember gratefully about Halvorson was the suddenness of his departure ("right in the middle of our move!"). They were sad that he was gone. Were they happy I was here? For the first time in my ministry, I felt as if I were in competition with a predecessor. For the first time, others saw me as an 'older fellow.' Once a youth pastor, now an old man! It was a strange, unsettling sensation. Sue felt it more strongly than I. In more than one conversation, she felt the prickliness that comes with being evaluated with an unfavorable verdict. We prayed regularly for patience and wisdom.

The initial area of greatest anxiety among those who were doubtful about me was the area of worship. "We have two distinct kinds of worship service," the call committee made clear to me. "The early service is traditional. For that we use the hymnal liturgies. The late service is contemporary. We have a praise team that often plays in that one." They asked if I would agree to maintain that format.

"I'm the servant, not the master," I replied obligingly, though with some misgiving. I still subscribed to Professor Caemmerer's view that worship was an exercise in mutual submission. In Sequim, everyone had learned to appreciate and participate in a variety of styles. That was healthy, wasn't it?

In the early months at Oregon City, I planned the services as they directed, though no one told me exactly what 'contemporary' meant to them.

I began to get questions about the hymn choices I made, usually second-hand. And when I chose, once in a while, to use the same format (one time traditional, the next time contemporary) for both early and late services, it produced tremors of anxiety. The way some saw it, I was pulling the congregation back from the cutting edge of relevance into more dependence on the hymnal. On the defensive, I suggested that a class on Lutheran worship practices might get us on the same page. The class was well attended. It was obvious that people felt strongly about their preferred worship style.

A large positive in the area of worship was the presence of a trio of competent (and friendly) organists. The senior organist was Irene Rubin, who had been at the organ bench for decades, and at Trinity since 1989. She was capable, hard-working, pleasant, and respectful at all times. Every phone call I made to her was answered the same way: "Yes, pastor?" Irene seemed ready to do anything I asked.

Our second organist was Earlene Wagner, a vibrant woman, formerly Pentecostal. Having become a Lutheran, she appreciated our liturgical heritage, perhaps more than some of our lifelong Lutherans. She was passionate about music. Less experienced, but more proficient at the keyboard, she enrolled at Marylhurst University to get a Bachelor of Arts in music and a certificate in pedagogy. In her we found an enthusiastic acceptance which we very much needed.

Janet Moeller was the youngest of the three and still in her twenties. She played only as a substitute for the others on an occasional basis, but she had charge of Trinity's choir, which she directed with enthusiasm. Together the three made quite a team. I had no complaints about the music staff.

The second shadow on the wall was a concern about my health. Late in my time in Sequim, I had experienced a sudden weakness that made it hard to climb stairs or even cross the street to retrieve mail from our box. I was sometimes short of breath. After failing an EKG at the doctor's office, the doctor dispatched me to Swedish hospital in Seattle for a battery of tests, including a stress test and a lung function test. I did not do well on the stress test, and the doctor kept me for a coronary arteriogram. The results were all negative. "It's not your arteries," he told me with a puzzled shake of his head. "You're clean as a whistle."

Back home, the symptoms faded for a time. Whatever it was seemed to have passed. In the meantime, we had moved to Oregon City and plunged in, feeling fine. But within a few months, the exhaustion returned. "I feel like an 80-year-old smoker," I told Sue as I climbed Trinity's stairs. One Friday morning I awoke to what I thought was a heart attack. Pains across my chest and down my arms. Such shortness of breath that I could not even make it to the bathroom. "Call the doctor," I whispered to Sue. How often I had heard stories from parishioners about a spouse's death that began with just these symptoms. *Is this how life ends for me?* As I lay on the bed, there washed over me an unexpected peace. God had been good. I had no complaints. I was ready to go if He wanted it so.

To the doctor I went, and as he examined me, he said, "I have a hunch." He sent me to Willamette Falls Hospital for a spiral CT scan. That test confirmed what he suspected. Not heart trouble but pulmonary emboli – dozens of small blood clots in my lungs. He could not determine the site of origin, he explained, "but we don't need to know that. We can control these with medication." I began taking blood-thinning medication, a regimen that would have to last the rest of my life. The symptoms disappeared.

With that diagnosis and subsequent medication, I looked with new appreciation on the sign on my office mirror someone had placed there:

Only one life, 'twill soon be past;
Only what's done for Christ will last.

My childhood's preoccupation with mortality took hold of me again, coupled with the realization of my aging. I was 52 years old. How was it possible that 27 years had passed since that June day we seminarians were launched into our first assignments?

There came help for me in a sort of comforting synchronicity. Just as God provided three capable organists, so He provided three pastors to supply wisdom and help as I began at Trinity. Paul Schmidt had been the official interim, a man who could look with some objectivity at Trinity's strengths and weaknesses. I consulted him on several occasions in those early months.

Paul Heinlein, a younger pastor who stepped away from full-time ministry to take a secular position due to family concerns, preached and led worship on most Sundays during the prior vacancy. He and his family lived in nearby Gladstone, and he told me he was glad to help wherever he could. I employed him regularly during Advent and Lent when we held Wednesday as well as Sunday worship.

Trinity's former pastor, Lornell Ruthenbeck, who had served from 1968-88, was still a member too. When I initially worried that having a former pastor around might prove awkward, Paul Schmidt reassured me, "Pastor Ruthenbeck is peacefulness personified." That proved true. Lorrie took pains to give me room to operate and as much encouragement as he could. There came little typed notes of appreciation on my office door and gracious words at the door after service. He and his wife Lois also proved to be a great asset in visitation of shut-in members. Since there were eighteen shut-ins, their visits saved me several days of time each month. Later on, as the Ruthenbecks slowed down, the elders and I agreed to set up a team of lay visitors to do what the Ruthenbecks had done. The visitors made monthly stops and distributed Holy Communion, using the elements already consecrated at the altar.

A beginning was made. With the move to the new location would come more opportunities and challenges, some new shadows, and new channels of help and grace.

FARMING THE FIELD

We bade farewell to the old building and our friends at RCC on July 8, 2001. Using Psalm 84 as my text, I invited the congregation to reflect on the memories associated with 'this old house,' but also to anticipate the doors about to open on our new facility. "Remember," I told them, "not to get too comfortable anywhere, for we are always a pilgrim people, on the road to a better home."

The move went off without a hitch and almost without a backward glance. Like a weary worker settling into warm bath water, we settled into the new place with a pleasurable sigh. So much parking space! No hills or stairs to climb! The large narthex felt like a Hyatt Regency hotel with its lofty ceiling and ample elbow room.

We set September 16 as the Dedication Sunday, and our fellowship groups, classes, and guilds busied themselves making banners to adorn the multi-purpose room which was to serve as our worship room. Brenda Bruce and I worked on the gilt-lettered bulletin. The choirs finalized their music.

The Tuesday before the dedication, Sue and I were awakened by a phone call from our daughter Christa in Kansas City. "Turn on the television!" she said with urgency. As millions of others were doing, we watched in horror the unfolding attack on the World Trade Center. That evening and the following day, as President Bush had requested, we opened the sanctuary to anyone who wanted to come in prayer. A solitary woman from the neighborhood came and sat in the mournful silence.

The following Sunday we cast aside sorrow and rejoiced in our wondrous new building. The new Northwest District President Warren Schumacher came to preach. A large throng gathered to sing and pray while video cameras rolled, recording the event.

Eugene Peterson wrote, "Pastoral work... is like farm work. Most pastoral work involves routines similar to cleaning out the barn, mucking out the stalls, spreading manure, pulling weeds..." In Peterson's terms, the barn had been raised. Now the fields had to be farmed.

The evangelism team and I started with a neighborhood canvass. We fashioned a tri-fold with 'An Invitation from your Neighbors at Trinity Lutheran Church' giving worship times, a simple statement of our confession of faith, a listing of groups and a map. Eighteen people assembled on a sunny Saturday morning. After a Scripture reading and prayer, Eddie Walters and Bob Lenhart distributed the handouts and assigned each team a territory. We scattered to meet our neighbors and invite them to church. More than 270 homes received our visits that day.

That outreach brought almost immediate opportunities to plant the message of God's grace. At one home I met a young woman who said, "You're right over there? I guess I don't have an excuse anymore!" Her name was Kim Rohrs, and within a short time, she, her daughter Chelsea, and her brother-in-law Cary appeared for worship. Cary was a single man who lived with his mother because he was very sick with Fabry's Disease, an inherited disorder that attacked the internal organs. His kidneys were failing, and his life was threatened. His sister volunteered to donate one of her kidneys, and the operation was a success. I visited them in the hospital, and prayed thanks for the gift of life.

Because of the uncertainty of his future, Cary was hungry to come closer to God. I began a sequence of home studies with him. Nearby in the kitchen, his mother Karen listened in. She told me later that she had become a Mormon a few years earlier, but lapsed because "they want me to tithe," something impossible because of the financial demands of her son's illness. She told me more. "Now I can't go to the temple either because of that rule." On the day Cary was finally baptized, Karen came along with him and joined Trinity.

Another opportunity to plant the seed, even more urgent, surfaced through a comment at the door after worship one Sunday. Joan Hagedorn, the woman who had come to pray alone in church on September 11, asked if I might pray for her brother-in-law Freddie. "He has cancer," she told me. "He's been thinking about getting baptized. Could you visit him?" In short order I arranged a home visit. I found Freddie at home, being cared for by his brother Mike, Joan's husband. Freddie was failing and told me he had only weeks to live, according to his doctor. It was January, and Lent was approaching.

"Have you ever heard the Easter story?" I asked.

"Well, can't say as I have," he replied.

So I told him the story – the Last Supper, the betrayal in Gethsemane, the trial and crucifixion. I told him about Dismas, the thief crucified next to Jesus, who came to faith at the very last moment of his life and was saved. I finished with that wondrous morning when life began again for Jesus, for the grieving disciples, for Dismas, and for everyone else who has trusted in Him. "It was for us he did all that, Freddie."

Freddie, who had made a mess of his life and had the reputation of being a 'bad' man from a family with a checkered history, listened with interest. He seemed especially interested in the part about Dismas.

"Have you ever been baptized?" I asked, remembering Joan's request.

"No, but I've been considering it."

A few days later I returned for the baptism. Freddie was not well enough to venture from his house, but he had donned a suit. "I didn't want to be baptized in my pajamas!" he grinned. Susanne Walters came along to help me, and she stood beside me, holding the basin of water as I spoke the sacramental words: "Freddie Hagedorn, I baptize you in the name of the Father and of the Son and of the Holy Spirit." Three times I poured the water on his head as he bowed over the basin. Then, after a brief instruction, we shared Holy Communion for the first and only time in his life. At the end, we all sat down while Susanne brought in a large birthday cake with a single lit candle on it. "Happy birthday!" we sang, and Freddie smiled happily. "I only wish," he added, "that I had more time to learn all this."

A week later he died. At his memorial service, I preached about the happy ending that had come to him, as once it had come to Dismas, the thief on the cross. What a difference the Gospel made for both of them! There was a hush in the room as scores of family and friends listened. I offered the grace of God to them all:

Today, here in this place, God has come very close to you, too. Because of Jesus Christ and His love, there is not a single story here in this room that cannot have a happy ending.

Jesus died for us... and rose again!

Because of Him, there are no quarrels that cannot be mended, no griefs that cannot be endured, no sins that cannot be forgiven.

The seed was planted in many hearts that day.

There were stalls that needed mucking out on our farm. The visits in member homes had revealed a plethora of divorced people and perhaps half a dozen live-in arrangements. Why were so many so troubled and fearful of commitment? What had eroded so many of our marriages? And what could be done to help when so many were hurting?

The same year we moved to our new church, I heard tidings that piqued my curiosity. Nationally-known columnist Mike McManus was coming from Washington, DC, to conduct a Marriage Savers' Conference in Clackamas County. It felt like more than a coincidence, coming on the heels of my anxiety about the state of our marriages. I enlisted two couples – Jim and Bev Harris and Dave and Beth Wilson - to accompany me and Sue to the meeting.

McManus outlined a pro-active approach to saving marriages. "People come to the church when they want to get married," he began. "Why not do more than simply tie the knot?" He went on to detail ways that pastors and churches could help people lay a better foundation for life together, including healthy sex education, requiring counseling prior to marriage, and providing training for couples to be marriage mentors to others before marriage and during times of distress. He shared pleasantly startling statistics of the help such an approach had provided in Fresno, California, and other places. He urged attendees to sign a community marriage policy and put it into effect back in our congregations.

Trinity was among 144 churches who eventually signed the agreement in Clackamas County. That was how our Marriage Savers program began. Eventually, six couples agreed to help plan marriage enrichment events and partner with couples that I assigned to them. Among the blessings that followed were 'Ten Great Dates,' recognition of golden wedding anniversaries and periodic marriage renewals in worship, and a sequence of marriage retreats at the Pacific City beach home of Tom and Sandy Rasch. Five years later, the divorce rate in the county had already dropped by eleven per cent. Among the marriages rescued or renewed were several in our own congregation.

A farmer must think ahead. What should I plant next year and the year after? Shall we purchase additional acreage or a new combine? The pace of life and ministry at Trinity was increasing. Should we stand pat, or should we add new programs and staff?

Late in the year 2002 the district offered special training for pastors and lay leaders called 'Tracking the Spirit.' It was designed to make us pastors more sensitive to the direction of the Holy Spirit and open to new ministry ideas. I attended and found myself nudged to do something. I wasn't sure what.

Within a month I convened a gathering of Trinity's leaders at the home of Peggy Baker. The home, sequestered in a woodsy rural area, was the perfect site for us to slow down, pray, and think together. The Spirit did more nudging. The day yielded two important agreements. The first was that we would devote the following year, 2003, to the theme of 'Renewal.' I would preach a 12-week series of messages based on the book *Twelve Pillars of a Healthy Church* by Waldo Werning. We would urge our members to take a spiritual gifts inventory and see how those personal gifts could be utilized. The second agreement was to add an assistant pastor who might give special attention to outreach ministry. We agreed that the fields around our church were 'white unto harvest.' But we needed more workers. Perhaps an outreach pastor and a newly-energized laity could bring a bumper crop into God's barn.

MULTIPLE STAFF MATTERS

Trinity's was the largest staff on which I had served. In addition to a secretary, the church employed three part-time organists, a part-time business manager, a full-time Director of Christian Education (DCE) who doubled as youth leader, and a preschool teacher. Over the eleven years I served the congregation, there were significant changes at almost every position. Each of the changes triggered a chain-reaction of programmatic and emotional responses.

DCE Larry Deyoe was a high-energy extrovert who moonlighted as a disc jockey at KPAM, a local Christian radio station. Under his guidance, our youth program seemed to be humming along nicely. Then, a year after I arrived, he received a call from a large church in Plymouth, Minnesota, to serve as their youth director. To the chagrin of many of our youth, Larry accepted and he and his family departed, leaving a hole both in our team and in our congregation's ministry.

My hands were too full to take on this responsibility, so the congregation commenced calling another person. My daughter Christa, a graduate of Concordia University in Portland, put a name on my radar. Dustin Kunkel, she said, was a Spirit-filled, gifted man who had impressed her during her student days. We added his name to the call list. After a lengthy time of sifting through information and praying, the congregation called Dustin and he accepted. Dustin, his wife Janette, and their daughter Lily arrived in the spring of 2001.

Dustin made a splash. I was surprised to discover that both he and Janette sported tattoos. Tattoos? In my growing-up years those were the mark of wild rebellion, of motorcycle gangs, of criminals! Obviously, the culture had changed while I was sleeping, for this young man was none of those bad things. His boyish good looks, lively guitar playing, and intense interest in people were a magnet for the church's youth and their friends. In a relatively short time, the youth group was renewed and growing. He even added a release-time class for kids from nearby Oregon City High School. Dustin made thoughtful contributions to our already-interesting staff meetings, and he held before the congregation an oft-repeated goal that we "feed, grow, and mature" in our discipleship.

During the Year of Renewal in 2003, he took the lead in helping our members get a bead on their spiritual gifts. He offered no rubber stamp of existing policies, but chose instead to challenge me to think about the traditional way I came at ministry. He echoed Waldo Werning's call that we empower the laity instead of doing things for them. I found that idea both thought-provoking and unsettling. My preferred leadership style was to be a benevolent autocrat. Dustin helped me loosen my grip.

Janette Kunkel, meanwhile, was searching for her niche. Trained as a teacher, she asked about the possibility that the church's early childhood program might add kindergarten to the existing preschool offerings. Just like that, it seemed, we added a kindergarten class, and the wiggling of more little folks and the squealing of additional voices made us glad we had a new and larger facility. No one realized at the time what new forces had been unleashed – forces that propelled us toward a new school and all its attendant complexities before we were quite ready.

Changes were coming also to the pastors who helped me so capably. Pastor Ruthenbeck and Lois encountered health problems, and their available time and energy was curtailed. Pastor Heinlein, who had played a key role in offering 'seeker' worship in midweek and assisting me in Advent and Lent, told me that he might not be able to continue helping for long. His wife wanted to make the move to another church for personal reasons. His availability became unpredictable.

The decision made at the planning retreat at the Baker home the previous autumn – that we begin the call process for an assistant pastor – now moved to center stage. A growing youth group and a growing school suggested that this was a perfect time for us to find a second pastor who could help me with the preaching load and help us focus on outreach.

The board of elders, who also served as the call committee, did its work. A self-study was completed and forwarded to the district. President Schumacher, in turn, sent us a list of potential candidates. We did our homework, solicited interviews, and finally held a call meeting. Bryan Schindel, a young pastor in British Columbia, was selected. He visited but ultimately declined the call. A second time we convened, prayed, and placed a call to Peter Kirby. But he too declined.

"Could we call a man from the seminary?" one of the elders queried. It was already springtime, and the assignment of new pastors was well underway. Were we already too late? Dustin Kunkel told me that his brother Kris, a seminarian, had two friends who were finished with their studies but still not assigned. One of them, Matt Henry, had not yet decided whether he wanted to be a sole pastor or on a team and had missed the interview process. With permission from the seminary's placement office, we interviewed him and shared our findings with the congregation. Late that spring, we extended him the call. Much to our relief, he accepted.

I had been in a multiple pastoral staff twice before. I worked for nine years with Win Schroeder in Vancouver and four years with Steve Eaton in Sequim. In each case, though of differing ages, we teammates were cut from the same cloth – studious, serious, and traditional in our approach to shepherding the flock. The teaming of Pastor Matt with me was a marriage of both different generations and different approaches to ministry. I laughed to discover that he liked Michael Jackson's music and Bart Simpson's humor. He could have made fun of my early appreciation for the Beach Boys and The Three Stooges. As in a marriage, there came a gradual unfolding of more basic differences.

We were a study in contrasts in our personalities and ministry styles. My seriousness contrasted with his appetite for fun. My meticulous soul care with his big picture idealism. Less than a year into our time together, we had an unexpected clash over work schedules. My day off was Saturday, but I did not adhere to it faithfully. Most Saturdays I would come in to practice my sermon and make a last check on preparations for Sunday worship. Sometimes I did more. One particular Saturday he discovered me giving private instruction to someone in the library – someone who preferred a Saturday meeting. Later that morning, when he found me free at last, he rebuked me.

"I'm angry with you!"

"What about?"

"Your day off is Saturday. WHAT are you doing HERE? You should be at home!"

I was taken aback. It was the first time a fellow pastor had laid into me so directly. A part of me felt guilty for my workaholic fudging. A part of me felt angry that this young pup of a pastor had scolded me, a hard-working veteran. The next Monday we met under calmer conditions. I agreed to honor the commitment. He agreed to be more respectful in addressing issues.

Our differences went deeper. I felt that most pastors would be more effective (and that their churches would grow) if only they worked harder, especially at their visitation of members. Matt was convinced that there needed to be a paradigm shift in the church's approach to ministry. He often cited a book entitled *The Present Future* by Reggie McNeal and urged Trinity's people to buy it and read it. In one memorable sermon he spoke in urgent terms against the word 'member' as indicative of a club mentality in the church. I sat up straight, for that word had always been a good word, even a biblical one to me, reflecting Paul's description of believers as organs (members!) in the body of Christ. In a note I told Matt: "It's like spending my whole life building a house, and then finding someone has put a 'Condemned' sign on the front door!" It led to still more talk about our understanding of the church and its mission.

We were so different! How could we work together harmoniously? We reviewed our designated assignments. He was called to be our outreach pastor. We agreed that my focus would be discipleship and soul care, while he would focus on the interface between the church and the community. We composed a joint ministry statement to help our leaders and parishioners understand our roles. As in a marriage, we benefited from hearing the emphasis the other brought. Matt's efforts led to 'JC in OC' (Jesus Christ in Oregon City), a special effort in Advent to touch the lives of people in the community. When a church construction project was on the horizon, he urged us to take our Vacation Bible School outside our four walls into Hillendale Park. Since he and Sally had three foster daughters, he arranged for a foster children's Christmas party at the church. At each new juncture, I felt tingles of discomfort as I tried to see new possibilities in places and programs I had never considered. I was an old dog trying to learn new tricks.

The music team also underwent changes. Our trio of organists was reduced by one when Janet Moeller took a call to a teaching position in Hong Kong. Irene Rubin remained as principal organist, and Earlene Wagner eventually took the reins of the choir and played most Wednesdays in Advent and Lent.

In 2005, Irene experienced some heart trouble necessitating surgery. I visited her and husband Carl in the hospital the night before her operation. Earlene would take good care of things, I assured her. She spoke with a calm smile about God's hand on her life and her trust in Him. "You know how some people may ask, WHY ME? Well, I don't," she told me. "I really mean it. I know my life is in God's hands, and I don't worry about it."

The surgery went well and for a couple of days she was recovering on schedule. Her daughter Ann and I even went in to the cardiac intensive care unit and sang her one of her favorite hymns, 'Holy, Holy, Holy.' Then came unforeseen trouble, and her condition worsened. Pastor Matt hurried to visit the waiting family and heard with them the frightful news that Irene had died. All of us were deeply shaken by her unexpected death. At her funeral I preached that she was "singing heaven's song now."

But the rest of us had still to do our earthly practicing. Of our three organists, only Earlene was left, and she now took on the whole task – the planning, the playing, the choir rehearsals, the inclusion of soloists. She did all of this while making a regular commute of nearly 20 miles each way for each event. She was promoted to Minister of Music and in that role coordinated the congregation's vocal and instrumental music. Sue, meanwhile, had continued with her children's choir ministry, and Ann Clack took upon herself the ministry of the praise team, which sang for our blended service. With all these willing helpers, the music ministry remained vital.

In 2002 Pastor Rick Warren, a dynamic evangelical pastor in California, launched a program of church renewal and outreach called 'Forty Days of

Purpose.' I was not in the habit of taking on such programs, partly because I was busy enough already and partly because I tended to view programs that originated in the Baptist wing of the church with some old-fashioned German Lutheran suspicion. But Matt and Dustin saw possibilities for outreach in it, and they brought it to the staff meetings and then to the church council for discussion during our Year of Renewal.

By late 2004, the congregation agreed to come aboard. We set about planning, and by Lenten season of 2005 we were ready to launch. The forty days of purpose would fit nicely into our six-week Lenten observance. The response was more than I anticipated. People bought Warren's book and signed up for the proposed small groups in such numbers that we finally had 33 separate groups involving 300 people, including 30-40 non-members. Sue and I hosted a group in our home and enjoyed the fellowship we shared. A closing service at Oregon City High School's new auditorium brought nearly 400 people together. At the same time we were enjoying a wondrous influx of new faces. Our new member Sunday that year brought 45 new communicants. For the first time in more than 30 years of ministry, I witnessed significant growth in a church that I was serving.

The next staff change, though we did not know it, would mark the end of that boom time and the beginning of an increasingly unstable period in the congregation's life and my own ministry. It began with the announcement by Dustin Kunkel not long after our forty days of purpose had concluded that he wanted to seek an advanced degree. Having been a camp counselor for a time earlier in his career, he had his eye on a degree in outdoor ministry. Where would he get it? At the University of Edinburgh... in Scotland!

In spite of my urgings that he slow down and consider how short a time he had been with us, he finally decided to resign his position in order to move his family to Edinburgh. It felt to me as if the bottom had suddenly dropped out. The burgeoning youth ministry was rudderless again. How would we replace his energy?

The congregation, feeling anxious, directed that we initiate the call process to replace Dustin as soon as possible. Once again we solicited a call list from the district. The list that came back to us was minimal. There were not so many DCEs available as there were pastors. And the man who seemed most qualified and most willing to come, John Zimmermann from Oklahoma, had just experienced a bankruptcy! Nevertheless, the congregation extended a call to him. It seemed, a few of us reflected later, a hasty decision, but when he communicated his acceptance, people were glad we had filled the vacancy so quickly.

John and Donna were in their forties, with two adolescent daughters. They had nearly twenty years of parish experience, and they were eager to begin. But John stumbled out of the gate. On his very first youth trip to Eastern Washington, there was conflict with the youth counselors, and one called me to complain. I tried to defend him, explaining that he and family were exhausted from their move and that he had agreed to go at the last minute with no preparation. "Cut him some slack," I urged. Inevitably, there were comparisons with Dustin. John would have to begin as I did, with a shadow on his wall.

Our new youth worker had made a very bad first impression with our youth and their parents. Some were already saying that we had made a mistake in calling him. "What have we gotten ourselves into?" I wondered privately.

SABBATICAL JOURNEYS

As if in preparation for the troubled times coming, Sue and I took a four-month sabbatical leave from our work at Trinity in the summer of 2006. Those months strengthened our marriage and renewed our spiritual lives. It was a break we sorely needed.

We both held on to a childhood dream of making a mission trip to some faraway destination. Sue's desire began with an answered prayer for a missing ring when she was a young girl. "If you help me find that ring, God, I promise I will be a missionary!" She later found the ring in a place she had already looked in vain. But she had not become a missionary, and the unfulfilled promise troubled her. My own adolescent dream of being a missionary to the South Seas was shelved in favor of a stateside ministry.

Now and then our hearts were pricked again. At a women's gathering at Seaside, Oregon, I heard a mission speaker named Gary Thies, the single most enthusiastic mission advocate I'd ever met. "Go on a mission!" he urged. At another gathering it was Pastor Clem Pera, urging pastors to take a sabbatical away from their parish work. "Why don't you go, Mike?" he asked me. I used all my customary workaholic's excuses to decline, but back home I began to ponder the possibilities, especially when another pastor described the blessings he experienced on a sabbatical leave.

I called Clem back to ask questions. "It's a biblical idea," he said. "It's often done in one's seventh year, and there are companies that give pastors grants to fund the experience. You've been a pastor a long time. I think you're due." I learned that both Eli Lilly and the Louisville Institute supplied such grants. Pastor Vic Hippe, my vicarage predecessor in Vancouver, offered to e-mail me the successful proposal he had submitted as a model. Sue and I decided to make a go of it.

Late in the year 2005 we assembled a tentative plan for a four-month sabbatical leave. I had just finished reading *The Cloister Walk*, a fascinating book by Kathleen Norris in which she described her experience of living at a Benedictine monastery in Collegeville, Minnesota. Why not begin, Sue suggested, with a spiritual retreat to such a place? Of course, we would want to take a short-term mission trip too, but where? I placed a call to Gary Thies in Iowa.

"Gary, do you have some places to recommend for a short-term mission trip?"

"Do I ever!" he exuded. "Kyrgyzstan. It's the best thing the Missouri Synod has going."

"Where in the world is Kyrgyzstan?"

"North of India. It's a former Soviet republic. We have two missionaries there starting house churches. That's where you ought to go!" There was nothing uncertain about Gary Thies. His enthusiasm stoked the fire already kindled in me. It was to be Kyrgyzstan.

Sue and I were excited. I shared our dream and a possible time frame with the church council, and they responded with an enthusiasm that surprised me. "Go for it," they urged. I selected three congregation members who knew me well to help make plans. At year's end I submitted a grant proposal to the Louisville Institute and spent a couple of anxious weeks waiting for a response. Then came the letter with news that I had been awarded a $15,000 grant. "Praise the Lord!" I shouted to my office staff. Later I learned with astonishment that there had been only 61 awards out of 295 applicants. God's grace again.

THE MONASTERY

We arrived in Indiana for a visit to our mothers, having left our home and our parish responsibilities behind. Pastor Matt was getting his first taste of solo ministry while I got a taste of retirement. I brought along a new Dell laptop computer purchased with my grant money and began journaling the 120 days. The first stop was in Indiana to see our mothers. Now widowed and in their eighties, both were living life in slow motion. Sue's mother was pitiably bent with osteoporosis. My own mother was fitted with a brace after suffering a compression fracture in her back in a fall. Weak in body but strong in faith, they radiated to us the sweetness of their lifelong love for the Lord. We had lived away from them for our whole ministry. How much longer would we have them?

Like wide-eyed freshmen, we drove into Collegeville two days later. St. John's Abbey occupied the southwest corner of the campus of St. John's University. The school was set among forest and fields beside a lovely blue lake. Guestmaster Roger Kasprick welcomed us and placed us in the care of a younger monk named Cyril Gorman who would be our personal guide to the life of the monastery. We were taken to a guestroom which was to serve as our home for the next two weeks. Guests of any religious faith or none at all were welcomed by the monks, though guests stayed in separate quarters and ate at a separate refectory. "Receive each guest," Benedict instructed, "as Christ Himself."

The Benedictines followed the rule of St. Benedict (born in 480 AD). As with other monastic communities, they took vows of celibacy and made a commitment to their common life under the rule of their abbot. The rhythm of the community was set to the metronome of the Daily Office, a sequence of worship times that punctuated each day. The eight traditional hours

(Matins, Lauds, Prime, Terce, Sext, None, Vespers, Compline) shrunk to five over time. At St. John's Morning Prayer at 7 a.m. preceded breakfast. There followed Noontime Prayer, the afternoon Eucharist at 5 p.m., Evening Prayer at 7 p.m., and Compline at 9 p.m. "To pray is to work," said Benedict.

Benedict's wisdom and guidance was everywhere. On one building we saw the letters IOGD. In answer to our inquiry, Cyril explained that it was an abbreviation of the motto of the Benedictines: *In Omnibus Glorificetur Deus* ('That God be glorified in all things'). We learned that there were 140 men in the community from very diverse backgrounds. They were priests, plumbers, teachers, bakers, and even a circus ringmaster! They were also an aging community. At least 30 were confined to the infirmary.

There were surprises around every corner. The monks, we found, did not simply pray. Each had some assigned work, and some went off campus to teach or follow other occupations, while others busied themselves on the St. John's campus working in the boiler room, the greenhouse, or the pottery shop. One, to my delight, was the curator of the monastery's extensive stamp collection. Cyril himself was a marathon runner who wedged his running in between other responsibilities. Blessed with a keen wit and a playful sense of humor, he pointed out a macabre metal statue in the nearby gardens. "There's scary Mary!" he whispered with a wicked grin.

We made a commitment to join the monks in their daily worship routine. In so doing, we were ushered into a life lived at a slower pace, one which accentuated listening more than speaking. The worship took place in the enormous college chapel. About 70 of the monks were there at any given time, along with a scattering of guests like us. We sat behind the altar in a semi-circle of wooden benches. Unlike the noisy gatherings at our home church, the setting here was sheer quietness. No ushers with bulletins. No buzz of conversation. No organ prelude. Instead the monks came as if on tiptoe, bowing slightly before they sat to pray and prepare. Psalm-books and other worship aids were spread before us. Always, at some signal unseen by us, the monks suddenly rose as one and began their worship. They used psalms and hymns, for the most part. There was a chapter from Revelation each morning and from the Acts of the Apostles each evening.

Since we wanted not merely a vacation but a spiritual retreat, Sue and I decided to take advantage of a service called spiritual direction. Our three sessions took place with Father Simeon Thole, a soft-spoken older monk. Instead of the sage advice we anticipated, Simeon told us that his role was simply to help us listen carefully to God. The chief questions to answer were, "What is God telling me? What is God trying to do with my life?" He could not answer that, of course. That was our task. In addition, he introduced us to the practice of *Lectio Divina* ('divine reading'), a dramatically different way to hear the Scriptures and apply them to one's life.

It proved to be a challenge for us. We were used to racing through our readings and then running off to the next task. One must, he told us, slow down. He outlined the steps:

QUIET yourself – Let the swirling mind settle. Prepare to listen.

READ expectantly – "What is God saying to me here, now?"
You may have to read more slowly, or re-read sections. When you hear something addressed to you, stop reading and write it down.

MEDITATE – Ponder what the words say, how it connects with your life experience (this too was written).

PRAY- specifically about these matters.

ENJOY – the presence of God!

This was to be undertaken with some selected part of Scripture. Sue chose Philippians for her study, while I chose Colossians. Quiet hours of each day were set aside for this discipline, which reminded me of the careful, conscious chewing of each bite of food. Among other things, God was telling me that I had been living at too fast a pace, especially in my spiritual life. "Slow down and listen," was His word to me.

There were other meaningful meetings in those two weeks. Roger Kasprick agreed to entertain my list of questions about Catholic teaching and practice. "Give me your list ahead of time," he requested, "so I can think about what to say." Abbot John Klassen was surprisingly transparent when I interviewed him about life at the monastery. His blunt answer to my inquiry, "What's the biggest problem you face here?" was "Handling the clergy sex abuse crisis. We're not insulated from that!" Richard Bresnahan ran the pottery shop and supervised a stable of apprentices. He provided us with a fascinating, though condensed, introduction to pottery-making. Most surprising was to learn that Kathleen Norris, whose book had made us aware of the abbey, was herself on campus. We met her in the refectory and again in the library and found her to be a thoughtful, somewhat reserved conversationalist. For her, writing was a truer voice than speaking.

We returned home feeling that our spirits had caught up with our bodies. Our pace had slowed. We had made a commitment to renew our daily time together, starting with a mutual reading of the Psalms. Only a few weeks into our sabbatical, we had already found a wider, deeper world. Our mission to Kyrgyzstan in the month following would transport us halfway around the world and all the way back to the Book of Acts.

MISSION TO KYRGYZSTAN

The flight to Kyrgyzstan consumed an entire day. The first leg, Portland to Chicago, was a misery, seated as we were at the very back of a jam-packed aircraft. The second leg to London in the first class section of a British Airways jumbo jet was pure luxury, an adjustment by the agent in Chicago when he heard about our discomfort on the first leg. There would be another stop in Yarevan, Armenia, before the final leg that deposited us at Manas Airport in Bishkek, Kyrgyzstan. The tickets for the trip cost $2200 each. I thanked God for the grant money.

We had prepared diligently. Passports were acquired, along with vaccinations for diseases we might encounter. Steve Cameron helped me learn the Cyrillic alphabet and some simple Russian words. The church's mission department sent us a survival kit of information to read about our destination. Kyrgyzstan, said the brochures, was a country about the size of South Dakota. The former Soviet republic, now independent, was home to more than five million people, an ethnic mix of Mongols and Russians. Though blessed with spectacular, mountainous scenery, Kyrgyzstan was the poorest country in central Asia. The people were 70% Sunni Muslim and 20% Russian Orthodox, with scattered other smaller groups. Despite our preparation, both of us felt anxiety about being so far from home in an alien land where most neither spoke English nor shared our faith.

Our church had begun mission work there just a few years earlier. Two missionary couples – Tim and Rita Nickel and Bob and Sue Pfeil – came to the country relatively late in their pastoral careers to take on the daunting task of planting a Lutheran mission in the country. They learned Russian and agreed to devote ten years to the task. I read Tim's e-mails with astonishment at the strides already made. There were nearly 1000 baptized believers in forty house churches and the beginning of a fledgling seminary. There were Bibles and catechisms in Russian. There was local opposition, too, and courage abundant in both the missionaries and the people.

I wrote Tim to ask what he wanted us to do while there. "Probably some teaching in the house churches," he replied. Hoping to be well prepared, I pushed for more details, but Tim had responded in words I rarely heard Lutherans use: "The Holy Spirit will take care of that." Waiting at Heathrow Airport in London, we came face to face with Tim and Rita, who were themselves returning to the country from furlough. We took an immediate liking to these energetic and warm-spirited people.

Our stay in Kyrgyzstan was divided into three parts. The first week at the mission quarters in the capital city of Bishkek was designed to immerse us in the culture, familiarize us with the mission staff and the work to be done, and introduce us to our translator. The next sixteen days would be spent visiting and teaching in four house churches in the eastern part of the country. The final week back in Bishkek was for de-briefing and reflection.

The need for an initial week of adjustment soon became apparent. On the ride from the airport into Bishkek, we saw trees with trunks painted white ("The Russians did that"), cows wandering in the roadway, and mosques that appeared to be made of enormous sheets of tinfoil. Physically, we felt like zombies with eleven time zones of jet lag to overcome. Within a day, as travelers often do, we both became sick. Meanwhile, our missionary hosts gave us a crash course about Kyrgyz money (40 soms to a dollar) and food like shashlik, kumyz (fermented mare's milk that smelled faintly of gasoline) and fried bread. We visited the money changer's shop to get a supply of local currency and then the grocery to purchase supplies for our week-long stay at the missionary apartment on the fourth floor of an apartment building.

Sue Pfeil took us for a visit to a nearby orphanage where the missionary staff led Bible study. On the way we picked up our translator, a tall young Russian woman named Irina Konkina. She and husband Vasily, a ruggedly handsome man who had served in the Russian army, took us on a sight-seeing tour the next day. We heard about recent political violence as they showed us the government buildings, saw a pair of newlyweds having photos taken in a park, and visited a Muslim cemetery. While Vasily drove, Irina fielded our questions and asked a few of her own. She was a knowledgeable woman with an almost child-like curiosity about us.

The mission in the country was two-pronged: to share the Gospel of Jesus in teaching and worship in a house church setting, and to minister to crying physical needs through a medical van that provided basic health care and an eyeglass clinic. The spiritual darkness of the people was evident in a high rate of alcoholism, spousal abuse, adultery, and an astonishing number of abortions. In rural areas many of the women had experienced half a dozen abortions each. Part of our first week's orientation was a visit to the van, which was clean and well staffed. Several local women lined up for exams that day.

The following week we made the 250-mile drive to the eastern part of the country where we were to conduct our teaching mission. The scenery with its mountains and farms reminded us of the North Cascades Highway in central Washington. The farming, we noted, was very 'old tech,' with scythes, hay wagons, and herders on horseback. Historically, the Mongol people were horse-loving. Along the way we enjoyed seeing many round yert houses, fruit stands, and even a pair of donkeys at a bus stop.

Our home base was a pleasant guesthouse in Karakol where we slept and took our meals with Vasily and Irina. After leaving our things there, we made a ten-mile drive to the house church in Ak Suu where the small congregation gathered to meet us. We found 17 people waiting in the meeting room. We sat in front facing them to get acquainted while they displayed shy smiles. After Tim introduced himself and thanked them for hospitality, it was our turn to share about ourselves. The room warmed with gentle laughter. They asked questions ("How long have you been believers?" "Do you have children?"). Then they shared. We heard stories of deliverance and healing and persecution. Kenjibek described his deliverance from alcohol and wife beating. Nurisa, once an obstetrician, told of her revulsion with abortion, her conversion, and the hostility of once-friendly neighbors. Tim surprised me by announcing, "Pastor Mike will preach about baptism Sunday and will baptize any that need to be baptized."

Afterward Tim and Rita met with people individually for prayer – a common ministry practice after each gathering. A heavy-set woman named Rachat begged for prayer against the demons that came by night. "They pull at my arms and legs and I get no sleep," she said with tears. Tim, Rita, Irina, and Kenjibek surrounded her, laid hands on her and prayed simultaneously in three different languages. Sue and I watched, spellbound. It felt as if we had stepped into the Book of Acts. We convened in another room around a long table laden with special doughnut-like bread to be dipped in sugar, plates of spiced noodles, fresh cherries from trees along the road, and more.

Before departing, Tim instructed me, "You'll be visiting four different house churches over the next two weeks. Spend a couple of hours and teach whatever you can."

"Where do I start?" I asked.

"Start with the Ten Commandments and the Apostles' Creed. Keep it basic. Answer questions. Make sure and pray with anyone who asks. If anyone wants to be baptized, baptize him! Confirm those who are ready. God will give you the words."

I was thrown into the pool to sink or swim. Feeling overwhelmed, I prayed for wisdom and for the right words. The next day we commenced our round of visits. The team consisted of six people crammed into a very small car - Sue and I, Irina, Vasily, Nurisa, and a quiet man named Kuban who was converted to Christianity through Baptist missionaries. Each week for two weeks we made a teaching visit to all four house churches at the villages of Vasnyesenovka, Cholpon-ata, Shakty, and Sari-kamush. Tim's assurance proved true. The Holy Spirit took over and words simply came, measured out sentence-by-sentence as Irina translated. After introductions and brief story-sharing, I explained our use of the Bible and then explored the Ten Commandments with them one by one. Questions came often. If there was an abortion, who was more guilty – the doctor or the woman? Are we to eat the food offered at a Muslim funeral? Irina's knowledge of local customs often rescued me when I did not know how to answer.

At the end of each meeting, which normally lasted between two and three hours, there came a meal at a low table around which we sat cross-legged on the floor. The generosity of our impoverished hosts was humbling.

The women who came outnumbered men three to one. Our work was not without obstacles or opposition. In Cholpon-ata we had gathered on the beach at giant Lake Issyk-kul. In the midst of the lesson, I found that I was seated on an anthill and the ants had commenced biting! On two occasions women had to leave, summoned home by husbands who did not want them there.

A greater obstacle was the presence and power of Satan, manifested in some unhealthy interactions between the missionary couples and an unexpected attraction that I sensed between me and my translator as we worked together. One night I woke to find Sue tossing uneasily beside me, muttering under her breath in anger, for she could sense the attraction too. We talked, but the distress remained. She phoned Rita in tears, and Rita, well accustomed to the working of the Tempter, calmed and comforted her with a listening ear and a reminder that evil was evident in certain strongholds in our lives – areas where Satan saw a weakness and established a beachhead for further attack. All of us had them, she said, and she lifted us both in prayer.

Beset as we were with the struggle against that temptation, our work was blessed. As Tim had predicted, there came requests for baptism. At the Sunday service in Ak Suu, after preaching a sermon explaining baptism, I baptized a grandmother and a small child. In Vasnyesenovka later that week came the baptism of three children. Two days later ten adults and children presented themselves for baptism on the beach at Cholpon-ata. Sue and I took the group to a secluded spot, waded into thigh-deep water, and immersed them one by one while Irina translated and Vasily snapped photos. "Hallelujah!" someone on shore shouted in the midst of the baptisms. From then on, after each, we all chorused "Hallelujah," a joyful word understood by everyone, regardless of language.

The final Sunday at Ak Suu brought the confirmation of six adults who had willingly endured an hour-long examination. I felt a mixture of joy and anxiety for these new believers. I was anxious because there was so little time, so little instruction for them. When would the missionaries have a chance to return to teach and deepen their understanding? On the other hand, I was joyful at their hunger for God, their openness to the Gospel, their willingness to commit in the face of Muslim neighbors' disapproval, and their transparent affection expressed in many ways toward us. I wrote the people back home to pray for all these concerns.

On the flight home we were reflective. The journey to Kyrgyzstan was more than we had dared hope. We walked in missionary shoes, experienced missionaries' joys, and felt the power of the Enemy working against us. We watched the grace of God touch other lives and our own in a powerful way. How could we bring God's gracious touch to others back in Oregon?

Sue and I baptize a Kyrgyz woman in Lake Issyk-kul in July of 2006

MISSION FITS AND STARTS

Trinity was a mission-minded church with a long history of support for mission work. Steve Henderson, son-in-law of Pastor Ruthenbeck, lived in China and made periodic visits to Trinity to report on work being done there. Carl and Melody Knight, workers for Lutheran Bible Translators in Sierra Leone, also came on furlough to encourage support for translation work. Our people received them warmly and gave generously.

In the years before I arrived, Trinity decided to do more. The congregation planted a new mission church in the town of Canby, Oregon, about twelve miles south of Oregon City. The mission was named 'Church of the Master,' and it began strongly. Several families pledged their support and presence. New people were reached. Then a conflict surfaced between the mission planter and Pastor Halvorson. I asked several old-timers what the conflict was about, but their stories diverged and left unanswered questions. I didn't see a need for me to ferret out more details. It was clear that a bad taste was left in many mouths, not for missions generally, but certainly for any other new church plants we might make. I still wanted to start a mission, but I could see that there was plenty for me to do as I settled in. I tabled the idea until a more opportune time.

In my first year at Trinity the focus was on providing 'seeker services' for people who might not like traditional worship. Larry Deyoe advocated for these before he left. A group of lay people expressed a willingness to staff the endeavor. Pastor Paul Heinlein's guitar playing and informal manner seemed a perfect resource, so a Wednesday evening seeker service was launched. It lasted a year. Then a dwindling attendance forced us to give it up.

Interest remained. Had we done this on the wrong night? Two years later, with the Heinleins less involved, I asked that we try again. This time we offered worship on Sunday evenings. Head usher Gary Hoffman cheerfully helped with the weekly setup of chairs. Earlene Wagner and others rotated in to play the keyboard. We used contemporary songs. I delivered sermons standing free of the pulpit and employing a more folksy manner. All with the same result. There was a good initial response, mostly from members who had been away or worked Sunday mornings. But after nine months, we pulled the plug again. Later attempts on Saturday nights (dubbed 'Saturday Night Alive') met the same fate.

Our mission spirit had not been doused, however. A new mission outreach came thanks to the vision and hard work of Valerie Vanderford. She proposed taking groups on short-term missions, something the national church was encouraging many to do. Already in 2002 she began praying and planning for a two-week trip, and she gained a solid hearing. A group of thirteen people signed on, and Valerie met with them to organize and to inspire them with Bible study and prayer.

The first trip took place in the summer of 2003. The destination was the island of Helene off the coast of Honduras. The group endured muggy weather, the attacks of insects, and some sickness, but they soldiered on with a variety of projects – the construction of a school classroom, the hosting of a Vacation Bible School, visits for tutoring at a local school, outdoor games for kids and sharing and singing at worship. Our daughter Melanie, home for the summer from her teaching post in Las Vegas, went along. A slide show of the group's experiences brought smiles, questions, and the determination of others to be part of the next mission.

Trips were planned at two-year intervals. In 2005 there came a mission to Trinidad. A visitor from Trinidad named Pastor Bachew (a former Hindu who had come to Christ through a vacation Bible school) came to Trinity months ahead of time to share his story, whet our appetites and encourage us. This second group had fourteen including Pastor Matt and his wife Sally. Their report to us included stories of visits to a prison, schools, orphanages, and a home for developmentally-disabled adults. They described encounters with some of Trinidad's other religious groups – a visit to a Hindu temple with its prayer flags, the witnessing of a Hindu funeral, and the meeting of a Muslim imam at a mosque where the tour bus had stopped.

In each country our mission visitors met people who were kind, outgoing, and hungry for the Good News of Jesus. The special connection with Pastor Bachew later brought a visit from him and a steel pan band that played for us at Trinity. More trips followed – to Belize in 2007, then to Trinidad again in 2009. Dozens of Trinity's people had eyes opened and hearts encouraged by these mission journeys.

When Sue and I returned from Kyrgyzstan in late 2006, we too were newly inspired to do something more with missions stateside. Soon we saw that God had been moving in His mysterious way in other hearts to provide help with the hoped-for mission planting.

"Is there something in the water there at Trinity?" asked a district official after hearing that over the span of three years, five different men emerged expressing interest in pastoral ministry and/or mission work. The first was Mike Behnke, a single young man on our board of elders. I recruited him to assist me with confirmation instruction, and he proved a capable and responsible helper. He began to speak of interest in the pastoral ministry. Not wanting to leave the Portland area or his job at Southwest Airlines, he enrolled at Multnomah Bible School to begin study for the ministry. I served as his mentor and offered him opportunities to teach the new member class and assist in worship.

Tom Arnold had been a mostly inactive member of Trinity. He and his wife Amy called to ask if their two-year-old son Taylor could be baptized. "Let's talk about it," I said. That week I made an evening visit at their home. I used the opportunity to encourage a return to church and Amy's instruction in a new member class. Privately, Amy chafed at the request, but she agreed. God went to work in Tom's life in an unexpected way shortly thereafter, and I was surprised to learn that he was thinking of becoming a pastor. He told me a story most strange of how the idea had come to him while on a bicycle ride. In a very short time, he enrolled in the pre-ministerial program at Concordia University in Portland. Amy would be a pastor's wife!

The surprises kept coming. One morning, a young man strode into the office to meet Pastor Matt and me. It was Patrick Lovejoy, the son of one of our "missing" families. We had never laid eyes on him before that day. Patrick was back from going to school in Alaska. "I'm going to the seminary!" he announced. Matt and I were astonished. God, it appeared, had been working overtime. So Patrick also began his studies.

There was more. A man named Marty Bergstrom brought his five-year-old son to our church for a visit. Father and son were more than just casual visitors, it turned out. "Say the Apostles' Creed," he prompted the boy, who proceeded to recite it flawlessly. I was impressed. Marty, it turned out, was a product of Trinity's old mission in Canby. He liked the Lutheran Church and asked if he and family might attend. The family plunged in to our parish life with gusto. Marty and his wife Janeen and their two boys were musically gifted, friendly, and articulate. It was no surprise when, a few months later, they enrolled in my new member class and brought another couple, good friends of theirs, with them. Marty volunteered that he was interested in becoming a Lutheran pastor. Within a month of his joining Trinity, Marty began study with the district's Lay Assistant Program (LAP) to prepare for churchly service. Mike, Tom, Patrick, and Marty made four.

A fifth was Brad McInnes, a man who began attending Trinity with his wife Jennifer and children after a time away from church. He was an attentive student in the new member class, and later he too expressed a desire to study for the ministry. I recruited Brad to enroll in LAP with Marty. In the course of time, both Brad and Marty took a pre-entrance exam from Concordia Seminary in St. Louis, and both passed. Brad and Marty eventually completed their work in LAP and were licensed as deacons, which gave them authorization to do 'word and sacrament' ministry under my supervision. The position of licensed deacon had been created to meet a need for ministry in our large district, especially in Alaska, where there were many scattered small groups who needed pastoral care but could not afford a pastor. I gave each man opportunities to preach and to teach. Their availability proved helpful to Pastor Matt when I left on my four-month sabbatical.

While I was away on sabbatical, a new opportunity arose for Marty. Ken Schauer, a pastor who worked with the Alaska Mission Committee, called Marty to see if he might be interested in serving a small Tlingit village called Flint Creek. The Missouri Synod already conducted vacation Bible schools there each summer. A month later, Marty and Janeen made the long flight to Juneau and the short hop to Flint Creek for a visit. They were captivated and made hopeful plans of returning there to start a mission. But much needed to be done first. Marty and I learned of openings in the seminary's 'Distance Education Leading to Ordination' program (DELTO) that prepared men for service in just such situations. He could become a DELTO vicar under my supervision and would be able to serve at Flint Creek. In short order he began his distance learning course work. Both of us were excited at the prospect.

Then came a serious check to our plans. I learned of trouble in the Bergstroms' marriage that might derail our Alaska mission endeavor. Both Marty and Janeen admitted inappropriate interaction with another couple, but both assured us it was behind them. I took Marty for an urgent conference with former district president Erhard Bauer, a man I depended on for wise counsel. Marty was up front and sincerely repentant. Bauer counseled that we continue to talk about this and delay the Alaska start as a period of probation.

Brad, meanwhile, spoke with me about making a local house church plant. He read some of the literature I had read for my sabbatical and we gathered a church planting team to advise and support the venture. We decided to attempt a house church plant at our home, with Brad and Jennifer teaming up with Sue and me to host. We invited half a dozen people who were not connected with a church anywhere. We prayed and prepared for the gathering. But no one came. More invitations went out. Again, no one came. After another week, we admitted defeat. It was back to the drawing board with the church planting team.

By the fall of 2007, I judged that it was time to move forward with Marty's mission to Alaska. He continued to work at his studies. He and Janeen seemed to be in harmony. They had assisted willingly and capably with playing and singing for worship, and there had been improvement in his preaching. In October, he and I flew to St. Louis for an orientation weekend with the DELTO vicarage program. Marty would be commissioned as a vicar accountable to the seminary and be under my supervision.

The congregation agreed to sponsor the mission outreach in Flint Creek. Funding would come from a variety of sources and be administered through the Alaska Mission Committee. Agreements were negotiated with the Presbyterian Church for the use of their vacant church building and parsonage in Flint Creek. District President Schumacher told me, "You're in charge, Mike. The district will provide funds for you to go up there for some on-site visitation as needed." At year's end, we commissioned Marty and Janeen as our missionaries to Alaska and sent them off with prayer. Outside, there was a lovely Alaska-like snowfall.

The year 2008 brought encouraging news on all fronts. The Bergstroms had arrived safely in Flint Creek, a tiny village of 800 souls. The arrival was an occasion of rejoicing for the native Tlingit people, and the Bergstroms made a fine first impression. The church was prepared, a new sign went up outside announcing the 'Harbor of Faith Lutheran Church,' and an initial worship service drew fifty people. It was better than I had dared hope, the answer to many prayers. Janeen made connection with women in the village and offered a cake decorating class. The boys were making a good adjustment in school. Janeen even prepared an occasional newsletter with pictures. Within months there came seven baptisms, all done in the local pool. All of us back at Trinity rejoiced.

Brad McInnes made a new start too. At the urging of Earlene Wagner, we turned our attention to Wilsonville, the Portland suburb where she and Mark lived and for which she carried a burden. Aside from a couple of mega-churches in southwest Portland, which drew from the town, Wilsonville was under-churched. Earlene's own neighborhood, she told us, had many de-churched and un-churched people. The mission planting team gave its blessing to our re-direction of energies. The Wagners agreed to team up with the McInneses, and a beginning was made in May. This time people came, bringing children and a few friends too. Brad led worship. Earlene and Jennifer provided music and child care. Though attendance was irregular, lives were being touched. Brad rejoiced to report two baptisms in the fall. Two others were baptized the following year.

These missions were not without significant cost. The Missouri Synod offered grant assistance through its ABLAZE program, and I made application. I researched demographics on Flint Creek and Wilsonville, described the plan of outreach, and listed the expected financial needs. Because the Bergstroms were living on site at Flint Creek, their costs would comprise the lion's share of expenses. The application was sent, and there ensued a hopeful season of waiting for a grant we prayed might supply $25,000. The letter that came from ABLAZE surpassed even that high hope. We had been awarded a $50,000 grant that would come in stages. After each I was to supply a progress report. Several congregations called to add their support. It all proved doubly important when Marty reported in March, "Someone stole our heating oil right out of the storage tank."

Then came more troubling news. An e-mail from Janeen in late summer informed me that they were experiencing 'issues.' In autumn that year I flew to Alaska for an on-site visit to assess and offer support. When I arrived, all seemed fine. The Bergstroms welcomed me warmly and Marty gave me a tour of the village. A man from the village took Marty and me out on a boat for some crabbing and whale-watching. I preached at the Sunday service attended by two dozen people and heard good reports from them. All seemed well, but Marty confessed some lingering concerns about their relationship with that other couple back in Oregon. Janeen added that the loneliness of Alaska was a significant challenge to overcome. She missed her friends in the 'lower 48.' These were troubling vibes. I promised myself to keep in closer touch with Bergstroms.

Early in 2009 I received a desperate phone call from Janeen that the marriage was coming apart and that she felt so fearful of Marty she was thinking of leaving with the boys. A phone talk with Marty revealed that he had a vastly different assessment of the issues. But there was no doubt their marital ship was sinking. With a crush of parish responsibilities, including several impending deaths, I wrote the Bergstroms a quick letter of counsel and pleaded with President Schumacher for help. We agreed that I would fly north again as soon as I was able. "Stay put until I get there!" I urged Janeen. I informed the seminary of the trouble brewing. "I don't see how we can continue the mission if they are in such trouble," I confided to the seminary's vicarage coordinator.

But Janeen did not stay. Alleging that Marty had renewed the relationship with the other woman that we all thought had ended a year ago, she packed and took the children to stay with her mother in Seattle. The first week in March, I flew to Alaska once more. This time Pastors Todd Roeske and Corbie Cross from the Alaska Mission Committee rendezvoused with me in Juneau and made the short flight to Flint Creek. President Schumacher had deferred to me in making a decision about Marty and the mission, and I felt a dreadful weight on my shoulders. I did not see how it could go on, but the other two men and I did our best to listen long and hard to Marty and the people of the mission. Marty denied Janeen's allegation. The people of the mission, uncertain who was at fault, simply hoped their little church might continue.

The mission and our support for it had to end. On that the three of us visitors agreed. With a marriage in such trouble, the seminary's policy was to end the vicarage so that the couple could work on their relationship. I wrote a detailed report of our findings for President Schumacher. Back home, I was stunned to receive a phone call and then a visit from the 'other woman,' who confirmed the relationship and provided copies of damning e-mails from

Marty. Sick at heart, I phoned Marty that the mission was ending and he must return home to see if the marriage might be salvaged. He refused, cutting off communication. I wrote to the mission church explaining my decision. They petitioned President Schumacher that the district continue to support the mission, but he declined their request. Marty was determined to go on without congregational or district support.

I summarized the frightful news at a congregational meeting. "You're in a no-win situation," Pastor Paul Schmidt had warned me. "Doing what you have to do will be like changing your car's oil in a white suit. There's no way you can come out of this clean." He was right. Several of Marty's friends, angered at the decision to suspend him and unaware of the whole story, were openly critical of me. Unable to divulge details, I felt hamstrung. It was the darkest time in my pastoral ministry. I prayed desperate prayers for wisdom and for courage to do what was right.

God's sustaining grace came to me in several ways in the following months. Brad McInnes took the preaching load during that Lenten season and provided a listening ear as well. Then came news that Tom Arnold had received a vicarage assignment and Patrick Lovejoy was placed in his first parish in Port Angeles, Washington. Paul Schmidt continued to be a caring listener. There were even steps to reconcile with Marty's angry friends.

The mission in Flint Creek was ended. The mission in Wilsonville, after moving to new quarters and struggling increasingly, was finally abandoned too. But there were those baptisms and many touches of the grace of God. Brad McInnes learned much and grew much and had proved to be a blessing to me in my need. Tom and Patrick were well on their way in ministry. Mike Behnke, though not an ordained pastor, found his niche serving fellow airline employees and assisting at local churches when the company moved him. Our congregation continued to be mission-minded, and God's grace kept reaching out.

I took comfort then, and I take it now, from St. Paul's promise: *"You know that in the Lord, your labor is not in vain."* The cause, I am sure, is the right one. In such a cause, even a failure is not in vain. God uses it all.

FIGHTING AND FAINTING

Was Trinity a healthy church? That was a question asked frequently as the years passed. On one hand, there were signs of vitality everywhere one turned. The customary barometers – attendance and offerings – showed increases in the early years of my service. By the year 2004, attendance had risen from 280 to 340 people per week. Our new pictorial directory was crowded with smiling faces. The budget met expenses, and we managed extras like the purchase of a grand piano for the sanctuary and the raising of money for a young woman's medical expenses. A generous donor contributed $10,000 to start an endowment for the school. New melody chimes, and later two octaves of handbells were purchased for our newly-formed handbell choir. Worship services continued to be broadcast on local cable TV.

The schedule was full too, with a variety of classes and groups offered. Jews for Jesus presented *'Christ in the Passover'* twice during those years. We served our community, painting the cafeteria at Gaffney Lane School and supplying the Backpack Buddies program at Mount Pleasant School. Vacation Bible School at Hillendale Park brought 170 kids and parents. Sue and I led four marriage retreats at Pacific City to grateful reviews. A group of women labored mightily to produce beautiful banners replicating the stained glass windows at the old church, and they were finally finished, hung high in the narthex, and dedicated with all the pomp we could muster one Sunday morning.

Trinity was healthy, wasn't it?

But I was not so sure. I felt as if I were riding a spirited horse, holding on for dear life to keep from being bucked off, for I was aware, as most parishioners were not, of a variety of forces in the congregation tugging against one another. There continued some unhappy rumblings about worship, an issue that never seemed to go away. There were increasing criticisms of staff members – our secretary and DCE were the most frequent targets of these. In addition, now that we were well settled into our new building, we held increasingly strident discussions about what to build next. There surfaced financial worries. With the addition of a second pastor, we experienced the first of several budget deficits. The salaries for our three called workers totaled more than $200,000. People were more anxious about the budget at Trinity than anywhere else I'd served. Matt and I also continued to lock horns over Trinity's future course. Were all these things merely growing pains, or were they symptoms of dysfunction, precursors of more serious conflict?

They were growing pains, we hoped. In a series of sermons in 2003, I challenged the people to consider 'Twelve Pillars of a Healthy Church.' In an attempt to understand that growth and pilot the congregation safely through any potential rocks and shoals, the leaders agreed to measure our strengths and weaknesses using the tools available through *Natural Church Development*, an inventory developed by two German churchmen and used in at least 70 countries. The initial survey revealed that our lowest scoring element of ministry was 'empowering leadership' (whether the leaders of the church empower all the people to be an active part of the church's mission). In due course I asked my friend, Pastor Mark Bertermann, to come and help me be accountable for doing more delegating and training of others. By the time the next inventory was done in the year 2005, scores in every factor rose.

Still, old shadows from my early days lingered to haunt me. The comparison with Mark Halvorson persisted. I was criticized for lacking 'vision,' something he had plenty of. This came not from some habitual crank, but from chairman Don Nicola, normally a cheerful, supportive man. Now I felt Don measuring me against my new partner, Pastor Matt. Matt aspired to be a visionary leader, and he made a steady push for people in the congregation to read yet another book, *Winning on Purpose* by John Kaiser. This book was big on reorganizing the structures of the church and focused on the lead pastor as a 'visionary' person who could excite and inspire. Matt, trying to be helpful, told me that I was more a 'manager' than a visionary leader, and he suggested that it might be well to consider a reversal of positions and that he might be lead pastor. It was a most unsettling thought, for I had been called to the position of lead pastor, and I was not convinced that being 'visionary' as Kaiser described it was necessary for pastoring or even biblical at all. My old demon, pride, had taken a blow, and I struggled to make an appropriate response.

The other shadow was concern over my health. One morning, as I preached at the funeral service for Florence White, a sensation like a fountain of warm water rose through my body and I felt as if I might faint. I went silent, gripping the pulpit to stay upright. From her place in the congregation, Sue thought I had stopped for emphasis. The faintness passed, and I continued, but the experience shook me. This, along with occasional times of depression, made me quietly anxious about the state of my health.

The congregation's health was tested by a sequence of interlocking issues that grew more intense in the year 2004. That year we began Trinity in Action, a capital campaign to fund our facility expansion. It was generally agreed that we were outgrowing our initial structure. Originally, our hope had been to construct a new sanctuary, seating perhaps 450 people. Five or ten years after that we might add school rooms. But we had not counted on the growth of the school, which had added a kindergarten and grade one. The cost of a new sanctuary, too, was daunting. It might cost as much as $3 million, something well beyond our resources now that we had three full-time staff.

So we settled on a more modest addition. The current sanctuary would remain, but we planned to add another multi-purpose room of equal size for fellowship, along with some increased office space and a classroom or two. The building fund goal was $950,000, but the offering fell short, provoking considerable anxiety, along with some second-guessing of the plans. Some complained that the school had derailed their desired sanctuary.

The death of Joe and Arlene Donovan during my sabbatical was followed by the news that they had left the congregation a bequest of $370,000. Was this a solution to our financial dilemma? Instead of easing the burden, however, the money seemed to make things worse, for now many people with strong ideas of how the money should be used chimed in. Much of the emotion was connected with the school.

When the proposal came that we add still another school grade, tempers grew short. At a meeting with Don and Pastor Matt, I urged that we slow down and first do some further study, such as synod's 'Genesis Study,' which prepared congregations for school expansion. "You're pretty negative about the school, aren't you?" observed Don. "Not negative," I said, "but cautious. Shouldn't we plan before we leap?" At council meetings, there were gloomy predictions that this issue would divide the congregation, a prophecy that was fulfilled by open wrangling at subsequent voters' meetings. In addition, we now needed a principal for the school. DCE John Zimmermann volunteered to serve as interim until someone full-time could be called. But more staff would mean more expense. When Zimmermann requested extra salary to cover his additional duties, there was growing financial fear. Here and there complaints surfaced about his attitude and his work with the youth. Some people found him hard to approach. Those who had not liked him from the start and had wanted him removed began to say so again.

I asked Pastor Matt, Don, and elder chairman Brian Pierson to join me in seeking the district president's advice. He said, "If you are unhappy with job performance, hold performance evaluations and establish a paper trail to which you can later refer." This we undertook. Performance reviews were distributed for all the whole staff, both called and contracted. Matt and I received acceptable reviews, but John's reviews were marginal, with many overt criticisms expressed. Elder Pierson and I had the unpleasant task of sharing these with John and urging improvement. John tried hard to listen with an open mind, but he struggled to explain and to justify his performance. "We'll do this again after a while," I told him. "Meanwhile, there are some things for you to work on. I'll try to be helpful."

In 2007 the synod made available its new hymnal, *Lutheran Service Book*. Earlene and I went to an introductory workshop and later recommended that the congregation buy the book and employ it. When we proposed taking six months to familiarize ourselves with its content, a new round of complaining ensued. So strident were the voices of those who feared losing their contemporary service that we called a special meeting one Sunday morning to listen to the concerns. Some of the concerns turned into criticism of Earlene as music leader. She left the meeting in tears and later stepped away from her position as Music Minister. In the wake of all this I experienced a deepening depression.

It felt as if we were under spiritual assault. My recurring prayer over many months was for some of Solomon's wisdom.

The nation's precipitous recession in 2008 brought more trouble. Families unable to afford the school tuition began to pull their students. Within a month, eight students left our school, and its future was hanging in the balance. Budget deficits became the rule and there was talk about cutting salaries. We began to take another look at our building expansion to see if there was a more affordable plan. Don and I suggested getting another round of input from the congregation, and one couple accused us of hijacking the process to follow a personal agenda.

By the grace of God, a way was found through the impasse over the building, and just in time. At the very least, it looked as if we might spend $1.5 million for what was initially priced at $950,000. After our building committee resigned in frustration, Cary Martenson stood up at an evening voters' meeting and startled us with a cheery announcement: "I think there is a way we can do all the things we hoped for the original figure." He had consulted with his father-in-law, Leonard Sundberg, who had been the general contractor for the original move, and asked for thirty days to flesh in the plans. The congregation, as if in a dream, agreed. The boil of our cantankerous division was lanced, and work eventually commenced.

On the morning of my sixtieth birthday, April 20, 2007, the phone rang early. "Either that's my first birthday call or somebody died," I joked to Sue. It was my sister Natalie on the line. My smile died on my lips. "Mom died this morning..." My mother had collapsed suddenly in her apartment, Natalie told me. Maybe it was a heart attack, or some kind of hemorrhage. I wept, stunned at the news. Her birthday card to me lay still unopened on the bedside table. The small sixtieth birthday celebration at church, along with the table of pictures Sue had arranged to honor me, felt out of place. I mourned through that next Sunday morning and for a long time thereafter.

At about the same time my fainting recurred, this time in more dramatic fashion. Again I was preaching at a funeral. Beth Golston's husband Mike died suddenly and unexpectedly after a short illness. Though he was not a member, and had not even been baptized, I agreed to do the funeral because of an 'amazing grace' moment. Mike's son, Mitch, had made a visit to his father and shared his concern for Mike's spiritual life. Mike was open to Mitch's witness and prayed to receive Jesus as his Savior. Death came too soon for a baptism. As with Freddie Hagedorn, I alluded to the thief on the cross, who found a 'grace-full' ending that day with Jesus. I shared the story from the pulpit. I read John 3:16, and then made my own very 'un-graceful' ending. There came that familiar warm rush of faintness. I swayed for a moment and fell forward, taking the wooden pulpit down with me and falling heavily on it as 200 people gasped together. Some, I am sure, thought they were seeing another death before their eyes.

But it was not so. In a dreamy haze, I felt myself floating down to the floor. I felt no pain. I heard, as if far away, the gasp of the congregation. I stared dumbly at the funeral bouquets I had knocked over. *What am I doing down here?* Seconds later, when I emerged into full wakefulness again, there were people rushing to my side. Mitch Golston himself had come up. Pastor Matt made his way down from the AV booth. "I'm OK now," I told them, getting to my feet to resume the service. "Oh no you're not!" Matt said with conviction, and others gently restrained me, then led me to the office. A team of paramedics was on the way. Matt finished the service while they asked me a battery of questions and took my pulse and blood pressure. Daughter Melanie arrived and drove me to the emergency room at Willamette Falls Hospital.

The fainting sent ripples through the congregation and through me. It was a signal that could not be ignored. Something would have to change.

DECISION TO DOWNSIZE

The operative word in many businesses around the country in 2008 was 'downsize.' Workers were laid off or had hours reduced. The steep drop in the stock market made retirees anxious about their investments. The impact on Trinity and its school were evident in declining offerings and enrollment. The continued conflicts and uncertainty in our direction took a toll on attendance, which dipped below 300 per week. Lower attendance brought reduced offerings. Budgetary pressures mounted.

Trinity's school was on everyone's mind. A new arrival named Kara Kaufman, a trained teacher, offered to take the administrative helm of the school for a much-reduced wage. She brought a steady hand and new ideas. The Genesis study, now complete, was presented to the congregation by DCE John Zimmermann. Along with it came the recommendation of the study team that our school expand to grade six. In normal times, the study might have been a motivator for us to look ahead. In the throes of the recession we were weathering, it felt like an impossible mission. In addition, several of our council members complained that the business plan that accompanied the recommendation was altogether inadequate.

Another request by John for a financial bonus provoked further upset. Another phone call from Don Nicola wondering why I had not given John 'the axe' left my stomach in a knot. It had begun to sound like Don and his family might leave. John was not unaware of the feelings that swirled around the congregation. During my weekly meeting with John, I asked him to consider making his name available to the district for a call elsewhere. He agreed to do that.

Meanwhile, I pondered the possibility of my own 'downsizing' to a smaller, less stressful assignment. I spoke privately with my personal mentor, former Northwest District President Erhard Bauer, and with Paul Schmidt. What if I were to take an early retirement and serve a little church that couldn't afford a pastor? They listened and shared good common sense questions. It was one thing to daydream a new scenario, but another to request it. I had an aversion to requesting a move. God knew my situation, didn't He? Let Him move me if He chose. During my sabbatical I had read *Under the Unpredictable Plant* by Eugene Peterson, who urged pastors to stay put rather than trying to escape uncomfortable assignments. So I stood pat.

Late in the year Pastor Matt stopped in to my office. "I have a call from a congregation in Lacey, Washington," he shared. He would pray and seek counsel, of course, but I knew that he would accept. I would not blame him for going. We were two different animals under the yoke together, still pulling different directions. He needed to be free. But where would that leave me? Others were wondering as well. "If he goes," asked Dan and Terina Trappe, a couple I had married and whose children I had baptized, "what will you do?"

In early December, Matt made the decision to accept the call and announced it during a sermon. He appeared energized, eager to make the change. Many listeners were surprised, some shocked. Matt had a loyal following. A phone call from one council member informed me, "When Matt leaves, some other people are set to go too." Disturbed, I wrote in my journal: "Very distressing. Pray hard!"

Just then, winter weather brought things to a standstill. A storm dumped four inches of snow on us, and then a thick layer of ice. Then ten more inches of snow! Along with all the other churches in the Portland metro area, we were forced to cancel Sunday worship, then the children's program and all planned Christmas services, something no one could remember happening before.

During those dark and icy days, I met with several of the officers to begin addressing the question of staffing. Matt's imminent departure, I suggested, was a necessary time to take another look at our staffing. I summarized the criticisms of John that had surfaced over the past two years. I held up options: a) call another pastor and replace Matt, putting us back at three called workers, b) reduce in force to two and stand pat with a pastor and DCE, or c) reduce in force to two and replace the DCE with a second pastor. The elders, after some discussion, reached a consensus that the third option was best for the congregation in the long run.

The new year 2009 began with Matt's departure. A large, emotional sendoff complete with a video tribute, a 'roast' from a friend, and a gift from the congregation made for a full program after church. Afterward, John appeared very glum and asked what was happening with staff. "We'll meet about that soon," I told him.

With Matt's departure, I was once again the sole pastor. An already full schedule became a test of endurance. In the month of January alone, even as things were unraveling in our Alaska mission and the congregation was trying to reach a decision about the facility expansion, there came a blitz of meetings and e-mails about the elders' proposal to downsize the staff, a funeral for Clara Wagner, private instruction for a man with emotional illness, emergency counseling with yet another troubled marriage, new member orientation for four families, a conference with an upset couple to 'put out a fire,' and multiple visits to two cancer patients in swift decline.

One of those patients was four-year-old Chelsea Hicks, a tiny blond sprite of a girl who had spent countless weeks shuttling between her home and Doernbecher Hospital. Her parents, with two other children to watch and jobs to manage, were exhausted, but they held to a dogged hope that she might go into remission. It was not to be. Late one night in February came their phone call, "Chelsea's failing." I drove in the pre-dawn darkness to their home and kept vigil with a dozen or more others as her mother Alison held and rocked her. Chelsea died two hours later. Her funeral the following weekend was the largest I had ever conducted. More than 400 people jammed the sanctuary and spilled into the narthex. Sue sang our hope:

Jesus, I Heard You Had a Big House
Where I could have a room of my own...

My own health continued uncertain. The fainting spells, though less intense, had begun to occur more often. In the spring of the year came something new – a kidney stone attack with pain so intense that it doubled me over while riding to the ER and reduced my prayers to the simplest of utterances: "Help me, Lord!" The stone passed. The concerns did not. The elders wanted to know about my health. I composed a report to them detailing my work hours and a breakdown of responsibility areas. I told them honestly about the faint spells and the times of depression. I outlined steps that would keep me healthier, including reduced hours and increased reliance on them as a helping board. It reinforced their desire to replace the DCE with a second pastor "before you kill yourself."

The staffing question had to be addressed and resolved one way or the other. The Zimmermann family lived in uncertainty about their future, and John's meetings with me were punctuated with emotional outbursts. There seemed to be no congregations calling DCEs, and John doubted he'd be able to move anywhere. I could feel John's fear. Both of us were wondering what our futures held. Again I consulted with Erhard Bauer. Should I stay or go? Should I retire early? He floated the idea of calling a retired pastor to come and help me transition into retirement in a year or two.

The proposal the elders had originally made to the council – that we have a reduction in force and eliminate the DCE position – was approved by that group. It came before the congregation at a special voters' assembly in early May. More than 150 people attended, and passions ran high. There seemed general agreement that we could not afford to return to three full-time called workers. Many expressed concern that my work load was unbearable and that my health reflected it. More than one of the elders rose to make that point. Replacing the DCE with a second pastor was, for them, a regrettable but necessary step. Others defended the current alignment and expressed fear of what yet another change would do to our youth ministry. There was an outpouring of sympathy for the Zimmermann family. John would have a hard time finding another position, they said. "We can't have them out on the street!" In the end, their voices prevailed, and by an 87-55 vote, the proposal was declined. John would stay, and I would get no immediate help. Sue left the meeting in distress, anxious about the continued stress on my health. In the weeks that followed, I reluctantly concluded that I must seek a call. My personal decision to downsize had been made.

I sat with Paul Schmidt as I had done earlier with Erhard Bauer. "I'm caught between two impulses," I explained to him. "On one hand, I feel increasingly that I need to slow down. The burdens are too heavy. I'd like to go to a smaller congregation. On the other hand, I feel guilty about seeking to move. Doesn't God know what I need?"

Paul, always a patient listener, pondered what I had told him. "What would be wrong," he asked, "with writing a letter to some district presidents and telling them your situation? You're still leaving it in God's hands to answer the request. And even if you were to get a call, you could still pray over it and see if this is what God wants."

I accepted his advice. Sue and I discussed the matter further and prayed over it frequently. If we were to move, we agreed, we would like to be closer to our relatives in Indiana, and particularly Sue's mother, the only one of our parents still living. We'd also hoped to be closer to our six grandchildren, all currently in Kansas City. In early summer I addressed a letter to the presidents of five Midwestern districts – Indiana, Central and Southern Illinois, Missouri, and Mid-South. I shared my situation and asked if they had any positions for an older pastor who wanted to downsize.

I would not resign my position, nor take further steps. I was content to leave it there in God's hands.

GRACE NOTES

The pastoral work went on. Even during those tumultuous months, God added His grace notes. The hard work of Kara Kaufman and the school staff paid off at last with the notice that our school was finally accredited. That would be a feather in our cap as we publicized the school to families.

One of the more urgent visits I made in those days was to John Paullin, the father of one of our members. John was in poor health, with a heart that threatened to quit at any time. We sat in the sun, listening to a neighbor's tractor plowing long furrows, and we spoke of time and grace. Not much time left for him, I observed, but God had plenty of grace. "I think it's time for me to be baptized," he responded. He took the step and on a Sunday morning soon thereafter, he was baptized, to his daughter's delight. At age 85, John was the oldest person I ever baptized.

Early that summer construction commenced on the long-debated addition. It was a relief to have the wrangling past and the workers pouring concrete and raising beams. The large building in back would be a combination gymnasium and fellowship hall, with several sizable rooms for our youth and quilters and adult classes. In front our offices space would double. An outdoor play area would serve our school children. I was amazed at how God provided everything we needed, in spite of the economy. The finished product was larger than we had pictured and lovely with its new paint job. A naming contest was held, and the new room was dubbed 'The JADE Room,' a kind of acronym in tribute to Joe and Arlene Donovan (J. A. D.), whose bequest had helped make it possible.

But the happiest event in the year was the wedding of our daughter Melanie. She had moved back in with us a few years earlier after six demanding years teaching at a Lutheran high school in Las Vegas. For years she prayed for a husband, made search on E-Harmony, and was courted by more than one suitor, but, like Adam in Genesis, she found 'no suitable helper.'

Early on she looked admiringly on Gary Hoffman, our handsome and hard-working head usher, but dismissed the idea of dating him because Gary was my age. Gary, it turned out, noticed her too, but declined to ask her out for the same reason. At last he invited her to join him in a 'Walk for Life' event in honor of little Chelsea Hicks, and the courtship began in earnest. I respected Gary as a man of faith who loved children, and I enjoyed his company on our annual fishing trips to Lake Simtustus in central Oregon. Things progressed quickly, and Gary finally asked our permission to marry our daughter.

The family gathers for Melanie and Gary's wedding in June 2009 (front row – grandchildren Ryan, Eric, John, Brenna, Katie, and Emily, daughter Christa and husband Jeff Zellar; back row – brother Jeffrey Kasting, me, Sue, Melanie, Gary, Caroline and Peter)

They were married in June, and our whole nuclear family gathered. Christa, Jeff, and the children flew in from Kansas City, and Christa was her enthusiastic matron of honor. Peter and Caroline came from San Jose, and Peter stood up to read the Scripture lesson. I preached a message on the love God supplies, using 1 Corinthians 13 as my text. Once again, I struggled to overcome tears at this astonishing joy that trumped the collected heartaches of the past several years. I began:

What a joyful day this is!

We're gathered for the marriage of two people who love God, who love each other dearly, and who are dearly loved by us!

Melanie, I still see in my mind's eye the little blond girl who loved to twirl to music and sit in my lap for story time.

Now here you are a grown woman – a teacher, an organist, and, wonder of wonders, a beautiful bride!

I held before them a love that was patient and kind, and reminded them that 1 Corinthians 13 was the script for the life Jesus lived among us. He 'bore all things' and 'endured all things.' Because of Him, they could 'believe all things' and 'hope all things.' I was preaching to myself as well as to them.

Four months later, out of the blue, there came a phone call from Central Illinois District President Dave Bueltmann. He had received my letter months ago, but the crush of business and a summer convention had pushed it to the back burner, he explained. There was a little church in Illinois that was interested in a retired pastor. A tiny little Trinity in Casey, Illinois. "They'll probably contact you soon," he added.

The phone call came a week later from Pastor Dick Krenzke, then serving as interim in Casey. We talked easily. Sue and I had already made plans for a visit to our kids in Kansas City and a drive to Indianapolis to see other relatives in mid-November, just a few weeks hence. Our route would take us east on I-70, right past Casey.

The visit lasted little more than a day. Casey was a town of 3000 people in corn country, economically depressed, wild about its high school football team. Trinity was a tiny church that had been there 63 years. Many pastors had stayed briefly and left again, as if through a revolving door. Tiny Trinity, I could see, was vastly different from Big Trinity back in Oregon City. After a full day of meals and meetings with the people there, I told Dick: "This is like a first date. I guess I'd say I'm willing to have another date and take another look if they are. But I don't want to be an interim," I added. "If they want me to come, let them call me. If they'd help with my salary, I'd take a pension to supplement and make it work."

Back in Oregon City, I set to work once more, but now with the awareness of that little church in Illinois always in the back of my mind. Another *Life With God* class began. The Nicola family made their departure to another church official. A search for a new organist commenced, with elder Dave Wilson and I interviewing candidates. I presided at a fiftieth anniversary marriage renewal. I conducted funerals for Chuck Turner and Carrie Woody, both cancer victims, and for Ron Petersen, who loved cats and kept more than a dozen in his home. There was a visit to Paul Schmidt, having an aneurism repair at Adventist Hospital, and to old Bruno Lankow, who was as sleepy as Bilbo Baggins at the end of Tolkien's tale.

On Valentine's Day the folks at Casey extended me a call. Three weeks later, I accepted it, but not without 'some hesitance and uncertainty,' as I confided in my weekly journal. It would be a dramatic change of pace. As Sue and I made preparations to go, the congregation dedicated the new facility and prepared for a new chapter in its life.

Our farewell Sunday was April 25, 2010, nearly eleven years after our arrival at Trinity. The church was full, and among the worshippers came a contingent of folks from Memorial in Vancouver. Seeing them there was like a little foretaste of heaven, the reunion of people from different chapters of one's story, all together around the throne. One last time Sue's children sang (*"Wherever I Go"*) and each child had a solo line. The festivities, fittingly, took place in the JADE Room, over which there had been so much wrangling these past years. But today it was joy and thanks, eye-popping tables of food, and music to thrill the ears and heart, sung by Sue's Harmony octet and played by Trinity's worship team.

One last time I spoke to them. After a string of thanks, I left them with a book and a Bible passage. The book, I told them, was *The Unnecessary Pastor*, given me years earlier by Dustin Kunkel. It was a reminder that we pastors are useful, but not indispensable. Remembering Mark Bertermann's installation sermon for me about the clay pot, I told them it had been a privilege to hold the treasure of the Gospel and pour it out. But God would provide another pot. For a Bible passage, I shared 1 Corinthians 3, which describes Paul and Apollos, men with different gifts, each useful for a time in God's plan. Trinity had known pastors Messerli, Ruthenbeck, Halvorson, Henry, and Kasting. Who were we? *"Only servants, through whom you came to believe."* We were, I said, a construction team like the one that just finished this new addition. "The changing of pastors," I added, "means that God is ready to start the next phase of constructing what He wants to make of Trinity."

I believed what I preached. God is faithful. He would do it. It was time for Sue and me to lay this ministry down and turn our hearts toward a new home in the Heartland.

Trinity Lutheran Church

Casey, Illinois

(2010–Present)

THE RHYTHM OF THE HEARTLAND

It was a Saturday morning in early May. The Stevens moving van sat beside our new brick home on Delaware Avenue in Casey. Four volunteers from the church finished helping us pile cartons, crates, and boxes in the garage, bedrooms, and kitchen. We sat talking after a hard morning of work. We faced a lengthy task of refurbishing this place, which needed new floors, a paint job in and out, and some new appliances. Tomorrow after church we'd pause to take the two-hour drive to Franklin, Indiana, where we'd visit Sue's mom, our last surviving parent.

The phone rang. It was Sue's brother Phil. "Sis, mom died early this morning at the home in Franklin." A thunderbolt. After all these years away, we were finally close enough to make regular visits. Now she was gone. Today, of all days! Sue gave voice to her lament, "Why couldn't God have waited one more week... even one more day? I don't understand His timing."

One final time we made the trip back to Indiana to lay one of our dear parents to rest. A thunderstorm forced us to move the committal indoors, and I sat beside Sue and our daughter Melanie, giving thanks through my tears for these godly parents of ours.

Once more, we have started over. We're back in the heartland. Living life in a new rhythm. The daily rhythm of the trains that pass through our little town, horns blaring. The seasonal rhythm of cicadas screeching in the trees, so familiar from our Midwestern childhood. The social rhythm of rural Illinois, with suppers at the VFW hall, the end-of-summer Popcorn Festival, and high school football fever through the fall. The town loves its Warriors. Their names and jersey numbers line Central Avenue.

We're impressed with the kindness of our neighbors. Everyone here waves. Greg Ramsay, the farmer who lives next door, brings a sack of sweet corn. Ron and Donna Hudson, neighbors a block north, pedal by on their tandem bike and stop to get acquainted. They too have a sack, laden with green beans and tomatoes. Ron invites us to sing in the community college choir Tuesday evenings and ride-share with him. The college is 33 miles northwest of Casey. We accept. For the first time in years, Sue and I sing together in a choir.

We have moved not only to a new location but into a new season in our lives. Our parents have all gone home to the Lord. We've taken their place at the top of the family ladder. Now 'grandpa and grandma' is no longer our parents, but us. That's what we hear when we make the seven-hour drive to

Kansas City to see our grandkids. In our mid-sixties now, we've entered the realm of Medicare, arthritis, and degenerative joint disease. After eleven years on Highland Drive, knowing where everything was, we are having trouble finding our glasses, our pill bottles, our keys, and that prayer poster we thought was behind the cabinet.

It's more than that. We spend more than a little time trying to answer the question "Who are we now?" In moving, Sue has left behind her role as intake volunteer with Love INC, her voice in the Harmony octet, and her children's choir. There just aren't enough children here at little Trinity in Casey. She volunteers Thursdays at the local Crisis Pregnancy Center. That's a start, but she says she still hasn't found her niche.

As for me, I'm trying to wrap my mind around being 'semi-retired.' I get a pension, to be sure, but I'm also the full-time pastor of a little church of 115 people. I can work as much – or as little – as I want. I've left behind a district in which I'd served for 30 years, along with deep connections to brother pastors. I'm the new kid in town once more, trying to find a place in a new circle of peers. There's time to read, to fish in a farm pond as I did in my teens, fuss with my stamp collection, and sponsor the chess club at the Roosevelt Middle School. Almost too much time. Both of us have dipped our toes into the cyber-fellowship of Facebook. We've bought a pair of bicycles to cruise the tree-lined streets and feel the wind in our faces.

Over the 65 years of its existence, Trinity Lutheran Church in Casey has had 37 different pastors, vicars, and interims come and go. I am number 38. Perhaps the short stays were because young fellows wanted to move on to a congregation larger, more prestigious, or with more growth potential. Some, so old-timers tell me, were frankly ministerial misfits. In my early days here I have the sense of being examined to see whether I'll stay or choose to move on as did so many others.

The great Swiss theologian Karl Barth cut his teeth in ministry in a small parish and observed that even a small church has enough of the human dilemma to challenge any pastor. He was right. Ministry in our small town of 3000 people has brought some new challenges. After serving four congregations with hundreds of members, the sheer smallness of this congregation was a call to creativity. Storage space in the office was minuscule when I arrived. Several men took time to answer my call for help and install shelves and files.

I work alone now, with no secretary on site, though Zeena Christopher, the parish organist, helps finalize the bulletins I prepare and runs them on Saturdays. About 50 worshippers attend the single Sunday service and half stay for Sunday School. The same faithful folks are perpetually on deck to sing in the choir, staff the Sunday School, and supply food for the

Wednesday night meals. "After a while we get burned out," one woman told me.

People in large cities sometimes picture rural America in idyllic terms. They imagine farmers on their John Deere tractors, housewives chatting over the back fence, and rosy-cheeked kids frolicking at the old swimming hole. They envision bonfires and barn dances with fiddles wailing, bus drivers who know the students by name, and a life marked by wholesome values, peace and tranquility.

One can see such things here, of course. But the actual conditions in our small town more often manifest the 'quiet desperation' Thoreau once described. The only large factory here closed down a dozen years ago, leaving 300 people out of work. Our once-booming town is a shell of its former self. There's a sadness that lingers among the vacant storefronts. The town is down to a single IGA store, one barbershop, and one remaining hardware store, though there is still enough business to sustain two funeral homes. The schools are struggling with shrinking budgets and unavoidable staff cuts. Big box stores are 20 miles away and more. Hospitals are even farther away.

Trying economic times have left many in our town mired in poverty. The once-a-month distribution at the local food pantry serves 150 families. There are high rates of alcoholism, drug use, and divorce. The churches in town receive regular requests for help paying rent and utilities, buying groceries, and providing emergency shelter. For many, life is hard and hope elusive. My fellow pastors and I meet together monthly to compare notes, to pray, and to plan ways in which we might join hands to help people hold on in faith. Every fifth Sunday the churches join hearts and voices in a 'Fifth Sunday Sing' with an offering that goes to support the food pantry. The music is a soul-lifter, the laughter and talk a real tonic.

At Trinity, we set aside the year 2011 as a 'Year of Outreach' to our community. We went on a walk to meet our neighbors, took our turn staffing the food pantry, organized and ran a vacation Bible school, invited neighbors to a Hallowed Eve Open House with games and treats, and volunteered to mentor students at the local junior high. I hope that, increasingly, we'll look at our town with mission eyes and servant hearts.

Although it's smaller, this congregation is no different than the others I have served when it comes to the human condition manifested among us. The same kinds of fears, temptations, and heartbreak play out everywhere. A leader in our congregation has a marriage broken by alcoholism. A nurse who administers chemotherapy to others is diagnosed with cancer and struggles to cope with her fear. A mother and father grieve with their son who is unemployed and experiences suicidal depression. How can we incarnate the grace of God to these people and others when they hurt?

On a bright July morning, a throng of children bounce with energy around our tiny narthex and chatter excitedly as their parents sign them up for the week's Vacation Bible School. Xavier, a 6-year-old boy with a Mohawk haircut, and his younger sister Addie, an irrepressible fountain of noise, are among the newcomers. Our registrars have only their names and ages and a phone number, so I call the number to learn more about these two and their family.

Their mother, Valerie, tells me, "This is the first time the kids have ever been inside a church." As we talk, I hear a spiritual hunger in her words. She used to go to church years before. She misses it, and she's fairly bursting with questions. Late in the week I meet her and Allan, the man she's been living with for the past three years, when they come to pick up the children.

"When we have *Life with God* Class this fall, is it OK if I send you an invitation?"

They look at one another. "Sure," she smiles.

They make the decision to come and try the class, if 'class' is the right word. There are no other students who have signed up. Sue and I invite the two of them to our home to make it more like a family gathering. Over the next ten weeks they decide to be transparent about the history of hurts in their lives. Valerie tells the story of her fractured home, of abuse by her grandfather and her residual anger toward her grandmother who stood silently by and would not help. In tears she pours out her shame over dark episodes of promiscuity and meth use. Then the sadness of a failed marriage suffocated by alcohol and lovelessness.

Allan, too, has sadness in his voice over a family history of mental illness. He's a shy man who fears coming to church because he wonders what the people there will think of him. "Everyone in town knows us," he says quietly, with emotion. He is unemployed, and both of them fear their relationship will not survive. But they keep coming. We read the Bible together. Sue and I listen, share, and pray with them. We hug them, and they hug us back. Then comes a joyful surprise – Valerie and Allan come to church in spite of their fears. Afterward he says, "That wasn't so bad." They ask about baptism for their children.

"May I talk with the kids?" I ask. A short, but lively gathering in my office to explain about "God," "sin," "Jesus," "faith," and "baptism" is followed by a walk to the baptismal font, where I show the children how we baptize. They are willing and ready. The following Sunday is a day of joy for this little family and for the congregation, and our people welcome them warmly.

Then something more. "We want to get married," they tell me. I administer the PREPARE inventory and use it to talk about the areas of strength and areas in need of growth. More tears. Some struggling. Always a willingness to persist and keep working. One night Valerie comes alone and lays out before Sue and me the dreadful struggles she is facing. How can she forgive? How can she BE forgiven for all the sordid history she carries on her back? In a time washed with all our tears, we share the sweetness of Jesus, the fullness of His pardon, and the promise of a new beginning.

EPILOGUE

Many years ago our family was traveling through New Mexico on vacation. Dad pulled our '53 Ford off the road and stopped. We'd been climbing a long, upward grade and were nearly at the top of a rise. We got out of the car and took a few minutes to look back where we'd come while Dad snapped a picture. A valley stretched out behind us, the two-lane highway cutting through it like a long, straight ribbon. It was eerily quiet. The empty immensity of the desert landscape was breath-taking. That journey introduced me to the astonishing dimensions of our vast country. "People who stay home all the time never get to see this!" I told myself. I often reflect on how those long, long trips enriched me.

Writing this book proved to be a similar experience. I've stopped to look back over my miles and years to appreciate the array of faces and places and emotions stored in my memory. In looking back I realize the 'breadth and length and height and depth' of God and the persistence of His love for me.

Looking back enables me to see the consequences of the choices I have made and evaluate those I must still make. A constant in my pastoral experience is the sense of life as a quiet, daily warfare as I wrestle with those choices. The battle front has shifted with the passing of time. The seven deadly sins have all taken their turn with me. Some were stronger in my youth, others as I have aged. The powerful lusts of my younger years have been replaced by a growing weight of sloth, the temptation to waste my time on empty, inconsequential things and use my age and ebbing energy as an excuse. My old nemesis, pride, has not relented. It keeps shifting its point of entry.

It's easy to become cynical doing what I do. The ministry brings a weekly dose of disappointments, broken promises, and just plain ugliness. I'm reminded regularly of Dietrich Bonhoeffer's warning in *Life Together* that a pastor dare not become the accuser of his congregation, but always remain its intercessor. That is still a mighty challenge.

Do we pastors think we don't need help with our own selfishness and sin? Lately at a wellness retreat I was reminded of the necessity of staying accountable in that daily warfare. Accordingly, I have made agreement with a trusted brother pastor to be my accountability partner and confessor, something I have too long neglected. I'm afraid not many of us pastors do this anymore, and many of us pay the price.

There is a lesson in that for congregations. Very simply, I would urge them not to take for granted a pastor's strength and faith. It would be far safer to assume their pastor is beset with the same weaknesses, silly habits and sins they experience. The challenge they face is caring for their pastors, like a caring spouse who says, "What can I do to strengthen, encourage and cherish my mate?"

"What is God teaching you just now?" Father Simeon asked Sue and me in our spiritual direction sessions at St. John's Abbey. His question still echoes. Just now I'd answer by saying that I have come to trust the promptings I feel. I do not need to wait for God to send an angel or shout through a giant megaphone. Over the years, I have increasingly sensed His urgings: "Contact that person. Write a note. Make a phone call. Stop by to listen!" I have ignored some of those promptings and heeded others. I have almost always been glad I obeyed the prompting and almost always regretted it when I did not.

God also continues to teach me the urgent importance of family ties, especially the witness a pastor makes by the way he treats his own family. I recently heard another pastor ask his congregation to complete this sentence: "If I had it all to do over again, I would spend more time..." He offered three options – 'at the office,' 'on myself,' or 'on my family.' As a listener to that message, I knew without a moment's deliberation that I would choose 'on my family.' I learned the lesson late, but at least I have learned it! So my wife and children tell me.

A theme in my life has been 'fathers and sons.' With the ancient creed, I confess my faith in God the Father Almighty. But I would not know Him so well without His worldly stand-ins. My own father bequeathed to me not only a genetic endowment, but a spiritual legacy and a pattern to imitate. I owe him more than I can repay. When I moved away from home, others fathered me too, most notably Pastor Schroeder, who provided me a living template of pastoral care, and C. S. Lewis, who fathered me intellectually by opening the doors of my mind like no other writer.

Then it was my turn. I too became a father, first to my own three children, who even now bring me the profoundest of joys and tears. Though one could not ask more, I have been given much more. In 40 years of ministry I experienced the humbling mystery that I have become a father to others in the course of my pastoral work. There are sweet children who hug me round the knees, "I love you, Pastor Mike!" or ask, with solemn faces, "Are you God?" I remember the generations of white-robed confirmands and the new adult believers who have emerged from the struggles of anger and shame to a faith they can live by. Most pointedly I remember the vicars entrusted to me for a year, some uncertain of their faith or their vocation, who came to some certainty as we worked and prayed together.

My vocation has forced me to face death on a regular basis, and my aging body can FEEL its impending arrival. "Make the most of your time," my mother liked to remind me. Thankfully, I have become less fearful, certainly through constant contact with people who are dying, but even more through the ministration of the Word of God I am called to speak to others and then find that I am preaching to myself. Pastor Schroeder, in the midst of his cancer treatments, told me how glad he was that the message he preached to others he found good for himself too. I've made the same discovery. I recalled God's bracing words of promise when I learned recently of the sudden and unexpected death of my former vicar Keith Gravesmill, stricken shortly after his Good Friday service in Austin, Texas. I am confident he was ready for the summons. By God's grace I hope to be.

God's grace. I've mentioned it frequently in this book. I stand at the whiteboard and spell it out for my students in an acronym:

GOD'S RICHES AT CHRIST'S EXPENSE

It is the story of my life – God's undeserved kindness in the face of my arrogance, my rages, my fears and my follies. Grace seems to meet me everywhere. It lives in the ancient words I speak in worship, in the exquisitely deep old hymns and energetic new contemporary songs of the church, and in the eyes, and words and hugs of the dear people who have endured my weaknesses over these many years. Most tangibly I experience it in the steadfast love of my wife Sue, who knows my frailties and foolishness best of all. "You two are really each other's spiritual guides," said Father Simeon. That is perhaps one of the reasons St. Paul called marriage a profound mystery and then added, "I take it to mean Christ and the church" (Ephesians 5:32). I bless the Lord for such a woman, the daily embodiment of His patience and pardon for me.

By the grace of God, I am what I am,
and His grace to me was not without effect...
1 Corinthians 15:10

CPSIA information can be obtained at www.ICGtesting.com
Printed in the USA
LVOW080419131112

307071LV00001B/2/P